University of the
West of England

**ST. MATTHIAS
LIBRARY**

This book should be returned by the last date
stamped below.

UWE, BRISTOL   B1087.6.93
Printing & Stationery Services

Isabella Ford

To my parents, Vic and Hilda Hannam, for all their encouragement.

Isabella Ford

June Hannam

Basil Blackwell

Copyright © June Hannam 1989

First published 1989

Basil Blackwell Ltd
108 Cowley Road, Oxford, OX4 1JF, UK

Basil Blackwell Inc.
432 Park Avenue South, Suite 1503
New York, NY 10016, USA

British Library Cataloguing in Publication Data
A CIP catalogue record for this book is available from the British Library.

Library of Congress Cataloging-in-Publication Data
Hannam, June, 1947–
   Isabella Ford / by June Hannam.
      p.   cm.
   Bibliography: p.
   Includes index.
   ISBN 0–631–15068–4
   1. Ford, Isabella, 1855–1924.   2. Trade-unions – Textile workers –
   Great Britain – Biography.   3. Women – Suffrage – Great Britain –
   Biography.   4. Independent Labour Party (Great Britain) – History.
   I. Title.
HD8039.T42G75   1989
331.88′77′00924–dc19
[B]   88–36725

Typeset in 10 on 11.5 pt Bembo
by Vera-Reyes, Inc., Philippines
Printed in Great Britain by
Camelot Press, Southampton

Contents

List of Plates

Acknowledgements

MANY people have helped me in the course of writing this book. The critical comments and encouragement I received from all those who listened to my talks on aspects of Isabella Ford's life at conferences and post-graduate seminars, including my own students at Bristol Polytechnic, have been invaluable in informing my ideas and in convincing me that I should carry on with the project. I have gained enormously from discussions with Jill Liddington, Liz Stanley, Ann Wiltsher, and David Rubinstein. A special thank-you must go to Angela John for sharing her ideas on biography writing, for her constant encouragement, and for her friendship.

I am grateful to Steve Caunce for his generosity in allowing me to consult the papers of the late Gloden Dallas, who had long taken an interest in Isabella Ford's life and work. I should also like to thank the many librarians who have given me permission to quote from manuscripts in their special collections, and in particular David Doughan of the Fawcett library and Mr T. Morrish of the Brotherton Library, Leeds University, for all their help. Material from the M/50 papers held at Manchester City Library has been quoted with the permission of the City of Manchester Leisure Services Committee. Extracts from Isabella Ford's letters to Rosika Schwimmer have been taken from the Schwimmer-Lloyd Collection, Rare Books and Manuscripts Division, The New York Public Library, Astor, Lenox and Tilden Foundations. I am grateful to Miss Edith Wynner for permission to quote from Rosika Schwimmer's typescript 'Age of Innocence' and to E. P. Thompson for allowing me to use material from Alf Mattison's letter book.

Without the support of family and friends I would have found it impossible to write this book. I am grateful to Penny for giving me peace of mind and the space to write. I owe my parents a heartfelt thank-you for all their support and for the practical help they have given as grandparents. I must also thank my children, Hannah and Joseph, for putting up with all those Sundays when I was too busy writing to spend time with them. Chris Maggs has lived with the difficulties of researching and writing this book as long as I have, and it could never been finished without his advice and encouragement.

Abbreviations and Glossary

Dates in parentheses after the name of an organization refer to when it was established.

AUCO   (1894) Amalgamated Union of Clothing Operatives. Trade union for workers in wholesale clothing factories. Originally for men only, but women admitted in 1899. Centred on Leeds, but with branches in other clothing centres. General secretary: Joseph Young.

CC   (1909) *Common Cause*. Weekly newspaper of the NUWSS.

EFF   (1912) Election Fighting Fund. Formed by the NUWSS to raise funds and campaign in elections for Labour candidates who opposed Liberal anti-suffragists. Run by a 22-member committee.

GUTW   (1883) General Union of Textile Workers. This name was adopted in 1912. Before then the union had a variety of names, the first being the Huddersfield and District Power Loom Weavers' and Operatives' Association. Organized wool and worsted workers, largely in the West Riding of Yorkshire. Led by Allen Gee and Ben Turner.

ILP   (1893) Independent Labour Party. A socialist group with the immediate aim of securing independent labour representation in Parliament. Affiliated to the Labour Representation Committee and then to the Labour Party.

IWSA   (1890s) International Woman's Suffrage Alliance. Brought together women suffragists from all over the world. Held annual conferences in the pre-war years.

LL   (1894) *Labour Leader*. Weekly newspaper owned and edited by Keir Hardie, until 1904 when it was acquired by the ILP.

LRC   (1900) Labour Representation Committee. Aimed to establish a distinct labour group in Parliament. Became the Labour Party in 1906.

LNA   (1869) Ladies' National Association. Fought to repeal the Contagious Diseases' Acts. Led by Josephine Butler.

LDN   *Leeds Daily News*. A Liberal newspaper which was sympathetic to working women during the labour unrest of 1889.

LLEA   (1869) Leeds Ladies' Educational Association. Established to promote higher education for women in Leeds and to arrange and supervise Cambridge examinations.

LM   *Leeds Mercury*. Leading provincial daily newspaper supporting the Liberal Party.

LWC   (1911) *Leeds Weekly Citizen*. Weekly newspaper of the Leeds Labour Party.

NAC   (1893) National Administrative Council of the ILP. An elected group charged with carrying out the policies adopted at the annual conference.

NUWSS   (1897) National Union of Women's Suffrage Societies. A non-militant, constitutionalist women's suffrage group which demanded the vote for women on the same terms 'as it is or may be granted to men'. President Millicent Fawcett, 1897–1919.

NUWW   (1874) National Union of Women Workers. Aimed to establish women's unions and benefit funds and to monitor legislation affecting women's employment. By the late 1890s it had become more philanthropic in outlook.

SDF   (1884) Social Democratic Federation. Socialist group influenced by Marx. Led by Henry Hyndman.

TUC   (1868) Trades Union Congress. Established as a forum of debate for affiliated trade unions. Later became a pressure group for, and voice of, trade-unionism.

WCOU   (1889) Wholesale Clothiers' Operatives' Union. Trade union for male workers in the Leeds wholesale clothing factories. Renamed the AUCO in 1894 when branches were established in other towns.

WFL   (1907) Women's Freedom League. A militant suffrage group established by former members of the WSPU. Led by Charlotte Despard and Teresa Billington Greig.

WIL   (1915) Women's International League. Founded after the Hague Peace Congress to link women from different countries who were committed to seeking a negotiated peace. Membership based on IWSA suffragists.

WLL   (1906) Women's Labour League. Aimed to encourage women to become more involved in labour politics; to increase representation for women on public bodies; and to improve the work and home lives of working-class women. Founded by Mary Middleton and Margaret MacDonald.

WPC   (1917) Women's Peace Crusade. A movement aiming to involve women at a grass roots level in the campaign to secure peace by negotiation.

WPLL   (1894) Women's Protective and Provident League. Umbrella group offering assistance to working women in setting up their own organizations and carrying out propaganda for female trade-unionism. Led by Emma Paterson.

WSPU   (1903) Women's Social and Political Union. Militant women's suffrage group. Members known as suffragettes. Demanded the vote for women on the same terms 'as it is or may be granted to men'. Led by Emmeline and Christabel Pankhurst.

WTUA   (1889) Women's Trade Union Association. Aimed to establish self-managed and self-supporting unions of women workers, in particular in the East End of London. Led by Clementina Black.

WTUL   (1891) Women's Trade Union League. Promoted trade-union organization among female workers. Any union with women members could affiliate. Grew out of the Women's Protective and Provident League founded by Emma Paterson in 1874.

WTUR   (1891) *Women's Trade Union Review*. Quarterly journal published by the WTUL.

UDC   (1914) Union of Democratic Control. Aimed to achieve a negotiated peace and to develop structures to prevent future wars. Members drawn from ILP, radical liberals, and anti-war suffragists.

YEP   *Yorkshire Evening Post*. Conservative evening paper published in Leeds.

YFT   (1889) *Yorkshire Factory Times*. Weekly newspaper written by local trade-unionists. Supported the movement for independent labour politics. Published in Huddersfield.

YLCE   (1871) Yorkshire Ladies' Council of Education. Formed to promote the education of women and girls. Local committees were run by women from leading professional and manufacturing families in Yorkshire. By the 1890s the Council took an interest in more general social and economic questions affecting working-class women and girls.

Chronology: Isabella Ford, 1855–1924

1855	Born in Leeds.
1878	Death of father, Robert Lawson Ford.
1885	Isabella helps Emma Paterson, President of the Women's Protective and Provident League, and members of the Leeds Trades Council to form a Machinists' Society for tailoresses in Leeds.
1886	Death of mother, Hannah Ford. Isabella sets up a Workwomen's Society for Leeds tailoresses and textile workers.
1888	Takes part in a strike of weavers at Wilson's, Leeds.
1889	In October establishes the Leeds Tailoresses' Union and takes part in the tailoresses' strike at Arthur's.
1890	Made honorary life member of the Leeds Trades Council. President of Leeds Tailoresses' Union (to 1899). Publication of first novel, *Miss Blake of Monkshalton*. Founder member of Leeds Women's Suffrage Society.
1890–1	Takes part in Manningham Mills dispute, Bradford.
1893	Joins Independent Labour Party.
1895	Publication of novel, *On the Threshold*. Elected Parish Councillor for Adel-cum-Eccup. Delegate to International Textile Workers' Congress, Ghent.
1896	Delegate to Trades Union Congress. Delegate to the Congress of the Second International, London.
1897	Delegate to International Textile Workers' Congress, Roubaix.
1898	Member of the executive committee of the Humanitarian League. Member of the executive committee of the Women's Trade Union League.
1900	Delegate to International Textile Workers' Congress, Berlin.
1901	Publication of novel, *Mr Elliott*.
1903	Delegate from ILP to Annual Conference of the Labour Representation Committee. Elected to NAC of the ILP (until 1907).
1904	Delegate from ILP to Annual Conference of the Labour Representation Committee.

Publication of pamphlet *Women and Socialism*.

Delegate to International Textile Workers' Congress, Milan.

1905   Delegate to Annual Conference of the Labour Representation Committee.

1907   Elected to executive committee of the National Union of Women's Suffrage Societies (until 1915).

Vice-President of Leeds Women's Suffrage Society.

1908   Delegate to IWSA Annual Congress, Amsterdam.

1909   Delegate to IWSA Congress, London.

1911   Chairman of the West Riding Federation of Women's Suffrage Societies.

1912   Member of the Election Fighting Fund Committee.

1913   Delegate to IWSA Annual Congress, Budapest.

1914   Delegate to International Textile Workers' Congress, Blackpool.

Joins Union of Democratic Control.

1915   Resigns from Executive Committee of the NUWSS.

Member of executive committee of the British section of the Women's International League.

1917   Forms Leeds branch of the Women's Peace Crusade.

Joins 1917 Club.

1919   Delegate to Women's International League Congress, Zurich.

Death of Isabella's elder sister Bessie.

1920   Delegate to IWSA Conference, Geneva.

1921   Delegate to Women's International League Congress, Vienna.

1922   Delegate to International Peace Congress at the Hague.

1924   Death of Isabella at Adel Willows, Leeds.

Ford Family Tree

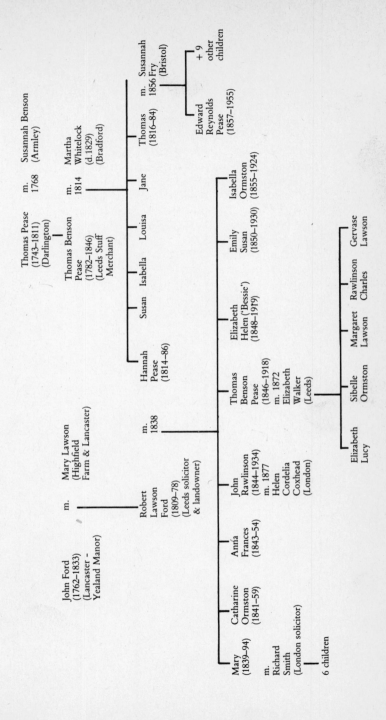

John Ford
(1762–1833)
(Lancaster –
Yealand Manor)

m.

Mary Lawson
(Highfield
Farm & Lancaster)

Thomas Pease
(1743–1811)
(Darlington)

m.
1768

Susannah Benson
(Armley)

Thomas Benson
Pease
(1782–1846)
(Leeds Stuff
Merchant)

m.
1814

Martha
Whitelock
(d.1829)
(Bradford)

Robert
Lawson
Ford
(1809–78)
(Leeds solicitor
& landowner)

m.
1838

Hannah
Pease
(1814–86)

Susan   Isabella   Louisa   Jane

Thomas
(1816–84)

m. Susannah
1856 Fry
(Bristol)

+ 9
other
children

Edward
Reynolds
Pease
(1857–1955)

Mary
(1839–94)
m.
Richard
Smith
(London solicitor)

6 children

Catharine
Ormston
(1841–59)

Anna
Frances
(1843–54)

John
Rawlinson
(1844–1934)
m. 1877
Helen
Cordelia
Coxhead
(London)

Thomas
Benson
Pease
(1846–1918)
m. 1872
Elizabeth
Walker
(Leeds)

Elizabeth
Helen ('Bessie')
(1848–1919)

Emily
Susan
(1850–1930)

Isabella
Ormston
(1855–1924)

Elizabeth
Lucy

Sibelle
Ormston

Margaret
Lawson

Rawlinson
Charles

Gervase
Lawson

Introduction

'I do not think anyone will ever fully know all that she did in framing the mental attitude and outlook of the founders of the Independent Labour Party . . . her power was in making the newly found party realise that a Liberalism which left out the claim to liberty of half the human race, was afflicted with fundamental defects which poisoned its very being.'[1] These words, written shortly after Isabella Ormston Ford's death, provide a key to understanding her life and her historical significance. Born in 1855, the daughter of well-to-do Leeds Quakers noted for their reforming zeal, she grew up determined to do something useful with her life. Committed to women's rights from her earliest years, she turned in the 1880s to the labour movement; from then on she combined propaganda for socialism and feminism,[2] always keeping to the fore the interests of the female worker. Never one to concentrate on a single issue, Isabella Ford was, at various times, a trade union organizer, a socialist propagandist, a suffragist, and a peace campaigner.

This biography focuses on Isabella Ford's work for the women's movement and the labour movement; it examines her attempt, both at a practical and at a conceptual level, to bring the two together and to develop a theoretical framework to link class and sex oppression. The book does not set out to provide a comprehensive account of her life – her novels and short stories, for example, do not get the attention they deserve. I have been deliberately selective in exploring a theme – the relationship between gender and class politics – that I believe was central to her own life and which is still unresolved for feminists and socialists today.[3] It is hardly possible, in any case, for biographers to know all that there is to know about the lives of their subjects. They can only provide fragments, glimpses of personality, some selected events. As early as 1871, Walt Whitman, one of Isabella Ford's favourite authors, expressed similar views about the prospect of a biography being written of his own life.

[1] M. Fawcett, 'Isabella Ormston Ford', *Woman's Leader*, 25 July 1924.
[2] Although contemporaries described themselves as members of the women's rights' movement, for the sake of convenience I have also used the terms 'feminist' and 'feminism'.
[3] For a discussion of the continuing difficulties in reconciling gender and class politics, see A. Phillips, *Divided Loyalties: Dilemmas of Sex and Class* (Virago, 1987).

When I read the book, the biography famous,
And is this then (said I) what the author calls a man's life?
And so will some one when I am dead and gone write my life?
(As if any man really knew aught of my life,
Why even I myself I often think know little or nothing of my real life,
Only a few hints, a few diffused faint clews and indirections
I seek for my own use to trace out here).[4]

I do not, therefore, intend that this biography should be seen as a finished piece of work or as a complete account of Isabella Ford's life. I am still coming across new references – to friendships or to issues in which she was involved – which give fresh insights into her life and work.

I have also not set out, as so many biographers do, to explore Isabella Ford's psychology as a way of explaining her actions, and I have avoided undue speculation about her innermost thoughts and feelings. As Bernard Crick notes in his study of George Orwell, 'none of us can enter into another person's mind; to believe so is fiction. We can only know actual persons by observing their behaviour in a variety of different situations and through different perspectives.'[5] My own approach has been to examine the way in which Isabella Ford was influenced by, and tried to influence in turn, external events in her life. She spent most of her adult years in the public eye and was concerned that her many talents – as a journalist, a platform speaker, a social investigator, a negotiator – should have a practical effect in helping to bring about changes in the lives of working women.

The shape of the biography has been determined to some extent by the nature of the sources available. If some aspects of Isabella Ford's life remain shadowy, this is partly because she left few personal papers – there are no diaries, journals, or letters to members of her family. Any insights into her personality, therefore, have been gleaned largely from the public statements of her political colleagues and must be seen as partial. On the other hand, as Crick again notes, we are all perceived differently by our contemporaries, whether friends, relatives, or colleagues, and in turn we relate differently to them. Biographers cannot hope, therefore, to describe the definitive personality of their subjects. In Isabella Ford's case, the silence of relatives and the absence of the private views of her friends add to the difficulties of the biographer. The lack of personal papers means that important questions must remain unanswered; it would have been interesting, for example, to know whether her relationship with family members who remained staunch Liberals was affected by her socialist beliefs. Letters to friends give fascinating insights into her private, as opposed to public, views about

[4]Walt Whitman, *Leaves of Grass, 1871*, quoted in C. Hill, *God's Englishman: Oliver Cromwell and the English Revolution* (Harmondsworth: Pelican, 1972), p. 11.
[5]B. Crick, *George Orwell: A Life* (Harmondsworth: Penguin, 1982), p. 30.

events, but these are few and far between. Moreover, the gaps in this correspondence can have a distorting effect; Isabella's views are recorded about some events, but not others, while the importance of particular friendships may be overemphasized because of the chance survival of letters.[6] On the other hand there is a wide range of sources on her propaganda work for socialism, women's rights, and peace, including pamphlets, letters to the press, committee minutes, and reports of organizations.

The absence of personal papers may explain why Isabella Ford has been neglected by biographers and historians. She is often accorded one or two sentences in suffrage and labour histories, but there is little assessment of her importance. And yet she was active at a national level in organizations which were at the forefront of socialist and suffragist agitation from the late nineteenth century; for four years running she was elected on to the National Administrative Council of the Independent Labour Party and at different times was an executive member of the Women's Trade Union League, the National Union of Women's Suffrage Societies, and the Women's International League. Her neglect is symptomatic of a wider failure by historians to recognize the role that women played in social and political movements.[7] Historians of the socialist and trade union movement, in particular, have concentrated on the role of men, but even studies of all-female groups have focused on a small number of leading women. Once a few 'great women' have been singled out for special mention, their names recur again and again in standard history texts, creating the impression that they were the only ones who had any historical significance and that they were in some way unique.

Isabella Ford made a distinctive contribution to the development of socialism and women's rights which deserves to be recognized. On the other hand, my intention in writing this biography is not simply to add yet another name to the existing list of 'great women'. Isabella Ford's importance lies in the fact that she was representative of a wider group of middle-class women who became involved in suffrage and labour politics in the late nineteenth and early twentieth centuries. The political and social context which encouraged Isabella Ford to challenge women's inequality, and which led her to see trade union organization and socialist politics as the only way to improve the lives of female workers, affected other well-educated women of her class and generation – Katharine Conway, Margaret McMillan, Enid Stacy, Clementina Black. After the turn of the century they were joined by a younger generation – Mary Gawthorpe, Ethel Snowden, Maude Royden – who campaigned as socialists and suffragists.

[6]Such a problem is not, of course, confined to a study of Isabella Ford.

[7]For a discussion of the neglect of women's contribution to labour politics, see J. Hannam, 'Usually Neglected in Standard Histories: Some Issues in Working on the Life of Isabella Ford, 1855–1924', in D. Farran, S. Scott, and L. Stanley, eds, *Writing Feminist Biography*, Studies in Sexual Politics nos. 13–14, Sociology Dept., Manchester University, 1986.

These women formed a broad leadership group, supporting the more well-known individual leaders of the organizations in which they took part. They were the ones who attended conferences, sat through interminable committee meetings, and disseminated propaganda as speakers and writers. Without their efforts, in the provinces as well as in London, it would not have been possible to build a popular base for socialist and feminist politics.

A study of Isabella Ford's life, therefore, will shed light on the activities, interests, and ideas of this much broader group. An examination in depth of one person's political work and ideas can yield valuable insights for the historian, revealing connections between movements and ideas that often appear as separate in mainstream histories. In Isabella Ford's case, for example, labour historians usually note her trade union work, and suffrage historians her contribution to the struggle for the vote. This serves to compartmentalize activities which she herself saw as 'branches of the same great tree'.[8] A trade union organizer, a socialist propagandist, a suffragist, and a peace campaigner, she never for one moment saw these activities in isolation from one another. Only when her life is viewed as a whole, however, is it possible to see the connections that she made between socialism, feminism, humanitarianism, and peace.

Historians have only recently begun to explore the richness of the links between all these movements;[9] in the late nineteenth century, working-class women as well as middle-class women demanded a voice in politics and urged the labour movement to take up their cause; many middle-class women who were interested in women's rights also became involved in the struggle for socialism and took their feminist ideas with them. They ensured that the 'woman question' was high on the agenda of socialist debate and that the needs of working women were not entirely neglected by the suffrage movement. By studying the lives of individuals it becomes far more difficult to draw rigid distinctions between different types of feminists and socialists.[10] The labels 'equal rights' feminists, 'industrial feminists', and 'social maternalists' can all be useful in helping us to make sense of the different priorities and ideas of members of the women's rights movement. On the other hand, individual women did not fit neatly into these categories. Industrial feminists, for example, may have agreed on the importance

---

[8] J. Arnott, 'Isabella O. Ford: An Appreciation', *Leeds Weekly Citizen*, 19 Feb. 1924.

[9] See e.g. J. Liddington and J. Norris, *One Hand Tied Behind Us: The Rise of the Women's Suffrage Movement* (Virago, 1978); J. Liddington, *The Life and Times of a Respectable Rebel: Selina Cooper, 1864–1946* (Virago, 1984); L. Garner, *Stepping Stones to Women's Liberty: Feminist Ideas in the Women's Suffrage Movement, 1900–1918* (Heinemann, 1984); P. Levine, *Victorian Feminism, 1850–1900* (Hutchinson, 1987); J. Rendall, ed., *Equal Or Different: Women's Politics, 1800–1914* (Oxford: Blackwell, 1987).

[10] For example, O. Banks, *Faces of Feminism* (Oxford: Martin Robertson, 1980), makes a distinction between 'equal rights' feminists and those who wished to take domestic virtues into the public sphere. For a discussion of the distortions caused by separating feminists and feminist thought into distinct strands, see Levine, *Victorian Feminism*, Introduction.

of trade union organization, but they differed in their views about protective legislation and married women's employment.

It was only through studying Isabella Ford's activities and ideas that I became aware that the attitudes of socialists and feminists towards specific policies were complex; that they derived their views from varied, and often surprising, intellectual sources, and that it is not always possible to draw a rigid distinction between them on political lines. Broad-minded and tolerant Isabella Ford developed a wide network of friendships with men and women from varied social and political backgrounds.[11] They were drawn together by a common set of interests – in women's rights, humanitarianism, and peace – which cut across formal political allegiances. Their shared beliefs enabled radical liberals, ILP socialists, and suffragists to take action together on a large number of issues in the pre-war years.

Throughout the study I have called Isabella Ford by her first name – using her full name seemed too cumbersome and formal. I have also quoted freely from her writings; her own words convey a much clearer sense of her humour, wide reading, and unusual insight into the lives of working women than any précis of my own, as well as explaining why she had such an impact on the views of contemporaries. Captivated by her wit, humour, and depth of knowledge about women's work conditions, both labour and suffrage audiences alike responded warmly to the burning intolerance of injustice and impatience to bring about change which came through so clearly in Isabella's speeches and writings. Never condescending in her attitudes towards working people, Isabella's guiding philosophy was that men and women must have control over their own lives: 'she has faith in the crowd, and urges with Diderot that we must never let our pretended masters do good to us against our wills'.[12] Rejecting philanthropy and its emphasis on rescue work, she chose instead to support trade-unionism and encouraged women workers to rebel on their own behalf. 'Only one thing is necessary for us all to remember, viz., that the industrial woman must work out her freedom for herself. . . . We cannot possibly know her needs so well as she herself can.'[13]

---

[11]I am grateful to Liz Stanley for first drawing my attention to the importance of friendship networks among women in the late 19th/early 20th cents. and for encouraging me to be critical of conventional approaches to biography writing. For her approach, see e.g. L. Stanley, *Feminism and Friendship: Two Essays on Olive Schreiner*, Studies in Sexual Politics no. 8, Sociology Dept., Manchester University, 1985.

[12]J. J. Mallon, 'Isabella Ford', *Woman Worker*, 7 Aug. 1908.

[13]I. O. Ford, *Industrial Women and How to Help Them* (Humanitarian League, c.1901), p. 11.

1

Early Years, 1855–1880

Never laugh at what is new.

> The Socialist movement, the Labour movement, call it which you will, and the Woman's movement, are but different aspects of the same great force which has been, all through the ages, gradually pushing its way upwards, making for the reconstruction and regeneration of Society . . . both the movements sprang from the common evil of economic dependence. Dependence on the owner of property is at the bottom of the woman's question as much as it is at the bottom of the labour question.[1]

So wrote Isabella Ford in 1904 in a pamphlet which sought to express in a systematic way the views which underpinned all of her public activities. She argued consistently, as a trade union organizer, a socialist, a suffragist, and a peace campaigner, that women's emancipation and the achievement of socialism were inextricably linked. Many contemporaries shared her views, but she was unusual in maintaining a commitment to both socialism and feminism, always refusing to put one cause before the other.

After 1900 she played a leading role in both movements and gained a national reputation for her talents as a speaker, writer, organizer, and champion of the rights of working women, and yet it was not until the late 1880s, when she was already in her mid-thirties, that Isabella Ford began to take a prominent role in public affairs in the West Riding of Yorkshire as a women's trade union organizer and a propagandist for socialism.

Isabella's involvement in the labour movement seemed a world away from the comfortable, upper middle-class environment in which she was brought up. She was not alone, however, in making the difficult transition from the radical liberalism of her youth to the socialist politics of her more mature years. Other members of her class and generation, including her own sisters and her cousin Edward Pease, made a similar decision. They were clearly influenced by recent developments in the socialist and labour movement, but their changing political commitment had deeper roots in the radical Quaker milieu in which many of them grew up.

[1] I. O. Ford, *Women and Socialism* (ILP, 1904), p. 3.

Isabella's parents lived in Leeds and were related to some of the most prosperous Quaker families in the north of England. The Fords had been farmers for generations, owning large estates in the West Riding of Yorkshire – at Ingleton, Bentham, and surrounding districts – and in Lancaster, Lancashire, where Isabella's father, Robert Lawson Ford, was born in 1809. Robert, despite having inherited land from his family, trained as a solicitor and set up a practice in Leeds: It was in Leeds that he met his future wife, Hannah Pease, a fellow member of the Society of Friends.[2]

Hannah's father, Thomas Benson Pease, was a Leeds stuff merchant, in partnership with his brother William Aldam. The main branch of the family lived in Darlington, where successful entrepreneurs had built up the Pease family wealth in the eighteenth century from wool-combing, banking, and coal-mining.[3] They intermarried with the Backhouses, substantial bankers in the town, and together the two families initiated and helped to finance the Stockton–Darlington railway. Hannah retained close links with her Darlington relatives, spending holidays on the Durham coast in the 1820s with her cousins Elizabeth Pease Nichol, Jane Gurney Fox, Ann Hodgekin, and Edward Backhouse, who were later to share her interests in political and social reform.[4]

Robert and the 24-year-old Hannah were married in 1838 at a time when Leeds was experiencing rapid population and economic growth. Their own relatives, the Arthingtons, Peases, and Aldams, who were noted for their business capacities and enterprise, were among those who took advantage of the changes brought by industrialization to make Leeds into a regional centre of commerce and industry. In the eighteenth century the town had relied on the woollen trade for its prosperity, but by the 1830s manufacturing had expanded to include engineering, clothing, flax-spinning, and printing as well as woollen textiles. From this diversified economy emerged a more varied middle-class elite which included manufacturers and professional workers – accountants, lawyers, and physicians – as well as the old-established merchant community.[5]

The Fords were firmly placed within this upper middle-class elite and the pattern of their family life conformed in most respects to that expected of their class. They set up home in Park Square, in the centre of Leeds, and six of their eight children were born here. Their first child, Mary, arrived a year after their marriage and was followed by Catharine Ormston, Anna

[2]J. Foster, comp., *Pease of Darlington* (privately printed, 1891); see also Census Enumerators' Books, 1871.

[3]For information on the Pease family, see A. M. Stoddart, *Elizabeth Pease Nichol* (J. M. Dent, 1899); and E. R. and J. H. P. Pafford, *Employer and Employed: Ford Ayrton & Co. Ltd.* (Edington, Wilts.: Pasold Research Fund Ltd., 1974), ch. 2.

[4]A letter and memorandum by H. Ford in S. A. Pease, 'Thomas Benson Pease', MS 369, Ford Family Papers, Brotherton Lib., Leeds Univ.

[5]For an overview of the economic, political, and social development of Leeds, see D. Fraser, ed., *A History of Modern Leeds* (Manchester: MUP, 1980).

Frances, John Rawlinson, Thomas Benson, and Elizabeth Helen, familiarly known as Bessie, who was born in 1848.[6]

By the time of Bessie's birth many well-to-do families had started to move away from the middle of town to the more rural surroundings of the suburb of Headingley. Years of unregulated urban expansion had brought health and environmental problems to the centre of Leeds, which was described in 1844 as 'a dirty and disagreeable town . . . perhaps the ugliest and least attractive town in all England'.[7] It was to escape this smoke-filled atmosphere that Hannah and Robert joined their contemporaries by moving to St John's Hill, Clarendon Rd, Headingley, shortly before the birth of another daughter, Emily Susan, in 1850.

The Fords' last child, Isabella Ormston, was also born in the new family home, on 23 May 1855, when her mother was in her early forties, and she spent her earliest years playing with Bessie and Emily in idyllic rural surroundings. The house was bounded on one side by fields, two of which were rented by Robert to graze ponies. According to Emily, their father had 'a gift for landscape gardening' and 'had made the garden with little hedges and paths, so that it seemed larger than it was'. Red and white hawthorn, laburnum, azaleas, pinks, pansies, and roses all grew in profusion, and 'there were wild hyacinths in the lawn . . . and a little pond with goldfish in it'.

The old house with its rambling garden gave the girls plenty of scope for their imagination. When the wind blew against the storm shutters on the bedroom windows they imagined they were out at sea, and sat in bed 'listening in ecstasy to the wind and full of fearful joy'. The lawn was inhabited by 'mysterious black cocks', and at the corner was a place for sticks. 'It was the home of robbers, a brood of terrible men, and we always walked quietly and as swiftly as we could past the entrance'.[8]

The three youngest sisters developed a very close relationship. They had to rely on each other for company during their early childhood years when their brothers were away at boarding school, and moreover two of their older sisters had died before reaching adulthood (Anna Frances at the age of only eleven, just a year before Isabella was born, and Catharine Ormston five years later at the age of eighteen), while the eldest sister, Mary, had left home when Isabella was only six to marry Richard Smith, a London solicitor, who was Lord of the Manor of Addingham, Yorkshire.[9] Mary had six children and was the only one of the sisters to conform to the Victorian ideal that women should marry and devote themselves to domestic con-

[6]Their birthdates were Mary, 1839; Catherine Ormston, 1841; Anna Frances, 1843; John Rawlinson, 1844; Thomas Benson Pease, 1846; Elizabeth Helen, 1848.
[7]Quoted in R. J. Morris, 'Middle-Class Culture, 1700–1914', in Fraser, ed., *History of Modern Leeds*, p. 200.
[8]E. S. Ford, 'The Old House', typescript, MSS 371/4, Ford Family Papers.
[9]Foster, comp., *Pease of Darlington*, p. 23.

cerns. Almost a generation separated her birth from that of Bessie, Emily, and Isabella, and the latter were influenced by very different ideas from those affecting their oldest sister. They grew up at a time when women were beginning to challenge their prescribed social role and could benefit from the greater independence afforded some girls of their generation.

When Isabella was ten the family moved once more, this time to Adel Grange, in the parish of Adel-cum-Eccup on the outskirts of Leeds, which was even further removed from the industrial environment of the town. The Grange was a large property, even by the standards of its day, and included a library, drawing room, dining room, eleven bedrooms, and spacious servants' quarters. Six indoor servants – a cook, a lady's maid, two housemaids, and a kitchen maid – were needed to run the house in the 1870s, and there must have been even more when the children were young.

The house stood in seven acres of grounds. Landscaped gardens and lawns led down to an ornamental lake, and rustic walks were laid out through the orchard and herbaceous and rose gardens. The large outbuildings housed a studio, stabling, accommodation for the coachman and his wife, and a cottage for the gardener, his wife, and the under-gardener. Beck Farm, which stood in a further seventeen acres, acted as home farm for the Grange, while Beck Farm cottage was leased on an annual tenancy.[10]

The children enjoyed a comfortable life-style at Adel. Growing up in a Quaker household, however, meant that their experience of childhood differed in many ways from that of other members of their class. Contemporaries claimed that the relationship between the family and its servants was one of 'esteem, equality and friendship', and that life at the Grange was unostentatious and based on 'simplicity of conduct'.[11] Hannah used the term 'thee' in correspondence, but did not follow the stricter rules of the Society of Friends which admonished members to wear distinctive clothing and to disapprove of music and dancing. On the contrary, the atmosphere in the household was a light-hearted one; all the children developed a strong sense of humour, which was used to good effect in their later writings and speeches, and were positively encouraged to seek pleasure from music, dancing, and painting.

Hannah and Robert were warm and affectionate, both to their children and to each other, although Hannah's first love had been her cousin Edward Backhouse, who shared her interest in sketching. As near cousins they were unable to marry and Isabella also pointed out that, in any case, 'our mother was then falling in love with our father and not with Edward Backhouse. . . . and *their* love letters are (we have read a few) *devoted*.' None the less, Edward Backhouse remained close to his cousin. In a note scribbled on the back of one

[10]'Particulars of the Adel Grange Estate', MS 370, Ford Family Papers.
[11]E. E. Crossley, 'Isabella O. Ford: Suffragist, Trade Unionist and Socialist', *Leeds Weekly Citizen* (*LWC*), 28 June 1929.

1. Adel Grange, a view of the house. (*Ford Family Papers, Brotherton Library, Leeds University*)

2. Adel Grange, a view of the gardens. (*Ford Family Papers, Brotherton Library, Leeds University*)

of his sketches Isabella recalled a visit that he made to Hannah just a few years before her death and 'how they sat talking on the garden seat here, so devotedly'.[12]

The bonds of affection between Hannah and Robert were strengthened by their common interest in politics, education, and culture, which also set them apart from the majority of their wealthy contemporaries. They were part of an advanced group within the Society of Friends who were radical liberal, internationalist, and humanitarian in their politics and sympathies. These families valued a broadly based education for daughters as well as their sons. Their children were taught science and philosophy alongside art and literature, and both sexes were encouraged to think independently and to develop a critical spirit. The Pease and Backhouse families in particular produced a number of intelligent, independent-minded female reformers who provided Isabella and her sisters with an alternative role model to the prevailing middle-class ideal of womanhood.[13]

The Fords had close ties of friendship with many of these radical Quakers, and also with members of the Unitarian Mill Hill Chapel in Leeds, with whom they shared a common intellectual, political, and social outlook. Members of both groups formed a constant stream of visitors to Adel Grange, which was described as a 'rendez-vous for reformers of all kinds and conditions', and intense political debate formed an everyday part of family life.[14] Hannah's own interest in politics had been awakened by her father's involvement in the political conflicts of the 1820s and 1830s in Leeds, when the 'Tory oligarchy of gentlemen merchants' was supplanted 'by a rival Liberal elite in all the political institutions of the town'.[15] Described as a 'stern Whig', Thomas Benson was one of the first aldermen on the reformed Leeds Corporation.

As members of a younger generation, Hannah and Robert were attracted to the more radical wing of liberalism. They supported fellow Quaker John Bright, MP for Manchester, in his campaigns in the 1830s and 1840s to extend the parliamentary franchise and to repeal the Corn Laws. A frequent visitor to Adel, he influenced the ideas of all members of the family; years later, at the end of a distinguished career as a Liberal councillor in Leeds, John Rawlinson used Bright's words to explain why he could not accept a knighthood. 'I feel as John Bright did when he said, after being offered an important post in the Government, "I dwell among mine own people". I don't want to be different from the rest of you.'[16]

[12]Sketches by Edward Backhouse Jnr (1808–1879) with pencil note by Isabella Ford, MSS 374/7, Ford Family Papers.

[13]For a discussion of radical Quakers, see G. Malmgreen, 'Anne Knight and the Radical Subculture', Quaker History, 71 (Fall, 1982), pp. 104, 108.

[14]'Isabella Ormston Ford', The Friend, 64 (1 Aug. 1924), p. 670.

[15]D. Fraser, 'Politics and Society in the Nineteenth Century', in Fraser ed., History of Modern Leeds, p. 273.

[16]Yorkshire Evening Post (YEP), 4 June 1913.

Along with many of their Quaker relatives and friends, the Fords also supported liberal and republican movements abroad. They were excited by the revolutions of 1848 that promised to overturn monarchical or absolutist rulers in favour of more democratic government, although they found it difficult to reconcile their pacifism with the violence that often accompanied such movements. Hannah's Darlington cousin, Elizabeth Pease, expressed these mixed feelings in an excited letter to William LLoyd Garrison, the American abolitionist, in 1848. 'We live in stirring times, and the blood of the slain is the only feature that checks the delight of contemplating the outburst of freedom which has filled Europe and the world with astonishment . . . the recent movement has given a powerful impulse to the onward march of Liberty throughout the world.'[17]

Both Hannah and Elizabeth admired the Hungarian revolutionary, Kossuth, and took a deep interest in the union and liberation of Italy. Mazzini, the Italian leader, stayed with the Fords on one of his visits to England and was a close friend of Elizabeth Pease and her husband, John Pringle Nichol, a professor of astronomy whom she married in 1853. For many Quakers, Mazzini seemed to embody all they held dear – peace, liberty, and the democratic spirit – and his writings were a source of inspiration for those who desired constitutional change.

The Fords were also part of the broad humanitarian movement of the period which sought prison reform, the abolition of slavery, and the protection of wild life. Their daughters inherited this outlook and were vegetarians, campaigners for animal welfare, and conservationists. In her later years, Isabella could still be seen planting flowers along the lanes of Adel, while at the age of sixty Bessie wrote to express her delight that the Independent Labour Party had set up a Children's Flower League. She hoped that this would teach consideration for flowers to 'prevent . . . the ruthless gathering and the digging up of roots which lead to the extermination of so much beauty', although she did not object 'to the time honoured daisy chain, of whose joys in childhood I have even now a vivid remembrance'.[18]

The anti-slavery movement was the humanitarian cause which had the widest support among members of the Society of Friends, and women again played an important role. Elizabeth Pease helped to form a women's anti-slavery group in Darlington and accompanied her father as a delegate to the World Anti-Slavery Convention of 1840, where she claimed to be raised to a 'white heat' by the exclusion of women.[19] It was here that she met and became friends with Elizabeth Cady Stanton and Lucretia Mott,

[17]Stoddart, *Elizabeth Pease Nichol*, pp. 172–3.

[18]Letter from Bessie in *Labour Leader*, 4 May 1906; see also obituary of Isabella in *YEP* 15 July 1924.

[19]J. Walkowitz, *Prostitution and Victorian Society: Women Class and the State* (Cambridge: Cambridge University Press, 1980), p. 44.

who went on to play a leading role in the American women's suffrage movement, a cause which also claimed Elizabeth Pease's attention in later years.[20]

Hannah Ford was less flamboyant than her cousin Elizabeth, but worked hard from behind the scenes for similar causes. Despite constant child-bearing in the 1840s, she did not allow herself to become weighed down by domestic concerns and was one of several Leeds women to organize a collection of items each year to be sent to the annual bazaar held in Boston to raise money for the anti-slavery cause. Hannah was also a member of the Leeds Anti-Slavery Society in the early 1850s.[21]

The Fords' sympathy for slaves and other oppressed groups abroad was also extended to working people at home. Their radical politics did not lead them to adopt the harsh liberal doctrine of individual responsibility for social welfare and they took an interest in the wages, work conditions, health, and education of working people. In the 1850s they helped to finance a night-school for mill-girls in the East End of Leeds which had been established by a shoemaker.[22] Hannah also taught in the school and encouraged her three youngest daughters to do the same when they reached the age of sixteen.

Given her own background and interests, it is hardly surprising that Hannah Ford was concerned that all her children should receive a broad education. The boys were sent to Quaker boarding schools at Hitchin and Tottenham and were then expected to train for a career. John Rawlinson worked as a clerk in his father's office before becoming a solicitor himself, while Thomas Benson was apprenticed to the engineering firm of Green-wood and Batley. He later decided to leave engineering because of its association with the manufacture of armaments and established a silk-spinning mill with William Harvey, also a member of the local Society of Friends.

Much less is known about the education of Isabella and her sisters; they appear to have been taught at home by governesses and not expected to train for a career. Hannah may have decided to keep her daughters at home because of her own 'sorrowful childhood'. After her mother's early death she was educated at three different day schools before being sent, at the age of seven, to a boarding school at Tadcaster where she experienced 'hard times'.[23] The scattered information that can be found on the content of the girls' education suggests that it was broadly based and did not suffer from taking place within the home. They became fluent in French and German,

[20] F. B. Tolles, ed., '"Slavery and the Woman Question": Lucretia Mott's Diary of Her Visit to Great Britain to Attend the World Anti-Slavery Convention of 1840', *Journal of the Friends' History Society*, Supplement 23 (1952), p. 23.

[21] *First Annual Report of Leeds Anti-Slavery Society, Mar. 1853–Mar. 1854.*, Leeds Reference Library.

[22] E. S. Ford, 'I. O. Ford', typescript, MSS 371/3, Ford Family Papers.

[23] H. Ford, 'Letter and Memorandum', p. 23.

played musical instruments to a professional standard, and read social and political texts as well as literature.

Emily's reminiscences of their work in the night-school for mill-girls gives an insight into their own education. She remembered trying to explain to the girls 'the boiling of a kettle, and we tried to pass on to them the chemical lessons we had learnt in the daytime, but I fear with very little result. We tried to teach them German folk songs and I had dizzy dreams of the whole of Leeds being converted to the Germans, great popular songs, such as the Lorelei.' But trying to teach the girls to read was hopeless; they just kept saying, 'tell us what you've been doin' yourselves – that's what we want to know'.[24]

The education of Bessie, Emily, and Isabella was very different from that experienced by most girls of their generation except those from a Quaker or Unitarian background. They were expected to develop enquiring minds rather than to gain accomplishments in the marriage market, and were fortunate in having parents who 'encouraged their daughters to cultivate mind and body to the best advantage'.[25] Ray Strachey paints a vivid picture of the intellectual concerns and excitement of such girls in her early history of the women's movement.

> If you were a Buxton, a Gurney, a Fry, a Wedgewood, a Bright . . . or a Darwin it was not such a very great misfortune to be born a woman . . . you would be allowed and expected to be educated and intelligent, and you would be considered an equal in family life, and might, if you chose, take up occupations and interests of your own. . . . In the journals and lives of the period we get charming glimpses of the intercourse of the young men and women of these families, talking, and talking earnestly, together about the semi-abstract subjects which youth enjoys . . . we see them reading German literature together and sitting at the feet of Carlyle, admiring Mazzini and attending scientific congresses and enjoying a companionship and an intellectual interchange which has a distinctly modern flavour.[26]

Education was not just a matter of formal lessons in such families. Informal discussions of political and social events also helped to shape the children's ideas, and, since most visitors to Adel were involved in public affairs at home or abroad, it must have seemed natural to the children that they should do something useful with their lives. Many years later, Isabella was to acknowledge the importance of this upbringing in shaping her interests as a mature woman:

> When did I begin to take an interest in working girls? I don't know. Some people are born that way. My mother was quite a revolutionist, a great admirer of Cossuth,

[24]E. S. Ford, 'I. O. Ford'.
[25]E. E. Crossley, 'Isabella O. Ford'.
[26]R. Strachey, *The Cause* [1928] (Virago, 1978), pp. 44–5.

and my father and a shoemaker named Greenwood . . . began more than 60 years
ago the first night school in England. That was in Spitalfields, down the Bank,
and it was for the benefit of mill girls . . . So you see, I am amongst those who
were born that way.[27]

Her brothers also became active in public life and shared Isabella's interest
in women's rights and the welfare of working people even if they did not
share her socialist politics. John Rawlinson spent many years as a councillor
and then alderman on the Leeds City Council and was elected as leader of
the Liberal Group in 1912. He was a patron of the Yorkshire College and
promoted various musical activities in Leeds, including two series of
subscription concerts in the 1880s and 1890s. Thomas Benson's activities
were at county level. In the 1880s he moved his factory and most of his
work-force to the small village of Low Bentham and took a leading role in
numerous committees concerned with sanitation, housing, and health in the
West Riding. He also sat on the West Riding County Council as a staunch
Liberal from 1889 until his death in 1918.[28]

Anecdotes repeated time and again in later accounts of Isabella's life
suggest that she had a moral earnestness and sense of social purpose while
still very young. During the Lancashire cotton famine when asked by her
father, 'What is an operative, baby?', Isabella is reputed to have replied, 'a
starving creature'. By the age of twelve she had already made an oath with
her friend Ellen Croft (later Mrs Francis Darwin) to dedicate her life to 'the
improving of the state of the world'.[29]

Other girls of Isabella's generation and social circle had a similar sense of
social purpose based on a strong religious fervour and the knowledge that
concern for the poor was a legitimate area of activity for middle-class
women, but Isabella was never satisfied with philanthropy as a solution to
social problems. Her mother's influence was crucial here. Hannah encouraged her daughters to adopt a critical approach towards social institutions
and prevailing values and taught them to 'never laugh at what is new'.[30] Her
sympathy with oppressed minorities and political exiles, in particular
Russian refugees, helped to give her children an international perspective, a
faith in democracy as the expression of the will of the people, and a hatred
of despotism, hereditary power, and war which they retained until the end
of their lives.

Of even greater importance was that Hannah was involved in the women's
movement just as her youngest daughters reached the impressionable age of
puberty and adolescence. An organized women's movement took shape
only slowly over the late 1850s and 1860s as a minority of wealthy middle-

[27]'Some Eminent Trade Unionists. no. 8, Miss Isabella Ford', *LWC* 12 June 1914.
[28]For John Rawlinson, see 'Portrait Gallery', *Yorkshire Owl*, 27 Jan. 1897 and *YEP* 4 June
1913; for Thomas Benson, see Pafford, *Employer and Employed*, ch. 2.
[29]*Yorkshire Factory Times*, 1 Nov. 1889; *New Leader*, 25 July 1924.
[30]J. J. Mallon, 'Isabella Ford', *Woman Worker*, 7 Aug. 1908.

class women began to question aspects of their prescribed social role. They challenged women's subordinate social and economic position and sought 'equal rights' of access to the public sphere. Early women's rights campaigns aimed to extend the provision of higher education for girls and to open professional occupations to women so that single middle-class girls could enjoy a degree of economic independence. These preoccupations were in turn linked to demands for the vote and for women to participate more fully on elected public bodies.[31] Quakers and Unitarians played a significant role in the leadership of these campaigns; they valued education for both sexes and were influenced by enlightenment doctrines of equal rights.[32] As an organized group the Society of Friends was not necessarily predisposed towards women's rights, but the fact that female members had the opportunity to speak at meetings encouraged them to see themselves as equal to their male co-religionists. They were often motivated by a sense of moral duty to take part in reform campaigns, where they hoped to take their domestic virtues into the public sphere. None the less, their experience in such campaigns often led to the development of a more feminist consciousness. The anti-slavery movement, for example, was particularly important in drawing attention to the unequal status of women.

Hannah's first interest was in the campaign to increase women's access to higher education and to establish their right to sit public examinations. She joined with other local women from leading manufacturing and professional families to set up the Leeds Ladies' Educational Association (LLEA) in 1865 which formed the core of a much broader group, the Yorkshire Ladies' Council of Education, established in 1871. The council's aim was to supervise examinations, to promote women's higher education, and to provide lectures for women of all social classes. One of Hannah's tasks was to help organize a series of health lectures for working women. She was joined in her educational work by Bessie, now in her early twenties, who was a member of the committee formed to establish the Leeds Girls' High School.

Involvement in the campaign for women's education brought Hannah and her daughters closer to some of the most well-educated and independent-minded women in Leeds . Many of them were Unitarians whose male

---

[31]For an account of the origins and aims of the women's movement, see Strachey, *The Cause*, ch. 5; O. Banks, *Faces of Feminism* (Oxford: Martin Robertson, 1981), ch. 3; and J. Rendall, *The Origins of Modern Feminism: Women in Britain, France and the United States, 1780–1860* (Macmillan, 1985), ch. 8.

[32]Olive Banks argues that Quakers demanded access for women to the public sphere so that their domestic virtues could have influence outside the home, whereas Unitarians were influenced by Enlightenment doctrines of equal rights and belief in the power of reason; see Banks, *Faces of Feminism*, pp. 26–7, 29–30, 46. It will be suggested throughout this book that Quakers, and many other women, used both sets of arguments at the same time, and that the contradiction between the two lay at the heart of the women's movement up to the First World War and beyond.

relatives were also interested in educational work. Fanny Heaton, a founding member of the LLEA, was the wife of a physician at the Leeds Infirmary who was 'actively involved with general social improvements and educational development in Leeds'.[33] She was supported by her sister-in-law, Miss Heaton, by Mrs Frances Lupton, the wife of a member of the Yorkshire Board of Education, and by Theodosia Marshall, a member of the famous flax-spinning family in Leeds, described by her close friend Emily Ford as 'very clever and educated'.[34]

Their participation in campaigns to improve women's higher education and in the parallel struggle to gain the parliamentary vote also extended the Fords' network of friendship with women from outside Leeds. One of these was Millicent Garrett Fawcett, who made her first speech on women's suffrage in Manchester in 1868, only a year after her marriage to the radical liberal MP Henry Fawcett. She was far less well known at this time than her older sister, Elizabeth Garrett Anderson, the first British woman doctor, but was to become the leader of the women's suffrage movement in the 1890s. Millicent and her sister Agnes were contemporaries of the Ford sisters in age and developed a very close friendship with Bessie and Isabella.[35]

Another friend was Josephine Butler, a founding member of the North of England Council for Women's Education. Influenced by her father, John Grey, an agricultural reformer and anti-slavery advocate, she grew up 'democratic in all her instincts'.[36] In 1851 she married George Butler, an Anglican clergyman and educationalist, and after the death of her daughter in the 1860s became involved in rescue work in Liverpool before turning to women's education.

The ties between the two families became even closer when Josephine Butler launched the Ladies' National Association (LNA) to fight for the repeal of the Contagious Diseases Acts. The Acts gave wide powers to the police in military towns to arrest women suspected of being prostitutes and to detain them in hospital if they were found to be suffering from a sexual disease. Josephine Butler added a feminist dimension to arguments against the Acts by claiming that they increased male power over women's bodies and reinforced the double standard of morality by punishing female victims rather than their male clients. It was at the Friends' Meeting House in Leeds that Josephine Butler held her first public meeting on the Acts in 1869.

[33]I. Jenkins, 'The Yorkshire Ladies' Council of Education, 1871–1891', *Thoresby Society Publications*, 56 (1978), p. 42.

[34]E. S. Ford, 'Josephine Butler', typescript MSS 371/2, Ford Family Papers.

[35]Millicent Fawcett was born in 1847, her sister Agnes in 1845. For biographical details, see A. Oakley, 'Millicent Garrett Fawcett: Duty and Determination', in D. Spender, ed., *Feminist Theorists* (Women's Press, 1983).

[36]J. Walkowitz, *Prostitution and Victorian Society: Women, Class and the State*, (Cambridge: CUP, 1980), pp. 115–16.

Hannah Ford attended the meeting and, along with many of her Quaker friends, signed a letter sent to the press shortly afterwards outlining the arguments of the newly formed LNA.[37] She helped James Stansfield, the Quaker MP and close friend of Mazzini, to fight the repeal campaign in Yorkshire, and remained a member of the Leeds LNA until her death in 1886.

The combination of moral and equal rights issues raised by the Acts had a particular appeal for Quakers, who were disproportionately represented in the repeal campaign. It required considerable courage for middle-class women to speak in public about questions of sexuality, and most of the active repealers were either married or middle-aged single women. Isabella and her sisters, on the other hand, were only in their twenties and unmarried when the campaign was at its height, which may explain why they did not join the Leeds LNA, but they were deeply influenced by the issues raised about the double standard.

Emily became a member of the LNA when she was older and in 1908 attended a congress in Geneva on the subject of whether state regulation aided the white slave traffic. In her work as a union organizer Isabella always drew attention to the sexual harassment suffered by women at the work-place and to the links between low pay and prostitution.[38] Moreover, her writings show that she was influenced by Josephine Butler's argument that women's oppression could not be understood simply as a question of civil and legal rights, but had to be located within a 'total economic, political and sexual power relationship'.[39] All three sisters must have been fully informed about the issues raised by the Acts since so many of their friends and members of their family were actively involved in the repeal campaign, including Hannah's brother Thomas and her cousins Elizabeth Pease Nichol and Katharine Backhouse, who were among the national leaders of the LNA. When John Rawlinson married Helen Cordelia Coxhead of London in 1877 she also became active in the Leeds LNA. Helen's interest in the welfare of female workers and in women's suffrage meant that she soon developed a close relationship with her sisters-in-law and helped to strengthen the Ford family's commitment to women's rights.

Life for the young sisters in the late 1860s and early 1870s, therefore, did not conform to the stereotyped picture so often presented of the unmarried Victorian woman filling up her time with empty pursuits until marriage. They were actively involved in women's rights campaigns and interested in political affairs. Their many friendships also ensured that they had an active

[37] *Daily News*, 31 Dec. 1869.
[38] E. S. Ford, *Women and the Regulation System: Impressions of the Geneva Congress of September 1908* (LNA, 1909).
[39] J. Uglow, 'Josephine Butler: From Sympathy to Theory, 1828–1906', in Spender, ed., *Feminist Theorists*, p. 146.

social life and they enjoyed far more personal freedom than many girls of their generation, mixing with young people of both sexes and leaving home unchaperoned.

Theodosia Marshall was one of their closest Leeds friends. At her dinner parties they met 'people of Intellectual distinction', including the Cambridge professors James Stuart and Fred Myers. Emily found these gatherings 'extraordinarily delightful', for 'it was a little centre of high culture which is rarely found. There was a glow that youth often gives to these things.' Josephine Butler was frequently there, accompanied by her sons, the youngest of whom had 'inherited his mother's wonderful beauty', but the young men 'were as shy as we were, with the antique shyness which used to afflict the young of that day'.

The Ford sisters often visited the Marshalls at their holiday home on Derwent Island. On one such visit Josephine Butler was also invited and she used to sit 'in the half twilight on the sofa with her three sons round her talking together in a low voice as if they were lovers'. Emily's most vivid recollection was of swimming expeditions in the early hours of the morning. 'Theodosia would insist that there should always be one swim by moonlight . . . I did not like it myself. I confess I was a little afraid . . . for only those who have tried it know of that mysterious feeling of awe which comes to us while swimming in the silver paths of the moonlight.'[40]

When they were at home, the young women spent much of their time reading, painting, writing, and playing music. Hannah and Robert always encouraged their children to be creative, and set a personal example in their own work; Robert had edited a school magazine, the *Bellford Gazette*, which contained articles on politics and international affairs as well as school events, while Hannah painted in watercolours and wrote poetry. Their son John Rawlinson followed in this amateur tradition, writing numerous skits about life as a solicitor's apprentice which gently poked fun at his father:

> Old Robert he sat on his high backed chair
> With his pen behind his ear,
> Whilst Austin his clerk did hook it away
> To play cricket and drink weak beer.[41]

Their daughters, however, were to adopt a more professional approach, exploring the philosophical issues raised by a study of art and literature.[42] They were also willing to hold up their work to public scrutiny. Emily published a series of plays in the 1880s and later distinguished herself as an artist, with several of her paintings being exhibited in the Leeds Arts

[40]E. S. Ford, 'Josephine Butler'.
[41]Satirical Verses Written by J. R. Ford and Others while Clerks at Payne, Eddison & Ford, Solicitors, c.1863; MS 367, Ford Family Papers.
[42]See e.g. E. S. Ford, *Rejected Addresses: An Episode* (Leeds, 1882), p. 13.

Gallery. Bessie was an accomplished violinist, owned a Stradivarius and, accompanied by Isabella on the piano , performed in a series of concerts for working people in the 1890s. Isabella's own talent lay in writing – three of her novels and several short stories were published in the 1890s and 1900s.

As she matured into a young woman of twenty, Isabella had already developed a critical intellect and an interest in radical liberal and feminist politics. There was little to suggest, however, that she would go on to achieve a national reputation as a propagandist for the rights of working women and independent labour politics, becoming the most well-known of the three sisters. Instead, it was Emily who took the first step to building a reputation for herself.

In the late 1870s, Emily became a student at the Slade School of Art. The Slade had been founded in 1872 by a series of endowments from a wealthy connoisseur, Felix Slade, and its first directors set out to challenge what they saw as stagnant Victorian traditions. With her own studio in London, Emily thrived in this environment and took a full part in the intellectual and cultural life of the city. She joined a small but growing minority of young middle-class women who were able to enjoy greater freedoms than their mothers' generation. Some, as in Emily's case, were encouraged by wealthy, progressive parents to pursue their interests away from home, while others took advantage of new opportunities for paid employment which enabled them to live independently of their families.[43]

After finishing at the Slade, Emily acquired a considerable reputation as a painter of church altar panels, although she was always surprised that anyone was willing to pay for her work. She painted numerous portraits of friends, including Josephine Butler and the Russian anarchist exile Stepniak, and her feminist painting, 'Dawn', was presented to Newnham College by Millicent Fawcett to celebrate the examination success of her daughter Philippa. In later years, Emily became a pioneer of the modernist movement in Leeds.

Emily's strong personality was suited to an independent life, and she was prepared for anything after the difficulties she had faced in the suffrage campaign: 'it was sufficiently terrifying to a young and highly strong girl like myself to have to get up and speak, sometimes with a paid bully lounging against the lorry ready to smash your meeting, if not your jaw'.[44] Emily had a dry sense of humour and entertained friends with her 'racy' impersonations of Leeds mill girls. On the other hand, she was also 'mercurial in temperament' and her intense enjoyment of life could quickly turn to the 'blackest despair'.[45]

The personalities of Bessie and Isabella emerge far less clearly in this

[43]See M. Vicinus, *Independent Women* (Virago, 1985).
[44]*Yorkshire Post*, 5 Mar. 1930.
[45]Ibid. 11 Mar. 1930. See also the comment on Emily's personality in P. Gunn, *Violet Paget: Vernon Lee, 1856–1935* (Oxford: OUP, 1964), p. 118.

period. As the youngest sister, Isabella had not played a prominent role in the local feminist campaigns and appears to have been too shy in her early twenties to make public speeches. Bessie was always the most introspective and private of the sisters, having a deep interest in philosophy and music. Throughout her life she rarely took a prominent part in public causes, preferring to work from behind the scenes. As the eldest sister she played a crucial role in ensuring the smooth running of the household after her parents' deaths and gave considerable emotional and practical support to her two younger sisters whose work took them so frequently from home.

The strong bond of affection and friendship between the sisters was never broken or weakened by marriage. A growing number of women in the late nineteenth century positively chose to remain single so that they would be free to pursue a career or to devote themselves to public affairs. There is no direct evidence that the Ford sisters made such a deliberate choice, although it is clear from some of their writings that they frequently discussed the difficulties women faced once they were married and the loss of freedom that this entailed. Emily's play, *Careers*, for example, concentrates on the difficult choice faced by Nora, an art student living with friends in a studio, between maintaining her independence or marrying the suitor suggested by her aunt, Lady Fel:

> NORA. But Lord Scareton gambles, and I don't like him.
> LADY FEL. I can't see what *that* has to do with the question. You should look at this merely as a question of establishment in life.
> NORA. Ah, well, I *don't* look at it so, that's just it.
> LADY FEL. And pray what *will* you do if you don't marry Lord Scareton!
> NORA. I don't know. Perhaps – let me see – teach.
> LADY FEL. Oh come now Nora, you are not only silly, but vulgar. I shall go, it is merely wasting words to stay.[46]

Because Isabella remained an essentially private person during the 1870s, later biographical accounts tend to ignore this period of her life. They follow a common pattern in pointing to her experiences at the night-school for mill-girls and then to her role in the tailoresses' strike of 1889 as providing an explanation for her conversion to socialism. And yet it was during the 1870s and early 1880s that Isabella and her sisters began to explore new ways of looking at the world which were to predispose them towards socialist politics and an involvement with the labour movement.

With their radical Quaker background, it is hardly surprising that the Ford sisters shared the dissatisfaction shown by many members of their class and generation with the crass materialism of their age, the relentless pursuit of wealth, and the harsh doctrine of individual responsibility. They read a wide range of political and social texts in this period, many of which

[46]E. S. Ford, *Careers: A Comedy* (Leeds, 1883), p. 10.

provided a critique of *laissez-faire* liberalism. [A character in one of Emily's plays notes: 'I have here a few authors without whose guidance life is indeed a chaos . . . The first I would mention are John Rae's "Contemporary Socialism", Marx's "Political Economy", Stuart Mill's "Political Economy", Herbert Spencer's "Sociology", Green's "Man Considered as a Block", Bastiat's "Works", also Prudhomme, Louis Blanc, Lassale and others.'[47]

Young people of the time were also plagued by uncertainties in their religious faith and yet were not convinced that science held the key to understanding man's place in the universe. In a reaction against materialism they sought to explore the inner self and to find new ways of relating to other people. The Quaker background and commitment to women's rights shared by Isabella and her sisters encouraged them to take an interest in such ideas. After the mid-1870s their tentative ideas were given a much firmer shape when they formed a close and lasting friendship with Edward Carpenter. Isabella was only twenty when they first met, but Carpenter was to be a guiding force for the rest of her life.[48]

Born in 1844 into an upper middle-class family, Edward Carpenter became a lecturer at Trinity Hall Cambridge in 1868. The following year he was ordained as a deacon. After reading Mazzini and other radical writers, however, he was so plagued with spiritual and intellectual doubts that he left the curacy in 1871. From then on he was concerned to challenge conventional views about masculinity, femininity, and sexuality and to explore new ways of living that would give freedom to the body and the senses.[49] Full of his new ideas, Carpenter spent the two winters of 1875 and 1876 in Leeds as a lecturer on astronomy for the University extension movement; the bulk of the pupils at this time, we are told, were 'of the young lady class', and some of the best scholars were from girls' schools, especially 'some very intelligent ones from the Friends' schools'.[50] It was at one of these lectures that he met the Ford sisters, and there was an instant rapport between them. [They were attracted by his attempts to develop an alternative notion of manliness and to gain self-realization through a closer communion with the natural world. He believed that 'knowledge would come not by taking overmuch thought, but by direct experience of life', in particular the 'unchanging life of the countryside'.[51]

After writing to the American poet Walt Whitman in 1874, Carpenter had become his devoted disciple. Whitman was seen by many contemporaries

---

[47]Id., *A Perfect Character: A Sketch* (Leeds, n.d.), p. 6.
[48]For Carpenter's life and ideas, see S. Rowbotham and J. Weeks, *Socialism and the New Life: The Personal and Sexual Politics of Edward Carpenter and Havelock Ellis* (Pluto Press, 1977).
[49]Ibid.
[50]E. Carpenter, *My Days and Dreams* (Geo. Allen & Unwin, 1916), p. 80.
[51]J. R. MacDonald, 'The Living Man', in G. Beith, ed., *Edward Carpenter: An Appreciation* (Geo. Allen & Unwin, 1931), p. 133.

as the 'prophet of a new democracy founded on the complete freedom of the individual and on the social instinct of man to share with others the joys and pleasures of life'.[52] The two poets shared a belief in the 'infinite possibilities of man',[53] but were different in their approach to nature. Whitman enjoyed the city and 'looked at the world from the outside; it was through his senses that he perceived the beauty of nature'. Carpenter, on the other hand, was happiest in the countryside and 'spiritualized' nature. He 'saw the world as it was reflected in his deep, vast soul, and he taught how it is man, or the spirit that in man becomes self conscious, that creates our world'.[54]

It was almost certainly Carpenter who introduced the Ford sisters to Whitman's writings, and they were attracted immediately by his ideas. Bessie found Whitman's *Democratic Vistas* to be a 'breath of fresh air'. She overcame her nervousness to write to the poet in 1875 because, she tells us, 'I believe in what you say in your book so much that I can hardly feel fear'. His ideas were like 'a great help coming from a long way off', and she was anxious to know whether Americans truly believed and cared about the democratic spirit which she hoped would one day grow in England. 'Your words that you have written are such a strength, it is so wonderful to find said things that hover in one. I mean, to read things that one's heart cries out in answer to. This is what makes me so that I cannot help writing to you.'[55]

Bessie, Isabella, and Edward Carpenter frequently sent gifts of money to the poet and received copies of his books in return, including *Leaves of Grass* and *Special Days*, and they continued to correspond with Whitman until his death in 1891.[56] Whitman's emphasis on democratic comradeship and the need to be close to the natural world, and Carpenter's own attempt to live a more simple life based on new personal relationships, exerted a profound influence on a whole generation of young people, including the Ford sisters, Katharine Conway, John Bruce Glasier, James Ramsay MacDonald, and Edward Pease, who later went on to play an important part in the socialist movement. Katharine Bruce Glasier claimed that 'it is no exaggeration for many of us inside and outside the political socialist movement to say that Walt Whitman's *Leaves of Grass* and Edward Carpenter's *Towards Democracy* have become as a kind of Twentieth-Century Old and New Testament, fulfilling rather than destroying the works of others that have gone before them in our lives . . .'.[57]

[52]G. Ferrando, 'Edward Carpenter As I Knew Him', in Beith, ed., *Carpenter*, p. 64.
[53]E. H. Miller et al., eds, *The Correspondence of Walt Whitman* (New York: NYUP, 1961), vols ii–iv, p. 13 n.30.
[54]Ferrando, 'Edward Carpenter', pp. 65–6.
[55]Letter from Bessie Ford to Walt Whitman, 16 Feb. 1875, Feinberg Coll., Library of Congress, Washington, DC.
[56]W. White, ed., *Walt Whitman: Day Books and Notebooks, vol. ii, Daybooks Dec. 1881–1891* (New York: NYUP, 1977).
[57]K. B. Glasier, 'Edward Carpenter's Influence', in Beith, ed., *Carpenter*, p. 86.

Bessie and Isabella were never provincial in their outlook, despite being based in Yorkshire. They had a flat in London, at 5 Hyde Park Mansions, where they frequently stayed for several weeks at a time. Here they could keep in touch with new ideas through their network of family and friends; their cousin Edward Pease, the son of Thomas Pease of Bristol, worked in London as a clerk and was part of a circle of young white-collar workers who gathered in the radical debating clubs which proliferated in London. Here they questioned prevailing social, political, and religious beliefs and avidly discussed the possibility of bringing about social reform.

In her play *Careers* Emily gently poked fun at the grandiose plans put forward by these many small groups;[58] she was familiar with them because she saw a great deal of her cousin Edward Pease in the late 1870s and early 1880s. They attended lectures and meetings, went boating on the river, and visited theatres and art galleries together. Emily also introduced Edward to psychic research. Along with many of her contemporaries who were dissatisfied with established religious doctrines but who still needed spiritual guidance, she spent a great deal of time wrestling with her faith and became increasingly interested in 'spirit influences'. Her mother held spiritualist meetings where attempts were made to communicate with the souls of the dead. She may have been prompted to do this by the death of her husband in 1878, although there is no direct evidence of how this affected any member of the family.

When she was in London Emily attended many spiritualist seances, becoming a member of the Society for Psychic Research, and encouraged Edward Pease to go along with her to meetings. On one occasion they 'sat in darkness singing hymns, till banjoes banged about the room, and spirit fingers touched one's forehead'.[59] It was at another of these meetings that Edward Pease met Frank Podmore, an upper-division clerk at the Post Office who was, for a brief period, secretary of the Society for Psychic Research, and who later joined with him in founding the Fabian Society.

Emily remained interested in the spirit world long after this period. An early critique of her paintings noted that 'her mind is in sympathy with spiritual aspirations of earlier centuries'. Her interest was less in the 'value and significance of externals' and more in the way in which she could use externals 'as a grammar to make vocal her thoughts'.[60] She was described as 'whimsical at times, sympathetic, deeply religious, and much interested in psychical research, she had a simple faith which, though clouded at times by her natural physical nervousness and fearfulness, yet never failed her'.[61] She eventually converted to the Anglican faith, the only one of her immediate family to leave the Society of Friends.

[58] E. S. Ford, *Careers*.
[59] N. and J. Mackenzie, *The First Fabians* (Quartet Books, 1979), p. 17.
[60] H. Ford, 'Emily Ford: A Painter of Religious Pictures', c.1909, pp. 3–4 MSS 378/1, Ford Family Papers.
[61] *Yorkshire Evening News*, 7 Mar. 1930.

Isabella and Bessie seemed to have been less troubled by religious doubts than their sister, although they too sought spiritual change and the possibility of living a 'new way of life' within the shell of the old society. None the less, the environment of reform in which they had grown up made all three sisters unhappy with an over-concentration on a personal, inner transformation alone. Instead, they sought to link such changes to more external, political reforms. Their concerns were still rooted in a radical liberal framework, but by the early 1880s those closest to them, including Carpenter and Pease, were becoming more receptive to those socialist ideas that subsequently had a strong appeal for the Ford sisters themselves.

2
Comradeship, 1881–1889

Women, it was said, were men's friends and helpers in the industrial world.

The growing discontent with mid-Victorian economic and social values was given a more organized focus in the early 1880s with the formation of two socialist groups, the Fabian Society and the Social Democratic Federation (SDF). The Fabian Society was established after a series of meetings, the first of which, attended by both Isabella and Bessie, was held in the London flat of Edward Pease on 24 October 1883. A conflict arose immediately between those who were interested in social and economic reforms, such as Edward Pease and Frank Podmore, and those who wished to concentrate on personal, inner change. After several more meetings, two groups were formed: the Fellowship of the New Life, which followed the precepts of Thomas Davidson that 'personal perfectibility could be achieved in the context of a fellowship', and the Fabian Society, which aimed to 'reconstruct society in accordance with the highest moral possibilities' through political means.[1]

Havelock Ellis, a medical student who was to write extensively about sexuality, his future wife Edith Lees, and James Ramsay MacDonald, later to be leader of the Labour Party, were keen supporters of the Fellowship and tried to put its ideals into practice by living communally in Bloomsbury. Edward Carpenter, Isabella, and Bessie, who were also among the earliest members of the Fellowship,[2] kept in close touch with the 'Bloomsbury group' when they visited London. They were not satisfied, however, with an emphasis on personal change alone. They believed that a transformation of personal life would take place alongside a change in political institutions, and that this could only be achieved though socialism.

Edward Carpenter and William Morris were particularly important in articulating contemporary longings for a new society. They argued that

---

[1] E. R. Pease, *The History of the Fabian Society* (Frank Cass, 1918), ch. 2.
[2] E. Carpenter, 'Preface' in Mrs Havelock Ellis, *The New Horizon in Love and Life* (A & C Black, 1921), p. viii.

changes in the relations of production would lay the basis for new personal relationships and create an environment in which individuals could fulfill all their potential. Morris used the Socialist League to develop his ideas more fully. Formed in 1885 by disatisfied members of the SDF, the League was short-lived. None the less, the broad ethical appeal of Morris's vision of a socialist future based on fellowship, co-operation, and an emphasis on the arts provided a common point of contact for socialists who were otherwise divided along tactical and theoretical lines. It had a particularly strong influence on Carpenter's circle of friends.

One of these was Tom Maguire, a photographer and poet of poor Irish Catholic parentage. He had established a Leeds branch of the SDF in 1884, when he was only seventeen, but the following year transferred his allegiance to the Socialist League. By October 1885 the League had sixteen members in Leeds, most of whom were later to become close friends of Isabella and Bessie.[3] In this early period, however, the Ford sisters do not appear to have been involved in the Leeds socialist movement. Their contact with socialism was still confined to the circles of radical, middle-class intellectuals who gathered around the Fellowship in London and Edward Carpenter in Yorkshire.

Carpenter was busy helping working-class socialists in Sheffield to carry out propaganda work, but he was also keen to change his personal life to reflect his new ideas. In 1883, therefore, he moved into a cottage at Millthorpe, near Sheffield, where he intended to live a simple life, based on manual labour and close to nature. In doing so he was following the example of many other middle-class intellectuals who were critical of materialism and urban values and who went to live in rural cottages or farming communities. Carpenter's friend Henry Salt, an ex-Etonian schoolmaster, and his wife Kate followed him to Millthorpe and rented a cottage nearby. Isabella had also long been attracted by the idea of living a new way of life and began to explore the possibility of forming a farm-based community at Adel. In the 1890s she submitted plans to Parker and Unwin, architects who pioneered the Garden City movement, for a community hall to be built on the site, but nothing came of the idea.[4]

Instead she spent many hours at Millthorpe, which became a 'social centre for socialists, anarchists, mystics and free thinkers'.[5] Here she could discuss the latest socialist ideas and explore more fully her interest in the social position of women. In this period, Isabella and Emily both expressed their ideas about 'the woman question' through fiction; they were concerned to explore the economic basis of women's oppression and were

[3]See E. P. Thompson, 'Homage to Tom Maguire', in A. Briggs and J. Saville, eds. *Essays in Labour History*, vol. i (Macmillan, 1960).
[4]I am grateful to Bill Berrett, Dept. of Civil Engineering, Leeds Univ., for this reference.
[5]S. Rowbotham and J. Weeks, *Socialism and the New Life: The Personal and Sexual Politics of Edward Carpenter and Havelock Ellis* (Pluto Press, 1977).

critical of a society in which women were forced to marry because they had
no means of support. The two sisters looked to paid work as a way out for
women. It would give them a purpose in life, as well as economic independence, although this was not to be seen as incompatible with marriage. In her
plays, Emily was also critical of contemporary definitions of masculinity
and femininity, and her female characters challenge, in humorous ways, the
equation of science and rational argument with the masculine mind.[6]

It was also at Millthorpe that Isabella formed a close friendship with
Olive Schreiner, the South African author of the feminist novel *Story of an
African Farm*, who lived in England during the 1880s. The two women
shared a common interest in exploring the interrelationship between personal and political life, and Isabella was particularly influenced by Olive
Schreiner's argument that 'women's oppressive situation was most obvi-
ously experienced in relationships, and that both men and women were
active in its perpetuation'.[7] She was to express these views most vividly in
her later writings on women and socialism. (eg ?)

Along with many other middle-class women socialists, they found it easy
to become friends with Edward Carpenter. They were attracted by his
rejection of conventional definitions of masculinity and his attempt to look
at the world through women's eyes; after reading one of his books in the
1890s, Isabella wrote to tell Carpenter that it 'makes the world seem so
much more beautiful . . . I believe you were a woman in some other
incarnation! . . . goodbye dear, re-incarnated woman friend.'[8] On the other
hand both Isabella and Olive Schreiner were aware that he had shortcom-
ings in relation to women and claimed that, although he could be close to
his female friends, he 'did not understand them'.

They also suffered from his unpredictability as a host. Isabella told Henry
Salt that once, when Edward 'had pressed her, rather against her convenience, to pay him a week-end visit, he announced calmly next morning
that he was going out for the day with a friend, and she was thus left to
spend a pious Sunday in solitary meditation'.[9] But such occasional disappointments were far outweighed by the stimulating company and relaxing
atmosphere of Millthorpe. Isabella spent some of the happiest times of her
life there, and when Carpenter finally moved in 1922 she wrote to tell him
that she felt 'sorry it is over – very. My 1st visit to you was in Albert's days
& Alice was there & how happy I was. It was all so wonderful . . .'.[10]

[6]I. O. Ford, *Miss Blake of Monkshalton* (John Murray, 1890); E. S. Ford, *Rejected Addresses:
An Episode* (Leeds: 1882); id., *Careers: A Comedy* (Leeds, 1883).

[7]L. Stanley, 'Olive Schreiner: New Women, Free Women, All Women', in D. Spender,
ed., *Feminist Theorists* (Women's Press, 1983), p. 232.

[8] Letter from Isabella Ford to Edward Carpenter, 28 Jan. –, Carpenter Coll. Sheffield City
Ref. Lib.

[9]H. Salt, 'Edward Carpenter', in G. Beith, ed., *Edward Carpenter: An Appreciation* (Geo
Allen & Unwin, 1931), pp. 188, 190.

[10]Letter from Isabella Ford to Edward Carpenter, 15 Jan. 1922. Alice was one of Carpenter's
sisters. Carpenter Coll.

Isabella moved easily between different friendship circles. At Millthorpe and Bloomsbury there were her unconventional socialist friends, experimenting with the possibility of living a new way of life based on greater freedom in personal and sexual relationships. At Adel Grange, however, she was still in contact with more conventional radical liberals who held 'advanced views' on women's rights and social and political reform. As we have seen, these included many visitors from abroad. The Ford and Pease families had strong links with American Quakers involved in anti-slavery and women's rights campaigns. One of these, the American suffragist Susan B. Antony, stayed at the Grange for a week in October 1883 with her cousin Fannie Dickinson. Her diary provides a rare glimpse of social life at Adel when Hannah Ford was still alive. Susan Antony did not meet Isabella and Bessie on this occasion, for they were in London, but she was introduced to local women's rights activists who were invited to dinner. They included Emily's friends Mrs Priestman Tanner, a member of the Ladies' National Association and the sister-in-law of John Bright; Alice Scatcherd, a suffragist from Morley with radical views; and Miss Carbutt, a Poor Law guardian. During the day Hannah took Susan Antony to a Liberal Party conference in Leeds and to Howarth, the home of the Brontë sisters. On 21 October she engaged in a 'spiritualism exercise' at Adel and the next day accompanied Hannah to a conference of the LNA in Birmingham.[11]

Europeans fighting for more representative, popularly based governments were also welcomed to the homes of Hannah Ford and her cousins. Among the more unconventional visitors to Adel were the Russian anarchist exiles, Stepniak and Kropotkin. Stepniak came to the Grange more frequently than the others and Emily thought that he was 'the most lovable of them all'. She recalled an afternoon walk when Stepniak argued that 'you must pay no attention to the individual, but must sacrifice him to the mass. We had contrary opinions on this subject, and were both deeply interested . . . when we returned I felt somewhat of a wreck, and when we got inside the house I immediately ordered tea and sank into an armchair. He sat down opposite . . . and said . . . "Now I want you to give me your opinion on the Christian religion in all its phases, from the very beginning to the present moment!" I feebly suggested that tea might come first!'[12]

All these visitors to Adel, and her radical friends in London and Yorkshire, exposed Isabella to a wide variety of political ideas and encouraged her to question established political and social beliefs. On the other hand, her contacts were still largely confined to men and women from the same closely knit group of well-educated and cultured middle-class families who based their ideas on wide reading and involvement in reform campaigns. At

[11]Susan B. Antony's Diary, 17–22 Oct., Lib. of Congress, Washington, DC. I am grateful to Gail Malmgreen for this reference.
[12]E. S. Ford, typescript, MSS 371/6, Ford Family Papers, Brotherton Lib., Leeds Univ.

the age of thirty, however, Isabella took a step that was to broaden her circle of friends and to change the direction of her life: she became involved in a far more practical way in the Leeds labour movement and was brought into closer contact with men and women from the working class.

Early in 1885 Isabella was persuaded by her mother's friend Emma Paterson, president of the Women's Protective and Provident League (WPPL), to become involved with the Tailoresses' Society that had recently been formed in Leeds. At the first meeting, helped by a women's rights' friend Mrs J. Marshall, she provided entertainment by singing and playing the piano. She also found the courage to stand up and deliver a short speech in which she argued that if music and business were combined, members might be persuaded to attend meetings more regularly, a philosophy which remained central to her later ideas on how best to organize women.[13]

Isabella carried on attending meetings throughout the year and drew closer to two members of the Leeds Trades Council, John Judge of the Boot and Shoe Makers' Union and John Bune of the Brushmakers' Society, both active supporters of the Liberal Party. As president and secretary, respectively, of the Trades Council they turned up at meetings of the Tailoresses' Society to give advice and support. Their own trade unions catered exclusively for male skilled workers, a pattern that predominated in the organized labour movement. The two men were willing, however, to help all-female societies whose emphasis on friendly benefits and cautious approach to industrial relations paralleled the concerns of their own organizations. John Bune became a particularly close friend of Isabella and supported all her later efforts to organize tailoresses.

The Leeds Tailoresses' Society was only one of many small, all-female societies formed in the provinces in the 1880s under the auspices of the WPPL. Emma Paterson hoped to encourage middle-class men and women to collaborate with skilled male trade-unionists in building up these societies so that the employment conditions of female workers could be improved. Isabella's own involvement in this movement arose almost naturally from her practical experience in the night-school for working girls, which had brought her much closer than many of her contemporaries to working women. Emily claimed that 'this constant intimacy with girls of our own age, but brought up in such different circumstances, has been an enormous help in life to us towards understanding others so differently placed and endearing them deeply to ourselves . . . we sometimes visited the girls at their work or in their homes and so became intimate with their manner of life, and all this helped as a training for her [Isabella] in her later social work.'[14]

Hannah Ford also had an important influence on her youngest daughter's

[13] *Women's Union Journal*, July 1885.
[14] E. S. Ford, 'I. O. Ford', MSS 371/3, Ford Family Papers.

trade union work. She took an interest in the conditions of employment of women workers at a time when it was more usual for members of her class to be concerned with the health, family life, and morality of working-class women. She subscribed to the *Women's Union Journal* and the *Beehive*, both avidly read by Isabella, who later recalled that 'in that paper [*The Beehive*] I saw that notice was taken of working women's industrial lives. In those days nothing was heard about women's wages in the papers!'[15] Hannah was also unwilling to see philanthropy as a solution for working women's problems and encouraged her daughter to look on trade union organization as offering a real possibility for change in employment conditions.

Isabella regularly attended meetings of the Tailoresses' Society, but was still too shy to take a very prominent part in public affairs. Towards the end of 1885 she had to withdraw from organizing work after suffering an accident to her shoulder when she was out riding with her mother in the pony carriage.[16] The death of her mother in the New Year was yet another personal blow, causing Isabella to give up her outside activities for a time. While she was still in mourning the Tailoresses' Society finally dissolved, but John Bune and the few surviving members acknowledged the contribution that she had made when they sent condolences on her bereavement.

After Hannah's death the three youngest sisters continued to live at the Grange, supported for the rest of their lives by the capital left by their parents. Bessie took charge of the day-to-day running of the household. Isabella, on the other hand, enjoyed supervising the farm and gained a considerable knowledge of agricultural methods. Years later she was confident enough to take part in a controversy about the best method of feeding milking cows. Her letter to the *Labour Leader* on the subject reveals not only Isabella's farming expertise, but also the way in which all areas of her life were guided by a strong moral code.

> Neither I nor our farm man can agree with all Mr Hicks says about the advantages of keeping milking cows indoors. We have both had practical experience of cow-keeping for over twenty years . . . and we supply many of our neighbours with milk . . . We find that when the cows are out of doors day and night during the summer months they give more milk, and better milk, than in the winter, when they are stall fed. They have a meal of oil cake and hay every day; in the summer the rest of their food is grass . . . we run our cows for use and profit, not for ornament, and we all are glad to find that the best economic treatment of our cows is also our best course morally. Morals certainly pay, even in farming![17]

Household affairs, while time-consuming, were not enough to satisfy Isabella's need to do something useful. Within two years of her mother's

[15] I. O. Ford, 'Why Women Should Be Socialists', *Labour Leader* (*LL*), 1 May 1913.
[16] Letter from Edward Carpenter to Walt Whitman, 23 Oct. 1885, Feinberg Coll., Lib. of Congress, Washington, DC.
[17] *LL* 25 Aug. 1905.

death she was active once again in the two causes which were to dominate the rest of her life, women's rights and the organization of female workers. It was in 1888 that she made her first major speech, at the opening of the Stanningley and Farsley Liberal Club which was part of a national network. In these early days, Isabella was clearly plagued with nerves. Speaking on the subject of women's suffrage, in the context that nothing could be truly national if women were not included, 'she referred to a report of a shipwreck which stated that "twenty one souls and one woman were saved". When her audience laughed at this Miss Ford gripped the table, lost the thread of her speech and sat down trembling.'[18] But despite her initial nervousness, Isabella's confidence soon grew. In July 1888 she took the initiative to establish the Workwomen's Society, a union for women workers. She had retained her contacts with the WPPL and asked its new secretary, Clementina Black, to speak at the society's founding meeting.[19]

The appearance of the Workwomen's Society was a timely one, for the pattern of women's employment in Leeds was about to change dramatically. Seven years earlier, at the time of the 1881 census, just over 18 per cent of the town's female labour force worked in the wool and worsted mills. A further 6.7 per cent, or 2,740 women, were employed in the tailoring trade, working either in small workshops or in their own homes, where they often assisted male relatives. In the late 1880s the rapid growth of ready-made tailoring was to transform women's experience of work as they increasingly found employment in large, purpose-built factories employing between 100 and 2,000 workers. Thirty-five such factories were established in the short period 1887–91. Young single women flocked into Leeds from neighbouring towns and villages in the hope of finding employment as machinists or hand finishers. Inside finishers could not keep pace with the output from the power-driven machines and therefore homeworkers, who were usually married women, were also taken on in larger numbers to finish garments. By 1891 at least 10,000 women, comprising 20 per cent of all female workers in the town, were employed in the tailoring trade.[20]

The reaction of members of the women's rights movement to these changes was a varied one. Most were primarily concerned with the moral and social problems that could arise from large numbers of penniless, homeless girls coming into the town. Helen Cordelia Ford was typical of

---

[18] E. E. Crossley, 'Isabella O. Ford: Suffragist, Trade Unionist and Socialist', *Leeds Weekly Citizen*, 28 June 1929.

[19] E. Mappen, *Helping Women at Work: The Women's Industrial Council, 1889–1914* (Hutchinson, 1985), Introd. The daughter of a Brighton Solicitor, Clementina Black was two years older than Isabella and shared her interest in writing fiction as well as in organizing women workers. She joined the WTUA in 1889 and was active in the Fabian Society.

[20] Calculated from the Occupational Census for Leeds, 1881 and 1891. For a description of tailoring in Leeds, see C. Collet, 'Women's Work in Leeds', *Economic Journal*, 1 (1891).

many in directing her efforts to providing temporary accommodation for such girls. She became a working associate of the Leeds Ladies' Association for the Protection of Friendless Girls and a committee member of the Girls' Night Shelter, both of which were established under the auspices of the Yorkshire Ladies' Council of Education (YLCE).[21] Isabella was more interested in employment conditions and trade union organization, an approach that was not acceptable to the majority of her contemporaries in the women's rights' movement. She did have the support, however, of her two sisters and a close friend, Diana Goodall, a fellow Quaker and member of the Women's Liberal Association, who worked in a mission in the East End of Leeds. They held a series of meetings in the hope of attracting tailoresses from the rapidly expanding factory sector into the Work-women's Society, but this proved to be an uphill task. After a year there were still only sixty members, drawn largely from two firms, Gaunt & Hudson's and Buckley's.

This failure to persuade more women to organize, coupled with the indifference or outright hostility shown by skilled male trade-unionists in Leeds towards the plight of female workers, made Isabella increasingly disillusioned in the late 1880s with trade-unionism as a whole. In an article written a decade later, she recalled her pessimism in these early years.

> Some unions excluded women, and others admitted them, mostly in order to prevent them from being blacklegs to men. 'The women must be got in because they undersell *us*, they injure *us*' — it was the old story of Rousseau and the sole object of women's education being to make women useful to men, over again. I was thinking of leaving the Trade Union movement altogether for the antagonism between men and women was widening and I could see no way of interesting women in the movement. Women resent this spirit of antagonism between them and men. Comradeship was the only thing, and who preached it, who understood it?[22]

Despair gave way to hope, however, as a wave of strikes in Leeds between 1888 and 1890 provided a catalyst for change; old ideas were swept away, and 'gradually' Isabella 'became aware of a stirring and lifting of the gloom'.[23] The unrest was part of a more general movement among hitherto unorganized groups to improve their wages and conditions of work. Strike actions went hand in hand with the formation of 'new unions', which were less exclusive in their membership policies than the craft societies and were often led by socialists. In catering for less-skilled workers who lacked a strong bargaining position, the newer unions set out to gain public sympathy and to raise funds to support their members' claims. Two London

---

[21]See the reports of both organizations in the YLCE papers, Leeds City Archives.
[22]J. Clayton, ed., *Why I Joined the Independent Labour Party: Some Plain Statements* (Leeds: ILP, c.1896), p. 5.
[23]Ibid.

disputes, the match girls' strike of 1888 and the dock strike of 1889, captured the public's imagination and came to symbolize the new mood in the labour movement. But similar actions also took place in all the major provincial centres.

The dispute which marked the beginning of Isabella's involvement in labour unrest took place at Messrs J. Wilson & Sons, woollen manufacturers, in October 1888, when 200 female weavers went out on strike to protest against the firm's system of fining and its recent proposal to change the prices paid for completed 'cuts'. After reading adverse reports in the press, Isabella was determined to find out about the strike from the weavers themselves. On hearing their side of the story she decided to stay and help.[24]

Her first task was to arrange for members of the General Union of Textile Workers' (GUTW)[25] and the Trades Council to speak to the women. Ben Turner and Allen Gee came on behalf of the union. Although Isabella was still somewhat nervous about speaking in public, they 'urged her on with a kindly word, the latter saying to her, "Just get up. Don't much mind what you are going to say, and it will be all right." Almost terrified she got up to speak, found that she had something to say, and went home with an excited enthusiasm for the cause of women.'[26] Isabella also gave financial assistance to the strikers, a practice that was to continue throughout the long years of her support for the labour movement. It was reported in the *Leeds Daily News* that 'Miss Ford, a Leeds lady, has offered £50 a week while the strike lasts.' The reporter's scathing comment was that 'this must be taken *cum grano salis*'.[27]

On this occasion the weavers were successful in their attempt to abolish fines and they all joined the local branch of the GUTW. The dispute also marked the beginning of Isabella's long association with the union, and her lifelong friendship with one of its leaders, Ben Turner, who shared her interest in poetry and Yorkshire dialect. Turner lived in Leeds during the period of labour unrest, formed a close relationship with local socialists, and later played an important part in the struggle for independent labour politics in the area.

The weavers' dispute may have been Isabella's first experience of a strike, but it was by no means the last. As unrest mounted among less skilled male and female workers she was repeatedly called on to address meetings, and her reputation as a speaker began to grow in the local labour movement. Early in 1889 she took part in another dispute involving female textile

[24] *Annual Report* of the WTUL for 1889, p. 10.

[25] The name General Union of Textile Workers will be used throughout the text when reference is made to the organization of wool and worsted workers, but the title was not officially adopted until 1912.

[26] *Yorkshire Evening Post*, 15 July 1924.

[27] *Leeds Daily News* (LDN), 19 Sept. 1888.

workers, this time at nearby Alverthorpe, where 140 female weavers had come out on strike against reductions in the piece rates. Isabella, Bessie, Emily, and Alice Scatcherd turned up with Turner and Gee to help the strikers, donating £35 to the strike fund. Isabella contacted Clementina Black, who appealed through the press for more public support.[28] Isabella also persuaded the *Leeds Mercury* to run a series of articles on the work and wages of textile workers, which gave the women extra publicity and won them more financial support. The money raised helped to ensure the strike's success, but it was more difficult to sustain union organization. When Isabella spoke to a meeting of weavers at Wilson's in July she found that many had already left the union and had to remind them that without greater unity progress was impossible. The need for collective action was a recurrent theme in Isabella's speeches to meetings of textile workers; recounting her experiences in Wilson's strike to a meeting in Lower Wortley, she claimed that the lack of trade union organization had made them 'like sheep without a shepherd'.[29]

In this early period of labour unrest Isabella was still involved in Liberal politics, and in February 1889 spoke at a meeting to establish a Leeds branch of the Women's Liberal Association. She concentrated on women's rights issues, noting that even among her own friends there was ignorance of the necessity of properly understanding the municipal vote. She abhorred the view that women should merely be home dwellers, with no rights beyond their own threshold, and argued that a woman's role as an educator made her more of a citizen than a man. The only remark which reflected her current involvement in the labour movement was when she urged women of the educated classes to associate to assist those who did not have equal advantages.[30]

But as Isabella took part in more and more disputes, involving male as well as female workers, so she formed a closer relationship with members of the Leeds Socialist League and moved further away from liberal politics. It is unclear when the Ford sisters first met members of the League. Alf Mattison claimed that it was as early as 1887 when 'I, Tom Maguire, Bill Allworthy and Frank Corkwell were deputed by the Leeds Socialist League to bespeak their interest in our local movement. We met with a cordial reception at Adel and their help was never sought in vain for the movement.'[31]

On the other hand it was almost certainly their role in the disputes which brought the Ford sisters closer to members of the League and to the movement for independent labour politics. They found that socialism raised the possibility 'that women and men should stand together as equals,

[28] *Yorkshire Factory Times* (*YFT*), 5 July 1889.
[29] Ibid., 26 July 1889. See also the meeting at Wilson's, 19 July 1889.
[30] *Women's Gazette*, 2 Feb. 1889.
[31] Alf Mattison's Diaries, Notebook B, 28 Jan. 1918, Brotherton Lib., Leeds.

in the industrial world, and even in the political world'. Isabella was attracted by the enthusiasm of Tom Maguire, Tom Paylor, and other League members for organizing all workers together, regardless of sex, race, or skill, on the basis of real comradeship. 'Trade Unionists I found, were beginning to preach that women must join unions because they were human beings. Women, it was said, were men's friends and helpers in the industrial world.'[32]

The escalating unrest gave socialists a chance to become directly involved in the struggles of working men and women, including bricklayers' labourers, gas workers, Jewish tailors, tramwaymen, and tailoresses, and their tactics began to change. Instead of preaching revolutionary doctrines on windy street corners, they turned to trade union organization and started to link industrial grievances with propaganda for independent labour politics.[33] The three Ford sisters took part with League members in disputes among less-skilled male workers; Emily was a member of the committee formed to help tramwaymen to improve their work conditions, and when the men went on strike she turned out after midnight with Isabella to give tea to those on picket duty. But it was the plight of women workers, in particular tailoresses, that had first claim on the sisters' time.

Until the period of labour unrest, owners of the largest clothing factories had received nothing but eulogies from the local press. Their five-storied buildings, depicted as being in 'renaissance' style, were described as 'palaces of industry' in which workers could enjoy dining and cloakroom facilities as well as light, well-ventilated conditions of work. The Leeds tailoresses, it was claimed, worked short hours for high wages, and this state of affairs was repeatedly contrasted with the 'sweated' conditions associated with the tailoring trade in London.[34] The image of the Leeds trade was tarnished, however, when in July 1889 the tailoresses expressed their grievances in a stream of letters to the press which claimed that employers gave a false impression of average earnings. The most common complaint was that wages were being systematically lowered by reductions in the rates paid for specific tasks and by regular deductions from weekly earnings. Tailoresses had to pay for the use of the dining rooms and other facilities, for thread, and for the power to run the sewing machines, while they were fined for lateness and damaged goods. In a typical letter, 'Underpaid' claimed that the manager of her firm 'says he has hands with 12/- but not how many have less than that. He doesn't say how much comes off for sewing, how long they sit idle, or that they are busy only seven months in the year.'[35]

[32]Clayton, ed., *Why I Joined the ILP*, p. 5.
[33]T. Woodhouse, 'The Working Class', in D. Fraser, ed., *A History of Modern Leeds* (Manchester: MUP, 1980).
[34]See e.g. *Leeds Mercury* (*LM*), 10 Jan. 1889 and *Bradford Observer*, 12 June 1888. For the growth of ready-made clothing in Leeds, see J. Thomas, *A History of the Leeds Clothing Industry*, Yorkshire Bulletin of Economic and Social Research, Occasional Papers no. 1, 1955.
[35]*Leeds Express*, 19 July 1889.

Until now members of the Workwomen's Society had adopted a cautious approach to industrial relations. Months earlier they had rejected Isabella's suggestion that the rules should be changed to permit strike action, arguing that they were well treated by their firms and might become subject to 'the special oversight of the foremen'.[36] As clothing workers openly began to express their discontent, Isabella was encouraged to try again. After consulting with Ben Turner and Tom Paylor she decided that a new women's organization, based on trade union principles, should be launched at a mass meeting to be held in October.

When plans for the meeting were well advanced Isabella took a break from organizing work. In September she joined Helen Cordelia Ford in accompanying fifteen girls from the Mill Hill night-school to London for a five-day holiday. They visited all the famous sights, including the People's Palace, the Tower of London, and the Kensington Museum. Isabella's nephews, Ford and Charles Smith, went with them to a Spanish exhibition and joined them for tea in Isabella's rooms. Her London friends Millicent Fawcett, Elizabeth Garrett Anderson, and members of the Women's Trade Union League also helped to entertain the group.[37]

Isabella arrived back in Leeds at the end of September to find that discontent in the tailoring trade was growing. The meeting to establish a Tailoresses' Union, held on 16 October, took place in a charged atmosphere. A large audience turned up to hear Clementina Black urge tailoresses to take heart from the London dock strike, where some of the worst paid, least skilled workmen had gained a victory by 'orderly combination'. Not only had their wages improved, but also 'the temper and spirit with which they were now looked upon by their employers and other classes'. Isabella's own speech also emphasized the psychological as well as the material benefits of trade unionism. She was followed by James Sweeney of the Socialist League, a boot-and-shoe worker, who moved a resolution to form 'a union among women and girls to improve the rate of wages and the conditions of labour'. Tom Maguire seconded with a stirring speech, and the resolution was carried unanimously.[38]

Only three days after this meeting, the newly formed Tailoresses' Union was unexpectedly faced with its first strike when 700 machinists employed by Messrs Arthur & Co. left work to obtain a reduction in the charge made for power which amounted to $1d$ in every shilling earned. Young women crowded into the streets uncertain what to do; according to Ben Turner, they 'immediately went to Miss Goodall to ask her to get Miss Ford to come down and advise them how to proceed. This Miss Goodall did, and

[36] *YFT* 21 Oct. 1889.
[37] H. C. Ford, *Short Diaries of Two Visits to London, May 1887 and September 1889* (Leeds, 1889), p. 26.
[38] *YFT* 18 Oct. 1889.

by noon she [Isabella Ford] was in Victoria Square, at the meeting held there, and also at the meeting held in the People's Hall in the afternoon of that date.'[39]

Having organized a strike committee – composed largely of tailoresses but with herself as secretary – Isabella then set out to refute statements made by the firm's manager that the tailoresses at Arthur's were paid high wages and that deductions were only made to simplify accounts. With Diana Goodall's help she compiled a list of wages, comparing Arthur's with two other firms that did not charge so much for power, and sent these to the press. The two women subsequently wrote a letter to the local newspapers which reminded the public that 'the strike is . . . solely about the power charge. No other firms charge above $\frac{1}{2}d$'.[40] Arguments about the strike were conducted very much in the public eye as management, workers, strike leaders, and journalists wrote letters and articles to the press throughout the dispute. Both sides aimed to get public support, but particularly the tailoresses as they needed money to remain on strike.

Some enterprising girls had already gone among the crowds at early meetings to collect money. The strike committee subsequently made this more systematic by distributing official collection boxes to be handed round at meetings or on visits to mills and factories. The gas workers, led by the socialist Walt Wood, were the most generous; they also helped the girls to guard the sheets spread out for the same purpose at local football grounds. Isabella widened the appeal for funds by contacting the new secretary of the Women's Trade Union League, Frances Routledge, who then wrote to the *Standard* to ask for aid. Over £400 was collected from fellow workers and a further £250 from public donations, which were distributed by the committee.[41]

The strike was unusual in attracting support both from the Liberal-dominated Trades Council and from socialists, although it was Isabella and members of the Socialist League who gave the most energetic leadership. At the many meetings held during the day and in the evening, some of which attracted audiences of 2,000, the inspiring speeches of Tom Maguire, James Sweeney, and Tom Paylor kept up the morale of the strikers. They urged workers from other firms to show unity and to join in the dispute. At the beginning of the strike Isabella and the socialists persuaded Jewish workers at a meeting in the Leylands to pass a resolution pledging not to do the work of the girls on strike. Tailoresses in other factories expressed their support but were wary of going on strike so close to the slack season, and the dispute remained a battle of attrition between workers and management in just one firm.

[39]Ibid., 1 Nov. 1889.
[40]*LDN* 29 Oct. 1889, *LM* 30 Oct. 1889.
[41]*Report of Strikes and Lockouts, 1889* (PP, lxiii, 1890), p. 126.

For the first two weeks there was boundless enthusiasm for the strike, and spirits were high when the manager agreed to see a deputation on 7 November. Diana Goodall, who accompanied the tailoresses, found that the manager, far from being conciliatory, was in a vindictive mood.[42] Taking down their names, he threatened that all those who had taken a prominent part in the dispute would be dismissed unless they signed a statement that allegations made about low wages were untrue. The manager clearly felt that he had the upper hand. He had been able to get uncompleted work finished by workshop and homeworkers just before the slack season began, while the skilled male cutters at Arthur's had shown no inclination to join the women on strike. In the eyes of the firm the dispute was already over by 7 November. As far as the committee was concerned, it was to last another seven weeks.

Isabella was tireless in giving help to the strikers, although the pressures on her increased when Bessie fell seriously ill and did not recover for several months. Ben Turner claimed that 'every day she has been on the scene of action, busy with pen and brain, ready to write out the names of the girls desirous of joining the Union, or ready to interview Mr Cobb, the manager for Messers Arthurs, as she has done on two or three occasions. The wonder is how she bears the burden of the struggle. Those who work with her wonder at this, and fervently hope no reaction will set in.'[43]

A further strain was created when Isabella found herself involved in a controversy between socialists and members of the Trades Council which resulted in the socialists withdrawing from active participation in the strike. The immediate cause of the controversy was a difference of opinion about how best to conduct the strike, but its roots lay in the political differences between the two groups. The strike was one event among many which convinced the socialists that they could not work with the Trades Council. After the gas dispute of 1890 they formed an alternative body, the York-shire Labour Council, to pursue their plans for independent labour rep-resentation in local and national government.

Isabella's response to the crisis was tactful. Refusing to comment on the split in any detail, she told one press reporter that 'the socialists found it better for one party to have the matter in hand and they withdrew from taking an active part'.[44] Although her own political sympathies lay with the socialists, she was concerned that the tailoresses should keep their links with the mainstream labour movement and with supportive members of the Trades Council such as John Bune. The role of conciliator suited Isabella's temperament and was one that she was to play often in subsequent years. Never afraid to take up controversial issues, in particular where women

[42]*YFT* 15 Nov. 1889.
[43]*YFT* 1 Nov. 1889.
[44]*Leeds Express*, 20 Nov. 1889.

workers were concerned, she sought none the less to reconcile conflicting views when labour unity appeared threatened.

The last few weeks of the strike were depressing. Many girls began to drift back to work, and the strike committee concentrated on raising funds for the relief of those still on strike and finding them alternative employment. By 4 December 400 tailoresses had returned to work at Arthur's, and the last relief payment was made on 28 December. Isabella had to accept defeat, but looking on the bright side commented that it was 'fine that 350 girls should remain true for six weeks'.[45]

Indeed, the strike did have some positive results, highlighting the problems faced by low-paid women workers and exposing their conditions of employment to public scrutiny. It also stimulated the development of trade-unionism among other groups in the tailoring trade; in November the Wholesale Clothiers' Operatives' Union (WCOU) was formed to cater for male cutters and pressers in the factories, while the Jewish Tailors', Pressers', and Machinists' Union, which had been demoralized by defeat in a dispute in 1888, now experienced a revival.

The dispute was also important for Isabella personally. It pushed her into the public gaze, and from then on she was acknowledged in the West Riding as the leading expert on women's work conditions. Her involvement in organizing women throughout 1889 meant that she was often approached by the local press to give her opinion about women's work and trade union organization; an article on 'Our Workgirls', published on 21 October 1889 in the *Leeds Daily News*, was based on information supplied by Isabella, who was described as an 'earnest and indefatigable worker'. The tailoresses' strike brought Isabella even greater publicity. In November her portrait appeared for the first time in the *Yorkshire Factory Times*. She is pictured leaning on the arm of a chair in a characteristically thoughtful mood, wearing simple and unostentatious clothing. Her hair is parted in the middle and pulled back to reveal a face full of character rather than conventional beauty. The portrait was accompanied by a biographical sketch written by Ben Turner. Explaining that her involvement in women's trade-unionism had arisen from her work in the night-school and from her parents' interest in social and political reform campaigns, he went on to describe her role in the strike and eulogized her contribution to the labour movement.

No flattery is needed in speaking of the good work done by the Ford family. All that Miss Isabella has done has been done through a sincere desire to benefit the workers . . . It is enough for us to state that in her the Leeds, aye, the Yorkshire workers have a valuable friend. The women workers of Yorkshire have in her a sister who can feel for them, who can sympathise with them, who can advise

[45]*YFT* 29 Nov. 1889.

them, and who is always willing to assist them if a desire is shown on their part to assist themselves.[46]

Turner's sketch established a version of Isabella's life which was to be repeated again and again in future biographies and obituaries. He not only laid down a chronology of so-called important events, but also provided an idealized view of her personality and motivation for helping others which persisted for the rest of her life. Turner was keen to distinguish Isabella from middle-class 'do-gooders' and philanthropists, but still managed to create an impression of 'saintliness', so common in biographies of middle-class women who helped the labour movement, which served to detract from their political astuteness and abilities. Isabella would have been of little help in the strike if she had turned up merely to express sympathy. Instead, she developed practical skills, such as mastering trade prices, technical, and working details, and finding out how to negotiate with management. She also learned from her experience in the strike not to take account of 'hearsay and rumour', whether from employers or workers, but to draw up 'papers containing an exact account of the condition, etc., of the home life of each worker'. Clementina Black taught her to do this 'for the purpose of deciding how the strike funds were to be divided'.[47]

These skills were useful, not only in the immediate dispute, but also in her future organizing work. The tailoresses' strike confirmed her role as a leading female trade union organizer and reinforced her commitment to the labour movement. According to Emily, 'it was then and there . . . that her decision to take the Labour side of life became final. She did not shrink from any of the disagreeableness of combat. She did not look back, but from that moment she remained faithful to her comrades.'[48] Once Isabella had taken up a cause she pursued it with enthusiasm, no matter what difficulties she encountered. She was remembered as having an 'indomitable will' and, we are told, in spite of her great sensitiveness 'she followed boldly where her convictions led her'.[49]

During the 1890s her convictions led her to commit herself to the slow, painful task of organizing women workers into trade unions and to building up support in the West Riding for independent labour politics. Her practical experience of industrial struggle ensured that by the 1890s her socialism would no longer be confined to theoretical discussions with middle-class intellectuals about how to live a new way of life, but would be directed to practical propaganda work among working-class people aimed at gaining their support for independent labour politics.

[46] *YFT* 1 Nov. 1889.
[47] *Tailor and Cutter*, 14 Nov. 1889, I. O. Ford, 'In Praise of Married Women', *LL* 2 Sept. 1904.
[48] E. S. Ford, 'I. O. Ford'.
[49] *Yorkshire Observer*, 16 July 1924.

3. Drawing of Isabella Ford from the *Yorkshire Factory Times*, 1889 (*British Library, Newspaper Library, Colindale*)

3

Pleading the Cause of Yorkshire Factory Girls, 1890–1895

There is no power so strong as combination.

Once the tailoresses' strike was over, Isabella committed all of her energies towards organizing female clothing and textile workers and carrying out propaganda work for independent labour politics in the West Riding of Yorkshire. Locally she was already acknowledged as a talented speaker and as an expert on women's work conditions. In the early 1890s her articles and lectures drew her to the attention of a much wider audience, and her reputation began to grow outside the West Riding.

Initially it was her talents as a novelist that brought Isabella public recognition. In the middle of the tailoresses' dispute her first novel, *Miss Blake of Monkshalton*, had appeared in serial form in *Murray's Magazine*. In 1890 it was published as a book and received favourable reviews. Edward Carpenter informed Whitman that the novel was 'quite a success', while Stepniak told Isabella that she had 'a fresh and most sympathetic and genuine talent as a novelist' and assured her that she would go far.[1] Spurred on by such encouragement Isabella continued to write, but fiction was pushed further into the background of her busy life as she increasingly gave priority to trade union organization.

The prolonged dispute at Arthur's had affected Isabella's health, and it was not until February 1890 that she felt well enough to resume her organizing work. More than 2,000 women had joined the Leeds Tailoresses' Union in the month after it was established, but numbers slumped to less than 200 once the excitement generated by strike action was over. Union officers now faced an uphill task in trying to convince tailoresses that they would benefit from more permanent organization. The painstaking, day-to-day organizing tasks were carried out by Isabella, the newly elected president, and a committee of women workers, many of whom had taken part in the strike at Arthur's.

[1] Letter from Edward Carpenter to Walt Whitman, 17 May 1890, Feinberg Coll., Lib. of Congress, Washington, DC; letter from Stepniak to I. O. Ford, 2 Jan. 1890, Leeds Archives.

A variety of methods were used to publicize the union and to make membership seem attractive; Isabella drew up provisions for out of work and sickness benefits, while the committee compiled a list of the rates paid for specific jobs and other useful information for members. Union officers tried to make direct contact with tailoresses, either by speaking outside factory gates during lunch breaks or by gaining access to the work-place itself. Given the hostility of managers, this was not always easy to achieve. On one occasion Isabella and Walt Wood managed to slip into Schofield's yard, only to be confronted by an irate manager. He argued that the girls earned enough wages and it was better to keep them quiet. 'Better for whom?', asked Isabella. '"For everyone"', he replied'. Isabella's defiant comment was: 'How long are they going to be kept quiet? I don't like being turned out of factories, it's not pleasant.'[2]

Business meetings were held regularly on Tuesday evenings, interspersed occasionally with more informal social events, where Isabella could be seen 'dancing and singing'.[3] Larger public meetings were also organized to give publicity to the union; Walt Wood, Ben Turner, and Tom Paylor were always willing to give their support and were often joined by members of the London-based Women's Trade Union League (WTUL). May Abraham, the League treasurer, was a frequent visitor to Leeds, while Miss Marland, a full-time organizer, regularly carried out either a week's or a fortnight's recruiting drive in the West Riding. Both women were close friends of the Ford sisters and stayed at Adel Grange when they came to Yorkshire.

The Tailoresses' Union was affiliated to the League, which had changed both its name and its policies since the death of Emma Paterson in 1886. Encouraged by the labour unrest and the willingness of more unions to take female members, the new president, Lady Dilke, argued that women could never hope to improve their conditions of work unless they co-operated with male trade-unionists and she urged them, whenever possible, to join mixed-sex organizations. She also took a more positive attitude than her predecessor towards the benefits of protective legislation for women, and during the 1890s the League actively campaigned to extend existing provisions.

The League provided an opportunity for middle-class women to give their services to the labour movement; women workers often lacked the confidence or experience to establish their own organizations, while male trade-unionists found the task of organizing women to be so difficult that they too looked for outside assistance in the shape of speakers, organizers, and general advice (see chapter 4). Members of the League may have had different political beliefs, but were able to work together through a shared concern to improve the economic position of working women and to

[2]*Yorkshire Factory Times* (*YFT*), 13 Sept. 1895.
[3]Ibid., 18 Mar. 1892.

'overcome inequalities' in their lives.[4] Their focus on the economic problems faced by female workers and their faith in trade-unionism as the most effective way to gain an improvement in conditions of employment distinguished them from contemporaries who concentrated on winning the vote or who sought to rescue women workers from moral danger.

There were times when League members could still display philanthropic attitudes, but the main thrust of their message was that women workers must organize independently. Isabella was particularly attracted by this outlook. She argued consistently that 'when the working woman does awake and desire her true salvation, she must, as all of us must, work it out for herself. All that can be done by outsiders – i.e. persons not of the proletariat class – is to help to awaken that desire, and to see that it is a desire for a true salvation, and not for some second rate form of it.'[5]

Isabella also agreed with the League's policy on co-operation between the sexes in the labour movement. The Tailoresses' Union was affiliated to the Leeds Trades Council and sent representatives to May Day rallies and other labour events. In September 1890 Isabella was made an honorary life member of the Trades Council in recognition of her role in the Tailoresses' Strike, and in the same year was also made an honorary member of the General Union of Textile Workers (GUTW).[6] Her association with the GUTW grew even stronger during the 1890s; she helped the local leaders – Ben Turner, Allan Gee, and William Drew – in their drive to gain more women members by speaking at recruiting meetings throughout the West Riding. In her speeches she drew attention not only to the low pay and poor working conditions of female weavers, but also to the way in which employers treated them with contempt, often referring to them as a 'pack of women'. At a meeting in Stanningley in July 1890 Isabella blamed women themselves for some of their problems: 'she would be frank with them, and tell them that experience had taught her that indifference played an important part in the low position they found themselves'. She had come to tell them that there was no power so strong 'as combination ... if she could get her sex to think the battle would be won'.[7]

As her involvement in the labour movement deepened, so Isabella found herself increasingly alienated from members of her own social class. Accused of 'mannish' behaviour for speaking on labour platforms and frequently greeted with the question, 'How are your strikes getting on?', she

[4]E. Mappen, *Helping Women at Work: The Women's Industrial Council, 1889–1914* (Hutchinson, 1985), p. 12. Mappen describes members of the WTUL and the WIC as social feminists because of their interest in the economic and social rights of working women. She argues that they usually wanted the vote, but were not willing to wait for it before demanding certain rights and a place in public life; p. 27 n. 1.

[5]I. O. Ford, *Industrial Women and How to Help Them* (Humanitarian League, 1901), pp. 1–2.

[6]Minutes of Leeds Trades Council, 3 Sept. 1890, Leeds Archives.

[7]Speech to Stanningley weavers, *YFT* 4 July 1890.

admitted that trade union work brought isolation.[8] It was often impossible 'to have honestly friendly relations with those on both sides of the gulf', and she joined hands with the oppressed in the realization that 'the interests of capital and labour are not identical at present. Some day they will be, but not yet.'[9]

In this context the League provided a much-needed source of friendship and support, although Isabella's feminist beliefs made her draw back from identifying too closely with all its aims and objectives. She was always prepared to defend the interests of female workers, even if this brought her into conflict with the League and with male trade-unionists. A particularly controversial issue during the 1890s was the question of married women's employment; both Lady Dilke and the leaders of the General Union of Textile Workers were critical of married women who worked for wages.[10] The GUTW was committed to increasing female membership. Its campaign took place, however, against a background of tension between men and women in the wool and worsted industry which highlighted some of the problems of mixed-sex trade-unionism for women. The onset of a depression in the industry led to short-time work, unemployment, and attempts by employers to replace male by female workers. Faced with a deterioration in wages and conditions of work, union leaders began to use married women workers as scapegoats for all the problems in the trade.

Turner and Gee were strong supporters of political equality for women, at a time when this was not a popular cause in the labour movement, but they were less willing to champion equality at the work-place or to challenge the existing sex division of labour. This encouraged them to criticize married women for causing male unemployment and led to considerable ambivalence in union policies; one moment union officials encouraged women workers to look on work as important in their lives, while at the next they urged married women to stop working.

Isabella's attitude towards married women workers was far more positive. She recognized that they usually had to work to make ends meet and argued that, far from being a problem, married women often made the best trade-unionists. She could also find no evidence that they were the cause of all the difficulties in the textile trade. On the other hand she did not want to exacerbate the antagonism that already existed between the sexes in the industry and was careful to criticize both male and female workers for their attitudes. At the Stanningley meeting in July 1890 she argued that 'men in

[8]*YFT* 5 Aug. 1892.

[9]I. O. Ford, 'Unsatisfactory Citizens', *Women's Industrial News*, Mar. 1898, p. 32.

[10]See Lady Dilke, 'Trade Unionism for Women', *New Review*, Jan. 1890 and speech at Bradford, *YFT* 17 Oct. 1890. For a discussion of the attitudes of Turner and Gee, see J. Bornat, 'Lost Leaders: Women, Trade Unionism and the Case of the General Union of Textile Workers', in A. John, ed., *Unequal Opportunities: Women's Employment in England, 1800–1918* (Oxford: Blackwell, 1986).

the old time earned enough to keep their wives at home, weavers especially; but now it took a whole family to keep the home going. Women must refuse to be "sat" on any longer – (laughter) – and must not undersell their brothers, husbands and fathers in the labour market. If a woman did exactly the same work as a man she ought to be paid the same wages.' Citing numerous examples of how employers 'grew wealthy' by cheating low-paid female workers, she concluded that 'it would only be altered when men and women were determined not to be pitted against each other'.[11]

Their differing views on married women's employment did not prevent Isabella and the leaders of the GUTW from working closely together. Isabella's conciliatory personality and the care she took to understand the fears of male workers were partly responsible for this. The depression in the wool and worsted trade and the set-backs faced by trade-unionists as a whole in the West Riding in the early 1890s also encouraged male and female organizers to forget their differences and to unite in trying to improve conditions of employment for both sexes. The last major dispute of the period of labour unrest, at Manningham Mills, Bradford, provided just such a focus for common action.

In December 1890, 5,000 textile workers refused to carry on working when they were threatened with a reduction in wages and they remained on strike for nineteen weeks. Leeds socialists were quick to lend support to their counterparts in nearby Bradford, and Isabella joined Tom Maguire, Tom Paylor, Walt Wood, and Ben Turner in addressing countless public meetings. 'Like a new Joan of Arc', she walked through the sleet and snow with the girls on strike, often taking insults from the crowds who lined the streets. With Bessie's help she served a breakfast of tea and bread and butter to the striking workers, and the two sisters used their contacts with League members in London to help raise money, as well as giving generously themselves.[12] The dispute gave Isabella furthur insights into the hardships faced by women workers. In later years she told a newspaper reporter: 'I have never felt absolute hunger . . . but these girls did. We found some of them desperate with hunger, and supplied a breakfast of tea and bread and butter every morning. One poor girl with a drunken father and an invalid sister collected 10s. and ran away with it. To her it represented wealth, and I was only sorry there was not more in the box. She had awakened to the right to possess something.'[13]

The textile workers were not successful in gaining their demands, but their defeat made Isabella more determined than ever to draw attention to the conditions under which women workers were employed. She began to give lectures based on her experiences as a trade union organizer to a variety

[11] *YFT* 4 July 1890.

[12] *YFT* 20 Feb. 1891; *New Leader*, 25 July 1924; E. E. Crossley, 'Isabella O. Ford: Suffragist, Trade Unionist and Socialist', *Leeds Weekly Citizen* (*LWC*), 28 June 1929.

[13] 'Some Eminent Trade Unionists, No. 8 Miss Isabella Ford', *LWC* 12 June 1914.

of groups outside the West Riding, and in doing so started to acquire a national reputation. In September 1892, while on holiday in London with nine members of the Tailoresses' Union, she spoke to a meeting of the Women's Trade Union League on the subject of women factory inspectors. A month later she travelled to Bristol to give a paper at the Annual Conference of the National Union of Women Workers (NUWW). The NUWW was established in 1874, under the trusteeship of Millicent Fawcett, to form trade unions and benefit funds for women and to monitor legislation affecting female employment. These original aims were later modified, with members seeking to promote 'the social, moral and religious welfare of women in general'.[14] In the early 1890s, however, the NUWW still showed an interest in work conditions, the subject of Isabella's paper.

At this stage Isabella was most familiar to her audience as 'a successful literary worker', but conference papers and articles were soon to make her better known as a leading trade union organizer. A report of the NUWW conference singled her out as one of 'the very remarkable speakers' whose paper 'deservedly attracted a good deal of attention . . . who could listen without being deeply stirred to the impassioned eloquence of Miss Isabella Ford pleading the cause of the poor factory girls amongst whom she lives and works?'[15]

The audience may have been moved by what Isabella had to say, but were less convinced by her emphasis on the need for trade union organization. The methods preferred by the NUWW can be illustrated by the campaign of the Leeds branch in the early 1890s to obtain seats for shop assistants. The active members, including Helen Cordelia Ford, organized a petition and then lobbied individual employers. There was no attempt, however, to encourage collective action by the women workers themselves. None the less, the interest taken by the NUWW in work conditions and social questions meant that women involved in the labour movement felt some sympathy with its aims. Isabella, for instance, often accompanied her sister-in-law to meetings of the Leeds branch, and chaired a session on the training of Christian workers at an NUWW conference held in the city in November 1893.[16]

Members of the NUWW and the WTUL were able to work together, despite their different approaches, because their main aim was to improve conditions of employment rather than to rescue individual female workers. One issue which involved both these groups was the campaign for female factory inspectors. An impetus was given to the movement in 1892 when a number of professional women were appointed by the Royal Commission

[14] P. Levine, *Victorian Feminism, 1850–1900* (Hutchinson, 1987), p. 91.
[15] *Shafts*, 1/3 (19 Nov. 1892).
[16] Minute Book of the Leeds branch of the NUWW, 1892–9; Official Handbook for Central Conference of Women Workers, Leeds, 7–10 Nov. 1893; papers, YLCE Leeds Archives.

on Labour to investigate female work conditions. This encouraged the WTUL to send a deputation on the subject to Asquith, the Home Secretary, early in 1893. Isabella ensured that the Leeds Tailoresses' Union sent a resolution in support of the deputation and joined Helen Cordelia in addressing numerous meetings in Leeds to explain why female factory inspectors were needed.

Isabella's views were developed more fully in an article published in March. She was particularly concerned about the embarrassment women suffered when they had to report inadequate sanitary arrangements to male inspectors; if the latter did inspect sanitary facilities 'the jokes and laughter are horrible . . . you cannot expect any high moral conduct from women over whom a watch is kept by a male overseer to see that they do not visit the lavatories too frequently (they are sometimes fined); such a watch may be necessary, for some of these women have scant sense of decency; but it ought to be kept by women over women.'[17] Arguing that women inspectors would be more likely than men to sympathize with the needs of female workers and to act impartially when given a job to do, Isabella claimed that they would be less likely to announce their visits beforehand and therefore there would be no time to cover up abuses. Her belief that women would behave differently from men when called on to play a role in public life reflected views that were widespread in the women's movement.

The first two female factory inspectors, May Abraham and Mary Paterson, were finally appointed in March 1893. As far as Isabella was concerned, this victory was only a beginning: 'in unorganized trades, like the laundry trade, the law and the inspector still have little power to help the worker – the women having no organization and no vote, have no way of expressing their opinion clearly and forcibly. Legislation is largely the result of organization – and legislation, in its turn, strengthens the hand of the unionists.'[18] This holistic approach to the needs of the woman worker, linking strong trade-unionism with women's suffrage and legislation, formed the basis of Isabella's arguments over the next three decades. On the other hand, she did shift the emphasis of her work and ideas in different periods of her life.

During the 1890s, trade union organization took priority; Isabella not only undertook practical organizing work in the West Riding, but also spoke to meetings of trade-unionists and women's groups on the value of trade-unionism for women. She was keen to address middle-class audiences as it meant they would become more aware of the problems faced by the female industrial worker. When she spent a month between May and June of 1893 in London, therefore, she opened a debate at the Pioneer Club on

[17] I. O. Ford, 'Women Inspectors of Factories and Workshops', *Woman's Herald*, 16 Mar. 1893, p. 61.
[18] Id., *Women as Factory Inspectors and Certifying Surgeons* (Women's Co-operative Guild, c.1897), pp. 7–8.

'Why Should Not Women Vote' and gave two lectures for the Humanitarian League on 'Women's Wages'. At the second meeting, presided over
by Clementina Black, Isabella urged the audience not to try and 'reclaim
women', but to look for the social causes of their industrial problems and to
seek scientific methods to deal with them.[19]

The ideas expressed in these lectures provided the basis for articles and
pamphlets; from 1893 onwards Isabella began to publish regularly, which
gave even greater publicity to her views. 'Industrial Conditions Affecting
Women of the Working Classes' appeared in the *Yorkshire Factory Times* in
March 1893, while *Women's Wages* was published as a pamphlet by the
Humanitarian League in the same year. A characteristic of her work was the
careful research undertaken before any argument was put forward. In
Women's Wages she set out to demonstrate the extent of low pay by giving a
series of case studies: 'One woman by working from 8 a.m. to 6.30 p.m.
(an hour off for dinner) in the factory, and then taking home bundles of
work to finish, and working until midnight, made a good average of 15*s* or
16*s* a week. Out of it she supported her parents, and at the end of the week
she had, when all was paid for, twopence left for personal enjoyment.'[20]

Such examples were used to underpin her main argument that low pay
was at the root of social problems. It was a waste of time, therefore, to try
and rescue women unless the cause of immorality was removed. Attacking
organized religion and philanthropists for denouncing strikes 'as if it were
in some way irreligious for women to do anything but submit to every kind
of injustice', and for teaching women that rebellion was 'unwomanly', she
urged women workers to take action collectively as the only way to achieve
an improvement in working conditions. Educated women such as herself
could only 'teach these women to rebel and not to submit,' she said. 'We
must arouse them to a better knowledge of their own worth, their own
infinite value.'[21] Scathing criticisms of philanthropists and an emphasis on
independent action by women workers were distinctive features of Isabella's writings at this time. So was her unique understanding, gained at first
hand, of the way in which women workers experienced their lives. Isabella
once said that 'it is far better . . . to understand these things from the actual
workers' own standpoint, sitting in back parlours of little inns, counting
our strike pay, listening to everyone and everything, and being taught
many things'.[22]

Her own willingness to listen to working women gave Isabella an
unusual insight into the way in which industrial work could have psychological as well as material effects on their lives.

[19]*YFT* 2 June 1893.
[20]I. O. Ford, *Women's Wages* (Humanitarian League, 1893), p. 7.
[21]Ibid., pp. 4, 15.
[22]A. J. R., ed., *Suffrage Annual and Woman's Who's Who* (Stanley Paul, 1913), pp. 243–4.

A premium is sometimes put on impropriety of conduct on the women's part by the foreman. That is, a woman who will submit or respond to his coarse jokes and language and evil behaviour, receives more work than the woman who feels and shows herself insulted by such conduct, and wishes to preserve her self respect. The pittance earned by some of these women is earned at the expense of more than only hard toil. Even when this coarseness is confined to language only, it causes deep suffering to some of the women. They feel, they know, that because they are women and therefore regarded as helpless and inferior, they are spoken to as men are not spoken to, and the sting enters their souls.[23]

She did not underestimate the practical hardships endured by women, but considered the effect produced on the general morality of the workers in same ways more important: 'the deadening and warping of their humanity, by the ordinary regulations imposed upon them in their industrial lives by most factories (with some few exceptions) good and bad alike'.[24]

The very real pleasure that Isabella experienced from being in the company of working women distinguished her from many other middle-class women involved in trade union work. Clementina Black, for example, disliked strikes and was distant in her relations with workgirls, finding their language 'vile and distasteful'. In the late 1890s, therefore, she moved away from the organization of female workers to concentrate instead on the investigation of women's conditions of employment. Joining the Women's Industrial Council she campaigned to extend protective legislation.[25] Isabella, on the other hand, could never be satisfied with the role of a social investigator alone; she wanted to be actively involved in women's day-to-day struggles and to find out about their problems 'from the inside'. Accepting that strikes brought 'great misery', she arued that they could also lead to the growth of trade union organization. This would substitute arbitration for disputes and would advance 'the moral welfare of the community'.[26] For Isabella, trade-unionism meant nothing less than a moral revolution; by fostering a sense of collective identity above individual competition, trade unions encouraged women to be comrades and to put a greater value on their own industrial worth.

Despite her emphasis on the need for strong trade-unionism, Isabella was clear that organization by itself was not enough to transform the lives of working women and must be accompanied by political change. She therefore combined her own work for trade-unionism in the West Riding with propaganda for independent labour politics. The labour unrest of 1889 had raised the possibility that socialists might be able to influence the political outlook of organized workers in Yorkshire and they took control of many

[23]I. O. Ford, *Women's Wages*, pp. 13–14.
[24]Id., *Industrial Women and How to Help Them*, p. 3.
[25]Mappen, *Helping Women at Work*, pp. 14, 17.
[26]I. O. Ford, 'Industrial Conditions Affecting Women of the Working Classes', *YFT* 17 Mar. 1893.

trades councils. In Leeds, Tom Maguire and his friend John Lincoln Mahon, a Scottish engineer, were so encouraged by these developments that they began to play down their socialist theory and to call for independent labour politics.[27] Socialist delegates to the Trades Council took every opportunity to promote an independent political stand; in July 1891, for example, Isabella reminded members of the iniquities of town councillors on the issue of fair trading and urged them to vote against such councillors in future elections.

The defeat of the textile workers at Manningham Mills gave a further impetus to the movement for independent labour politics, and labour clubs were established all over the West Riding. But the movement for independent labour politics made little headway in Leeds. Support was largely confined to members of the Gas Workers' Union, individual trade-unionists, and middle-class intellectuals such as Isabella and Bessie. The Trades Council remained committed to the Liberal Party and was alienated from socialist politics still further by the behaviour of Mahon. 'Vain, incurably quarrelsome, and given to intrigue', he stood as an independent candidate in the South Leeds by-election of 1892, against the express wishes of the Trades Council, and 'suffered a great deal of slander and physical violence'.[28] As a consequence socialists changed tactics once more and decided to work outside the council. Later in the year, Maguire, Mahon, and Mattison set up the East Hunslet Independent Labour Club as a focus for their political agitation. Six other clubs quickly followed, and in November it was agreed that they should form the Leeds Independent Labour Party.

While these developments were taking place, Isabella and Bessie were in London. Here they joined the Democratic Club, described as the home of the 'advanced Labour Party', and listened to their old friend Stepniak lecturing on 'Anarchism and Social Democracy'. As soon as they returned home at Christmas both sisters became members of the West Ward Labour Club. In common with many other middle-class women, Isabella and Bessie had initially been attracted to socialism by the writings of Whitman, Morris, and Carpenter.[29] It was their involvement in strikes among working women, however, which then confirmed their political sympathies. After her experiences in the tailoresses' strike Isabella was persuaded to give up any lingering connections with the Liberal Party:

> I found that it was quite impossible to obtain any help politically from either of the two political parties. . . . The Liberal Party was the avowed advocate of trade

[27]T. Woodhouse, 'The Working Class', in D. Fraser, ed., *A History of Modern Leeds* (Manchester: MUP, 1980).

[28]Ibid., pp. 372, 371. See also E. P. Thompson, 'Homage to Tom Maguire', In A. Briggs and J. Saville, eds, *Essays in Labour History* (Macmillan, 1960), vol. i.

[29]Katharine Conway and Enid Stacy, the Bristol socialists, were also affected by taking part in the 1889 strikes. See E. Malos, 'Bristol Women in Action, 1839–1919', in I. Bild, ed., *Bristol's Other History* (Bristol: Bristol Broadsides, 1983), p. 119.

unionism, but the Liberal employers were quite as bitter as the Conservatives against any of their female employees who dared to join a trade union . . . the insolent tone in which the working women who were daring to strike and daring to join unions were referred to showed that sex hatred, or what is even worse, 'sex contempt' on the part of men towards women, was underlying our social structure.[30]

No such 'sex contempt' appeared to exist in the Labour clubs. Recalling her first visit to Yorkshire in 1892 as a young Fabian lecturer, Katharine Bruce Glasier claimed that she had found an atmosphere 'of swift and eager welcome for every woman comrade and of settled conviction as to the women's equal rights of citizenship with men'.[31] Speaking at the opening of the West Ward Labour Club in January 1893, Isabella 'rejoiced to see women sitting there on terms of equality with men as members'. She joined the Independent Labour Party (ILP) in the same month, immediately after the founding conference in Bradford, because it stood for 'equality and opportunity for the whole race . . . women had never had such equality before'.[32]

When asked a few years later to explain why she had become a member of the ILP, Isabella recalled that she was impressed by the priority given in the manifesto to adult suffrage and to the demand that women should sit on town councils:

My last doubts were removed after a visit to a Labour Club in the Colne Valley, where the men had been giving a tea party to the women, and had poured out the tea, cut the bread and butter, and washed everything up, without any feminine help and without any accidents! A party, that included the education of men, which hitherto had been so much neglected, as well as the education of women, that gave the one such skill and dexterity, and the other wider and truer views of life, was the party for me I felt, and so I joined it.

Other women were also attracted by the way in which members of the Leeds ILP appeared to take them seriously. Barbara Lowrie, a young artist, felt uncomfortable at first when she attended meetings in the dismal rooms of the North East Ward Labour Club, but something fascinated her. 'Perhaps it was the inspiriting talk of men like Tom Maguire . . . The Comrades always seemed pleased to see me come in, and . . . I found that their object was to bring about a happier state of affairs for working men and women . . . Another thing, I believe woman has the right to her own individuality, and to be recognized as equally important with man, in all matters. In this club I found men and women who entirely agreed with me.'[33]

[30] I. O. Ford, 'Why Women Should Be Socialists', *Labour Leader* (*LL*), May 1913, p. 10.
[31] *LL* 9 Apr. 1914.
[32] *YFT* 20 Jan. 1983; Ford, 'Why Women Should Be Socialists', p. 10.
[33] Both Isabella and Barbara Lowrie gave their reasons for joining the ILP in J. Clayton, ed., *Why I Joined the Independent Labour Party: Some Plain Statements* (Leeds: ILP, c.1897), pp. 5, 7–8.

Sex equality and the link between the 'woman question' and working-class politics were avidly debated in the Leeds ILP. The importance of female labour in the town helped to bring such questions to the front, but the influence of Tom Maguire, Isabella, and other women members was also crucial in ensuring that these issues received prominence. It was the Labour clubs which provided a focus for such discussions, and in 1893 Isabella and Bessie put up the money to establish a central ILP club in New Briggate. Alf Mattison later claimed that 'the Misses Ford, who can never be thanked sufficiently for their help, became tenants of the property; they furnished it and decorated it; and Mr Walter Wood was installed as steward. Its rooms were open almost day and night, and great inspiration was drawn from the many happy meetings held there.It was a calling place for many notabilities in the Labour World as they passed through Leeds.'[34]

A 'band of idealists in a hostile or indifferent world which they were determined to convert and transform', the socialist pioneers were never to forget the comradeship, the 'dauntless enthusiasm' and the 'sublime faith' of these early years.[35] Looking back after Isabella's death Ben Turner recalled the atmosphere of the club in New Briggate: 'the late Tom Maguire would read his poetry and sing us his songs . . . the late Tom Paylor would regale us with Irish humour and sound philosophy . . . Alf Mattison and others would cling to organization and propose schemes and plans for our line of social progress. It was . . . the centre of the then left wing of the advanced Labour and Socialist movement.'[36]

Isabella's specific contribution to the early socialist movement lay in her emphasis on the needs of women workers, her humanitarianism, and her internationalist perspective, all of which brought her into conflict from time to time with members of the local trade union movement. In February 1893, for example, she became embroiled in a controversy with the Trades Council over its attitude to alien immigration. The position of a few political exiles in London had not been a matter of concern to the labour movement. The influx of Jewish workers in the mid-1880s, however, escaping the pogroms in Eastern Europe, caused alarm. Settling mainly in London, Leeds, and Manchester, they became associated in the minds of many trade-unionists with cheap labour and the threat of displacing native workers from employment. With the onset of economic depression in the early 1890s, demands for a restriction of alien immigration began to grow.[37]

Influenced by her parents' internationalist perspective, Isabella took a completely opposite point of view. While staying in London the previous December she had attended a meeting on 'Freedom in Russia' that had called for unrestricted alien immigration. In February she presided at a meeting to

[34]A. Mattison, 'A History of the Leeds Labour Party. Part V', *LWC* 8 Feb. 1918.

[35]J. Arnott, 'Isabella Ford: An Appreciation', *LWC* 19 July 1924.

[36]B. Turner, 'Miss I. O. Ford: An Appreciation, *YFT* 24 July 1924.

[37]J. Buckman, *Immigrants and the Class Struggle: The Jewish Immigrants in Leeds, 1880–1914* (Manchester: MUP, 1983).

form a Leeds branch of the Society of Free Russia, where Stepniak and Volkhonsky, editor of *Free Russia*, were the principal speakers. When the Trades Council introduced a resolution later in the month calling for a restriction of immigration, Isabella's vehement speech in opposition came as no surprise. As usual she tried to win her case by arguments based on facts rather than prejudice. She claimed that statistics showed that Jews were paid more than Christians and could not be accused of undermining wages. Her argument had little effect on the majority of members, for their minds were already made up, and the resolution was passed.[38]

In spite of such disagreements, Isabella continued to work closely with male trade-unionists in an attempt to increase union membership among tailoresses. She attended meeting after meeting, often with other local speakers in support. As an unmarried woman Isabella did not have to face a conflict between her organizing work and the needs of a husband and children. Moreover, she could rely on Bessie and the servants to take care of everyday domestic affairs at the Grange. On the other hand, the life of a trade union agitator was not an easy one. Every meeting held in Leeds meant a long journey from Adel, and if Isabella took the tram she arrived home late at night tired and exhausted. When she took a short holiday with Bessie in April 1893, therefore, Isabella found that she was having such a good time that it made her reluctant to return for a tailoresses' meeting. Other middle-class women involved in helping female workers also suffered from overwork and exhaustion; May Abraham, for example, fell ill in August after visiting a rag sorting works in Leeds and was nursed back to health at the Grange. With all the pressure of work, the two sisters were no doubt relieved to take their annual holiday abroad in the following month. They visited Norway, and Isabella's impression was that the 'peasants are very poor, but happy and free. They have no particular politics except to hate Sweden and no one has ever heard of a Labour Party.' It was a treat, she said, to be among such cheerful people.[39]

For the rest of the year Isabella was kept busy trying to organize tailoresses in Leeds and nearby Hebden Bridge; in November she arranged a series of meetings in the area to be addressed by Miss Marland, who had agreed to undertake a week of propaganda among clothing workers. But progress was very slow; by the beginning of 1894 the Tailoresses' Union had only 61 members, while the men's organization, now called the Amalgamated Union of Clothing Operatives (AUCO) was a little stronger, with 506 members, but these were drawn from Bristol and other towns as well as from Leeds. This prompted Isabella to seek a close relationship between the two groups. In January she arranged for leaders of the AUCO and the Trades Council to join Miss Marland and Agnes Close, a working

[38] *YFT* 17 Feb. 1893.
[39] *YFT* 15 Sept. 1893.

woman who was treasurer of the Tailoresses' Union, in addressing a public
meeting of tailoresses. A series of meetings followed over the next few
months at which Isabella urged male and female workers to act closely
together; in June, supported by AUCO officials, she spoke to tailoresses
who were on strike and exclaimed vehemently that 'she had had enough of
competition between the sexes . . . it divided families and cut prices'.[40]

After prolonged negotiations it was finally agreed in November that a
federation should be formed of all unions in the Leeds ready-made clothing
trade, including the Jewish Machinists', Tailors', and Pressers' Union.[41]
The aims of the federation were limited to watching over developments in
the trade and to encouraging members not to do the work of others on
strike. Member unions were not obliged to take joint actions or to provide
financial support during disputes. None the less, Isabella felt that it represented a step forward and was full of enthusiasm when she attended a
Women's Trade Union conference at Holborn Town Hall later in the
month. Here too she urged co-operation among trade-unionists and supported a proposal to establish an investigative committee which could
gather information about the conditions of women's employment in different parts of the country.

Returning home in December, she once again helped Miss Marland to
carry out a week of propaganda among tailoresses in Leeds. According to
the League organizer they 'held meetings every night, besides going
amongst the girls during the noon hour when they came out to snatch an
'airing' before going back to their machines'. Fining was the chief complaint; 'it is carried on to such an extent that I came across one case of a girl
who was fined threepence for coming out at the wrong door, although she
was a new-comer and did not know the rule'.[42]

In the same month Isabella took advantage of recent reforms in local
government to stand as a candidate for election to Adel Parish Council. Her
success was a double victory, both for women's rights and for independent
labour politics, and 'caused fearful excitement at Adel'.[43] She was more and
more convinced that women needed to take part in politics if they hoped to
change their social and economic position. Speaking to the West Ward
Labour Club in February 1895, she referred to the way in which women
were taught to be interested only in the home. It was no wonder, therefore,
that they became individualists who 'saw the world through prejudice', not
through the eyes of 'large-hearted citizenship'. If they had to vote, women
would be encouraged to 'think out questions affecting the well-being of the

[40] YFT 1 June 1893.
[41] YFT 23 Nov. 1894.
[42] Women's Trade Union Review, Jan. 1895, p. 9.
[43] Edward Carpenter to Alf Mattison, 3 Dec. 1894, Mattison Coll., Brotherton Lib., Leeds
Univ.

community', and then they would be likely to take an interest in trade-unionism. She was scathing of those who spoke of the 'sacredness of the home' and yet knew nothing of the conditions in cramped, working-class houses. A co-operative style of house-keeping was needed to give women time to think and to attend meetings, but Isabella realized that there were still 'strong prejudices against such matters' among women themselves.[44]

Her lecture was delivered just one week after Tom Maguire made his last appearance at the Club, debating with Ley Jones on 'will the ILP gain its ends sooner by remaining independent or by joining forces with the Liberal Party'. Less than a month later, aged only twenty-nine, he caught pneumonia and died at his home; friends found him without food to eat or coal in the grate. It was generally agreed that years of political agitation on a low, irregular income had led to his poor health and was the real cause of his premature death. With Isabella away in London, Bessie attended the funeral on behalf of them both. She provided a simple headstone for the grave and with some help from Alf Mattison paid the funeral costs.

It was also Bessie and Alf Mattison who were responsible for compiling *Tom Maguire: A Remembrance*. The book contained a selection of Maguire's writings and short appreciations of his work by themselves and Edward Carpenter. In her preface Bessie described Tom Maguire's vision of socialism which had been such an inspiration to Isabella and herself. Just before he died he had expressed the wish to write a book in which 'socialism was to be treated from its widest base, and set forth clearly as a living thing, entering into all the ways of life – as a great ideal and as something of far more . . . import than just another "party" or another cause of argument and "disputings"'.[45] After spending several days at Adel in August revising proofs for the book with Alf Mattison, Bessie felt 'proud' when she saw the advance copies. The proceeds from the sale of the book were given to Maguire's widowed mother, for Bessie had defrayed all the costs of production, and £80 was handed over in total, including donations from friends.[46]

Maguire's death left a void among the socialist pioneers in Leeds which was difficult to fill. The local ILP was having little success in municipal elections and still did not have the support of the organized labour movement. It was prone to the internal wrangling that Maguire deplored. In July 1895 Bessie complained to Alf Mattison that unpleasantness over Mahon was threatening to split the Leeds ILP. 'It's too terrible the ILP should quarrel amongst themselves; it's exactly what the Liberals expect them to do.' She later found members to be 'slow and dilatory' and thought it was

[44]*YFT* 1 Mar, 1895.
[45]A. Mattison and E. Carpenter, eds., *Tom Maquire: A Remembrance* (Manchester: Labour Press Society, 1895), pp. v–vi.
[46]Alf Mattison's Notebook 1: 18 Feb., 8 Mar., 7 and 11 Aug., 27 Sept. 1895, Mattison Coll.

no wonder they achieved so little; at the end of the year she accused them of being apathetic about Maguire's book.[47]

While Bessie was involved in the internal politics of the Leeds ILP, Isabella was continuing with her trade union work, but here too there were difficulties. Only a small proportion of the labour force in the West Riding textile and clothing trades, whether male or female, were organized, despite the efforts of local leaders to arouse interest in the benefits of trade-unionism. None the less, Isabella continued to have faith that men and women would be able to combine together to improve their conditions of work. It was with a sense of optimism, therefore, that she took part for the first time in the International Textile Workers' Congress, held in Ghent in August 1895.

Isabella went to Ghent with her close friends Allen Gee, Ben Turner, and William Drew as a representative of the General Union of Textile Workers. Finding herself to be the only female delegate, she was still able to muster enough courage to speak to all the men assembled in the vast hall. She urged them to send female representatives in the future, for women formed a large proportion of the textile labour force and their voice deserved to be heard. It was to be the first of many such trips for Isabella, and her fluency in French and German was a great help to the other English delegates. She used the occasion to find out as much as she could about local economic, social, and political developments, and the congress provided her with the first opportunity to make contacts at an international level with men and women who shared similar concerns to her own.

The congress marked the beginning of a period in which Isabella's talents as a speaker, a writer, and a trade union organizer were used to great effect outside the West Riding. Most of her practical propaganda work for socialism and trade-unionism still took place at a local level, but increasingly, she began to play a more prominent national role, in particular in the Women's Trade Union League. Although she continued to stress the importance of trade-unionism for women, failure to make any real progress led to a change in the focus of her activities. By the end of the century she had shifted the emphasis both of her analysis and her practical work away from trade union organization towards political action and socialist propaganda.

[47]Bessie Ford to Alf Mattison, 9 July 1894; 1 May and 18 Dec. 1895, Alf Mattison's Letter Book, in the possession of E. P. Thompson.

4

Yorkshire's Chief Women: Socialists and Trade-Unionists, 1895–1901

Every form of conventional thought must be fought . . .

As the century drew to a close, Isabella increasingly found herself pulled in several directions at once. In her practical work for the labour movement and in her writings she pursued the interests of all members of the working class, arguing that working people of both sexes must act together if they wished to achieve any real change in their lives. At the same time she recognized that women as a social group suffered from specific inequalities and maintained her contacts with members of the women's rights movement. Isabella's two objectives – the emancipation of working people and the emancipation of women from all social classes – were difficult to reconcile. Over the next few years, however, she saw it as her task to bring the two together.

There has long been a relationship between the ideology of female equality and radical and socialist politics, in theory if not always in practice. In the late nineteenth century, the growth of the women's rights movement went hand in hand with a revival of socialism. Individual women were members of both movements, and there was considerable interaction between the two. 'New life' socialists, in particular, were preoccupied with relationships between the sexes; it is hardly surprising, therefore, that the 'woman question' was avidly debated in socialist groups. The relationship between the women's movement and the labour movement was one of the key debates at the International Socialist and Trade Union Congress held in London in July 1896.

Isabella attended as a delegate from the Leeds Tailoresses' Union and joined female socialists from all over Europe to listen to speeches on women's work and political emancipation. Summing up delegates' views, Mary Foster, a graduate teacher and member of the Leeds ILP, reported that all were agreed that

> the bourgeois movement makes a great deal of noise, but its leaders demand mere palliatives . . . while the bourgeois women's movement in all lands . . . has

tended to open up the minds of women generally to an examination of the questions which especially affect their sex, it cannot be compared in importance and significance with the organizations for working women which exist in England and on the Continent, and with the efforts of individual women working with men in the ranks of Socialism to advance the cause of labour and political freedom.[1]

Isabella would have agreed with this overall analysis; although an active member of the Leeds Women's Suffrage Society during the 1890s, she was certainly not content to work from within the 'bourgeois' women's movement alone. Most of her energies were put into the local trade union and socialist movements, where she hoped to pursue the interests of women workers as part of a broad struggle for the emancipation of all workers. In practice, however, co-operation between the sexes was not easy to achieve. When there was a conflict of interest, female socialists were often inclined to put class unity above the specific needs of women. Isabella was also willing to make compromises if she thought that both sexes would benefit in the long run. She was unusual, however, in giving equal weight to her socialism and to her feminism, trying never to put one before the other. Convinced that class and sex oppression would only be overcome if men and women were organized in strong trade unions and were prepared to fight for socialism, she worked hard on behalf of both causes in the West Riding during the late 1890s.

Isabella often had to walk a tightrope in her trade union work, constantly acting as conciliator when there was conflict between the sexes. In the late 1890s, however, she remained optimistic that men and women could work together. She was now far more confident of her own abilities as an organizer and began to take a greater part in the trade union movement at a national level. In September 1896 she attended the Trades Union Congress for the first time, as a delegate from the Tailoresses' Union. In the same year she became a member of the Central Council of the Women's Trade Union League and started to write more regularly for the *Women's Trade Union Review*. Isabella tried to keep her own union members in contact with national developments by taking small groups on trips to London; in September 1895, for example, six Leeds tailoresses met trade union representatives from the East End in the offices of the League and afterwards visited local factories and workshops.[2]

Supportive accounts of the progress of the Leeds Tailoresses' Union appeared regularly in the *Review;* in April 1896 union funds were reported to be so good that £22 had been donated to Tom Maguire's mother and £50 to the Brushmakers' Society. But this apparent sign of health could not

[1]M. Foster, 'Women at the International Congress', in *Illustrated Report of the Proceedings of the Workers' Congress held in London, July 1896* (1896), p. 84.
[2]*Women's Trade Union Review (WTUR)*, (Oct. 1895), p. 20., Apr. 1896, p. 16.

disguise the fact that the union had only fifty-three members, a small fraction of the thousands of tailoresses working in the city. It was in this context that Isabella made a last bid to attract members by launching two new initiatives – the appointment of a full-time secretary and the establish-ment of a Women's Trade Union Club.

Until that time, a small group of women workers had represented the Tailoresses' Union on the Trades Council and carried out administrative tasks in their spare time. It was difficult, however, to find anyone with either the experience or the time to take on important roles, and individuals tended to hold office for only a short period. Isabella hoped that a full-time secretary would give some continuity. With Bessie's help she was able to offer a wage of £40 a year, and Agnes Close was appointed to the post in December 1896. Agnes had first met Isabella in the late 1880s when she was a pupil at the Mill Hill night-school, and the two women worked closely together on the strike committee during the tailoresses' dispute of 1889. Even at this early stage Agnes had showed some ability as a speaker, and once the strike was over she continued to be an active union member; she was a delegate to the Trades Council in the early 1890s and became union treasurer in 1894. She also joined the West Ward Labour Club and dissemi-nated propaganda for independent labour politics in Leeds.

Agnes was a frequent visitor to Adel Grange, and Robert Sherard found her there in 1896 when he was researching for his book on the *White Slaves of England*. Her health had broken down 'after trying for years to maintain her mother, three brothers and herself on the 15*s* a week she was earning'.[3] She was being nursed back to health by the Ford sisters, who must have hoped that the post of paid secretary would ease Agnes Close's financial problems as well as helping the union. Isabella described Agnes as 'well up in organizing work, hunting up girls in their homes, holding shop meetings, in the street during the dinner hour, and generally haranguing them at odd hours whenever she meets them. The girls were very pleased at her appointment, and we are very glad we have been able to find one who has worked in their own trade.'[4]

Part of Agnes's work was to help out in disputes. In two letters to Isabella she gave a detailed account of her actions in one strike which involved seventy machinists who had come to Agnes for help when their employer threatened to reduce wages. 'I got ten of the girls to go and see the manager and he would come to no terms with them. So I got a room at Lockhart's for 1/6 and I took the girls there, and we had nice meeting. Ben Turner was in Leeds, and I got him to speak to the girls, and then Walt Wood and I spoke to them. We told them what suffering it means to be on strike and not to be in a union . . . all the girls asked for you, and I told them that you were

[3]R. H. Sherard, *The White Slaves of England* (James Bowden, 1897), p. 130.
[4]*WTUR* (Jan. 1897).

away from home. I do wish you were in Leeds. I shall stick to them and help them all I can.' Then, on the Saturday morning, 'I and the girls went down . . . and stood about the shop. We did not stand very long before one of the clerks came out for 6 of the girls to go and see the manager in his office . . . and he gave them all they wanted.'[5] Agnes reported that a number of girls expressed interest in joining the union and that she intended to pay them a visit in the following week to remind them.

The second major departure at the end of the year was the opening of the Women's Trade Union Club in a four-storeyed building in Belgrave Street. Again Isabella and Bessie provided the initial finance, although they intended the club to be self-supporting. Agnes Close and her mother were to live there and pay rent. It was also assumed that trade union and socialist groups would contribute to the running costs by hiring rooms for meetings. Female lecturers visiting the town would be able to stay overnight in the club, and two rooms were reserved for the Tailoresses' Union. Isabella and Bessie hoped that any union admitting female members would make use of the club and that it would provide a focus for the organization of women workers in Leeds.

Sympathetic male trade-unionists gave their support to the new venture. John Bune provided some chairs, and Ben Turner launched an appeal from his column in the *Yorkshire Factory Times* for 100 books to set up a library: 'Good novels, useful social and political books, etc., will be thankfully received.'[6] The Club was to 'be open all day and every day, and will be a bureau for labour information; and, better still, tea and bread and butter will be obtainable at certain hours. There will be books, newspapers, etc.' It was Isabella's intention that the club should broaden the horizons of its members, and she took steps to ensure it. 'The whole place is painted white, and has yellow walls and a matting dado, and a wall paper covered with yellow daffodils or sweet peas – something nice. Beauty of all sorts is excluded from so many of our girls' lives, that it shall not be excluded from their club.'[7]

These objectives were entirely consistent with the Ford sisters' broad view of the meaning of socialism and trade-unionism; they always argued that members of the working class had spiritual as well as material needs, a view shared by many contemporaries – socialists, artists, writers, and settlement workers – who sought to introduce working people to the creative arts even in the midst of slum conditions. In the winter of 1893, Bessie organized a series of free concerts of music from the best composers in the poor quarters of Leeds, from a conviction that 'in the hearts of all men and women is the love of good music, only needing to be awakened and

[5]Ibid., p. 17.
[6]*Yorkshire Factory Times* (*YFT*), 5 Feb. 1897.
[7]*WTUR* Jan. 1897.

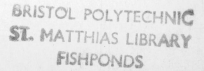

cultivated'.[8] The concerts were so popular that they became a regular annual event.

During her many trips to London with groups of tailoresses, Isabella made sure that they visited museums and art galleries, not just workshops and trade union offices. On one occasion she showed them pictures by G. F. Watts, an artist who had influenced the style of her sister Emily, and found that 'their appreciation of them was great'. When Isabella later met Watts she was able to discuss the tailoresses' response to his paintings, and he was pleased that 'they had understood the meaning of "Hope" and "Love" and "Death"'. In an appreciation of Watts written after his death, Isabella claimed that 'he wished Art to be a national thing, done by the People and for the People. He wanted free picture galleries; he wanted the People's homes to be beautiful, he said.'[9]

The house-warming party held in January 1897 to mark the opening of the Women's Trade Union Club also marked the beginning of what was to be one of Isabella's busiest years so far. She was to travel extensively at home and abroad, as well as taking part in national campaigns over protective legislation for women. Legislation was now being sought as an alternative strategy to improve women's work conditions as the leaders of the League, many of whom were Fabians, found that their attempts to organize women workers had made little headway. Isabella had mixed feelings about such a policy. As a suffragist she objected to the fact that women were rarely consulted about legislation which had a dramatic effect on their working lives. She opposed any attempt to restrict women's sphere of employment which seemed to be motivated more by the interests of male workers than any real concern for the welfare of working women. It was on these grounds that she had argued against a proposal in 1891 to exclude women from chain- and nail-making, a stand which had brought her into conflict with Ben Turner and the Leeds Trades Council.[10] Attitudes towards protective legislation, however, were complex. Alliances between individuals and groups varied over time, according to the issue under debate, and it is difficult to place men and women into neat categories of those who supported and those who opposed protective legislation for female workers.

In contrast to their disagreement six years earlier, Isabella and Ben Turner joined forces in March 1897 to oppose the recently revised Truck Act. Workers were now able to take employers to court if they were charged 'unreasonable' fines. Turner, however, argued that the Act legalized fines and should be repealed. He was sharply rebuked by Gertrude Tuckwell, secretary of the Women's Trade Union League, who claimed that the Act at

[8]Obituary of Bessie Ford by Rhoda Connon, *Common Cause* (*CC*), 25 July 1919.
[9]I. O. Ford, 'The Late Mr. C. F. Watts: The Recollections of an Afternoon', *Labour Leader* (*LL*) , 8 July 1904, p. 164.
[10]*YFT* 10 Apr. 1891.

least provided protection for the most helpless and disorganized workers, namely women. Entering into the controversy on the side of Ben Turner, Isabella pointed out that when the home secretary had asked her a year before to send information on the attitude of local unions to the proposed bill, both the Tailoresses' Union and the General Union of Textile Workers had expressed opposition to its provisions. She agreed with Turner that it merely legalized a 'hitherto illegal practice', and that it would be impossible for a working woman to take a case of unfair and unreasonable charges through the courts. Even if she were to win her case she would be subject to boycotting, in particular in the unorganized trades of Yorkshire. Her long letter in the *Yorkshire Factory Times* ended on a sarcastic note. 'But, not for one moment is the Home Office to be blamed for this tinkering kind of legislation. It is only natural that persons who know nothing except through those irrelevant and misleading things, books and official papers, of the intricacies and difficulties of industrial life, and especially of female industrial life . . . should pass a bill as the one of this year.'[11]

It was because she had canvassed the opinion of hundreds of non-unionists as well as trade-unionists in the tailoring trade, and therefore felt certain about the views of the workers themselves, that Isabella was prepared to support the extension of some areas of protective legislation, in particular when both sexes were affected. In 1897 she took the initiative in demanding that Section 40, the Particulars' Clause of the 1895 Factory Act, which directed employers to provide workers with details of the prices they were to be paid for specific tasks, should apply to the wholesale tailoring trade. The campaign began to gather momentum in March when the Leeds Tailoresses' Union sent a resolution to the home secretary asking for the inclusion of wholesale tailoring. In the following month the Leeds Trades Council decided to support the campaign after Agnes Close argued that tailoresses 'did not know what they would receive for work till they had done it. Often when work had been done extra well, they received a poor price for it.'[12] In an article published in April Isabella made similar points, noting that women were always uncertain about prices when they worked on samples – although as one said wryly, 'though I use the term "uncertainty" of price, there is very little uncertainty indeed – a sample is mostly an excuse for a low price – the best work turned out at even the lowest price'.[13]

The home secretary responded to the Tailoresses' Union by asking for details about the numbers working in the trade, including homeworkers, and the kind of particulars required. The president of the Leeds Trades Council received a similar request; he responded that it was rather a 'large

[11] *YFT* 12 Mar. 1897; for Tuckwell's arguments and Turner's reply, see *YFT* 9 Apr. 1897.
[12] *YFT* 16 Apr. 1897.
[13] *WTUR* Apr. 1897, pp. 9–10.

order', since employers were bound to refuse to give any details. Yet Isabella, undaunted by the task, had been hard at work collecting the information. She was able to reassure the president that she had 'drawn up a letter answering every question as far as possible', which only needed to be checked by the other clothing unions. As a result of such painstaking work the wholesale tailoring trade was finally included in Section 40 of the Factory Act in July 1898. Isabella's role in the campaign was acknowledged in the *Women's Trade Union Review*, which noted that the League, the Bristol Women's Trade Unions and 'above all Miss Ford' could congratulate themselves.[14]

In the middle of the campaign for the Particulars' Clause, Isabella began to have problems with her eyes. This did not stop her from speaking at the Leeds May Day rally with Edward Carpenter. Afterwards they went on to tea at the Central ILP club, the meeting place for the 'leading men and women' in the local movement. Carpenter stayed at the Grange for another two days; he reports that he found Isabella and Bessie 'groaning rather over the house and grounds and wishing they could simplify themselves into a little cottage'.[15]

The burden of looking after the Grange must indeed have been a heavy one. On the other hand, both sisters took pleasure in sharing their home with a wide network of friends, many of whom came from abroad. It was not uncommon for well-educated, upper middle-class women who travelled extensively and were fluent in languages to have such varied contacts, especially if they took an interest in public life or cultural pursuits. Where Isabella and Bessie were unusual was in developing close friendships with men and women from working-class backgrounds. They frequently entertained socialist and trade union groups to tea in their spacious grounds, and Adel Grange provided a place where working-class men and women could meet the national and international leaders of the movements of which they were a part.

The openness of the Ford sisters to new ideas, and their refusal to be bound by social conventions, drew a wide range of visitors to the Grange. Their guests tended to hold 'progressive' views on social and economic questions – including women's rights, the welfare of working women, and humanitarian causes – which cut across formal political affiliations and led to unusual friendships. Isabella was equally close, for example, to the Marxist Tom Maguire and to the moderate, pragmatic socialists Alf Mattison and Ben Turner. Her broad, well-balanced personality also helped Isabella to make friends easily with people from very varied social and political backgrounds. Free from the intolerance of the rigid doctrinaire, she

[14] *YFT* 7 May 1897; *WTUR*, July 1898. See also July 1897 and Gertrude Tuckwell's letter in the *YFT* 17 Dec. 1897 for more comments on Isabella's contribution to the campaign.
[15] Edward Carpenter to Alf Mattison, 4 May 1897. See also 19 Apr. 1897, Mattison Coll., Brotherton Lib., Leeds.

was always reluctant to let a disagreement turn into a quarrel. Impatient with anyone who was over-cautious, sluggish, or a humbug, she respected those who acted with sincerity, even if she disapproved of their methods.[16]

Friends could not help but be attracted by the sociability and tolerant attitudes of the Ford sisters. Bessie was responsible for the 'warm spirit of hospitality' found at Adel, creating a calm atmosphere with her quiet, selfless and philosophical temperament.[17] This complemented the more outgoing personality of her younger sister. Isabella was described as 'animated, frank and tender, a good fighter and a gay friend',[18] with a 'keen intellect'[19] and sense of humour – in short, a lively companion.

It was these same qualities that made Isabella such an entertaining speaker, and she was in great demand in the late 1890s to address local socialist and trade union groups. Her speeches always drew attention to the links between women's lack of political rights, their failure to take an interest in events outside the home, and their weak trade union organization. Speaking to a meeting of women at the Bradford Labour Institute, Isabella observed that men 'spoke of women as fools in regard to opinions on current questions', but this was because they were too committed to domestic duties. Although the vote would broaden women's horizons, Isabella also urged trade union fathers to 'help their daughters to understand the things pertaining to their class, and then the reproach of stupidity so needlessly fixed upon women would be taken away . . .'.[20]

The low trade union membership among female workers in the West Riding encouraged Isabella, Ben Turner, and Allen Gee, General Secretary of the GUTW, to appeal frequently to male trade-unionists to encourage their female relatives to join a union. At the May meeting of the Trades Council, Isabella pointed out that it would help the Tailoresses' Union if 'each man would preach trade unionism in his own home'. This was followed by an open letter to all male trade-unionists in the city, in which she claimed that many of them had daughters who did not belong to a union; 'this shows us', she said, 'that each man, who . . . might influence for good in this matter, has neglected to use his influence'.[21]

Because such appeals were addressed to men rather than directly to women workers, they have been seen as evidence of patriarchal attitudes in the General Union of Textile Workers.[22] On the other hand it could also

[16] J. Arnott, 'Isabella O. Ford: An Appreciation', Leeds Weekly Citizen (LWC), 19 July 1924.

[17] Ibid,. 18 July 1919. See also obituaries by Millicent Fawcett and Rhoda Connan in CC 25 July 1919.

[18] Obituary by Mary Sheepshanks in Woman's Leader, 1 Aug. 1924.

[19] E. E. Crossley, 'Isabella O. Ford: Suffragist, Trade Unionist and Socialist', LWC 28 June 1929.

[20] YFT 21 May 1897.

[21] Ibid., 7 May 1897 and WTUR, July 1897, pp. 19–20.

[22] J. Bornat, 'Lost Leaders: Women, Trade Unionism and the Case of the General Union of Textile Workers, 1875–1914', in A. John, ed., Unequal Opportunities: Women's Employment in England, 1800–1918 (Oxford: Blackwell, 1986), p. 222.

imply a recognition of the authority that men exercised within their families. A minority of socialists did make the connection between the oppression of women in the home and in the work-place; Tom Maguire, for example, suggested that men discouraged their female relatives from joining a union in case they neglected their domestic duties: '*My* Sarah Jane must stay at home and make *my* home comfortable for *me*! What else is a wife for!'[23] Isabella was also painfully aware of the pressures put on young women by male relatives. 'It is a common excuse amongst the girls with whom we have to do that they do not join the union because their fathers do not urge them or care for them to do so.'[24] She thought it was just as important, therefore, to change male attitudes as it was alter the views of women workers themselves.

In June Isabella took a break from union work and went off to London with Bessie to spend a month in their London flat. Their departure from Leeds meant that the two sisters missed a local meeting called to protest against proposals to reinforce the Cantonment Acts in India. Bessie felt so strongly about the issue that she wrote to Alf Mattison from London on 22 June 1897 to urge him to attend. The Cantonment Acts were based on the same principles as the Contagious Diseases' Acts, and Bessie referred in her letter to the part that her mother had played in the latters' repeal: 'my mother was one of the most ardent fighters & she used to tell us afterwards what a terrible & bitter fight it was. The women were helped most by the "working men of the North" – she always said.' Calling on working men to help the women's cause once again, Bessie thought it 'abominable' that 'native girls and women there should be bought and sold . . . into such an awful life, & all for the sake of our Army because men choose to say that a vicious life is a necessity to a soldier, most particularly in India'. Although Alf Mattison and other ILP members did go to the meeting, Bessie was not satisfied and felt that too little interest had been shown. In a subsequent letter she complained that 'in Leeds the ILP thinks of nothing but its little self, it can't take a large view of anything. But I feel ashamed of the ILP in Leeds.'[25]

The two sisters did not spend all their time in London worrying about the Leeds labour movement. They also managed to enjoy the latest concerts, art exhibitions, and plays. On one of their visits Isabella met up with Edward Carpenter and the Salts: 'We went to see Bernard Shaw's play – & tomorrow I have begged Mrs Salt to come & have tea with me & we will go to the opera together to hear Wagner's Tristan & Isolde. We go to unreserved seats high up – and it lasts more than 4 and a half hours & is boiling hot.' This letter to Alf Mattison clearly reveals Isabella's great sense of fun

[23] *Labour Chronicle*, 6 May 1893.
[24] *WTUR* (July 1897), p. 19.
[25] Bessie Ford to Alf Mattison, 22 and 29 June 1897. Alf Mattison's Letter Book, in the possession of E. P. Thompson.

and dislike of stuffy social proprieties. 'When we come out at midnight the public houses are emptying & the streets are like the infernal regions . . . London looks very beautiful & I keep wondering what it will all be like after the revolution. The rich people look very dreary & stupid as they drive along – they don't enjoy themselves half as much as I enjoy sitting humbly in the crowd watching them – as I enjoy a twopenny ride on the top of a bus along the streets. I am enjoying my stay here so much, I wish I could send you some of my enjoyment.'[26]

On the other hand, Bessie and Isabella also used their trips to London to attend political meetings and to keep in touch with the latest developments in the women's rights movement. Isabella belonged to three women's clubs. No alcohol was served on the premises, for the clubs provided education, not the 'sport, pleasure and dissipation' so often found in their male equivalents. The Writer's Club was for lunch, tea, and newspapers, while the Women's Institute 'embraces an educational programme of appalling size, to the frivolous mind'.[27] The Pioneer Club encouraged women to discuss political and social questions and to learn how to 'separate personal friendships from matters of principle'.[28] Such leading feminists and socialists as Eleanor Marx Aveling, Olive Schreiner, Dora Montefiore, and Isabella were among those who gave lectures at the Pioneer Club, and topics for debate included vivisection, the benefits of socialism for women, co-education, and Ibsen's plays.

It has been suggested that feminists in this period developed a network of female friendships in which 'personal political differences seldom intruded'. Women's clubs provided one way in which such friendships could be maintained and extended, enabling women to develop an 'alternative set of values' based on a new feminist political philosophy.[29] Some women then sought to carry through their ideas by organizing separately. Isabella, however, was always concerned to integrate her feminist politics into the mainstream socialist movement, and to change the attitudes of men as well as women.

After a brief return to Leeds in July 1897, Isabella went off once more to spend the second week of August in Roubaix, as a delegate from Bradford to the International Textile Workers' Congress. She travelled out with William Drew two days early in order to make preparations for the arrival of the rest of the Yorkshire delegation. She sorted out the other delegates' meals and used her expertise in French to help them make sense of what was often a disorganized conference. Ben Turner was full of praise for her efforts: 'Miss Ford of Leeds was very useful; in fact, many a time she kept us Englishmen supplied with what was going on when we were otherwise at a

[26]Isabella Ford to Alf Mattison, 29 June, n.d. Ibid.
[27]*Leeds Forward* (LF) Sept. 1898.
[28]*Shafts*, 3/2 (May 1893).
[29]P. Levine, *Victorian Feminism, 1850–1900* (Hutchinson, 1987), pp. 17, 23.

loss to know how matters stood.' Isabella not only acted as an interpreter, but also contributed to the work of the congress by seconding a resolution of support for Russian trade-unionists who were prevented from attending by the absolutism of their government. Her real sympathy with the problems of other nations contrasted with Ben Turner's chauvinistic account of the proceedings: 'the local committee had not made due preparations for a business congress . . . they do not understand a solid congress such as we

All through the congress, Isabella suffered from a pain her hand which made it difficult for her to write. As soon as she returned to England, therefore, she took a fortnight's holiday with Bessie in Whitby. Here the English like to see . . . and I am sure the English and the Germans are very much indebted to Miss Ford for her activity in helping them and us to understand what was going on.'[30]

sisters were so well known that a local fisherman had named three of his boats Bessie, Isabella, and Adel in their honour. Even on holiday Isabella did not relax completely; despite the pain in her hand she wrote articles for the newspapers in Roubaix to explain the importance of the congress that had taken place. Then, immediately after her holiday, Isabella attended the annual meeting of the Bradford branch of the GUTW to thank members for sending her as a delegate to Roubaix and report on the events there. She also told the audience that she felt encouraged by the appointment of Julia Varley, a young mill-worker, as a full-time organizer for the union, and concluded by giving an account of the work of the Leeds Tailoresses' Club: by 'sheer hard work and uphill fighting they had in a few weeks added 40 new members to the Tailoresses' Union'.[31] The credit for this, she said, had to go to Agnes Close, who had been busy holding meetings in the dinner hour and visiting the girls in their homes. Agnes was certainly responsible for all the day-to-day work of running the Tailoresses' Union, for Isabella was rarely at home during the last three months of the year. At the end of October she went to Paris for a few days and then stayed in London until Christmas, where at last, after six months, the pain in her hand appeared to be getting better.[32]

Despite her frequent absences from home, Isabella still made a major contribution to the West Riding trade union and socialist movements. Most notably, she helped to ensure that the 'woman question' was avidly debated in ILP branches and labour clubs throughout the area. Reminiscences by contemporaries mention the Ford sisters time and again for the role they played in creating an atmosphere of comradeship between the sexes in the West Riding; Ben Turner thought they were 'Yorkshire's chief women . . . with money and service [they] made the movement grow. They were

[30] YFT 13 and 20 Aug. 1897.
[31] YFT 15 Oct. 1897.
[32] YFT 3 Dec. 1897.

Trojans at the work.' Katharine Bruce Glasier, a close friend of the Ford sisters who often stayed with her husband at the Grange, also claimed that Yorkshire labour leaders were 'very influenced by the companionship which Isabella and Bessie Ford of Adel bore them in their efforts for full freedom of women and workers'.[33]

It would be misleading, however, to create the impression that Bessie and Isabella were alone in promoting the cause of sex equality in the West Riding ILP. They were joined by a much wider group of local female socialists. Although their names rarely appear in the histories of the movement, they formed a close network of friendship and mutual support. The Bradford ILP had several talented female members. Edith Priestman, a Quaker and the wife of a textile manufacturer, one of the first ILP councillors in the city, was a popular speaker and was elected to the Board of Guardians in 1898. Julia Varley combined her work as a trade union organizer with political activity and was also elected to the Bradford Board of Guardians (1901). The most well-known of the Bradford women was Margaret McMillan; a member of the School Board, she gained a national reputation through her efforts to improve the health and education of children and was in great demand as a speaker on women's rights, child welfare, and independent labour politics.[34]

Exchange visits were frequent between ILP members in Bradford and their counterparts in Leeds. These included middle-class activists like Barbara Lowrie, Mary Foster, Isabella, and Bessie but there were also working-class women who were active members. Some, including Mrs Walt Wood and Mrs Tom Duncan, were married to labour leaders, whereas others, such as Agnes Close, were themselves trade union activists. Despite their varied backgrounds, these female socialists shared one thing in common: a concern to improve the economic and social position of working-class women. The focus of their activities may have been different, but they all saw trade union organization, the demand for political equality, and the movement for socialism as part of the same broad struggle to achieve working women's emancipation.

Of all the female propagandists in the West Riding ILP, it was Isabella who was perhaps the most successful in drawing attention to the needs of working women. With her 'Irish wit' and wide knowledge of women's rights issues she was a popular speaker, and by the late 1890s had addressed audiences in most of the towns in Yorkshire. But she still found public speaking a nerve-wracking experience; writing to Millicent Fawcett about a suffrage letter which she hoped to send to the press, Isabella complained

[33]B. Turner, 'Looking Backwards', *Socialist Review* 23/125 (Feb. 1924), pp. 66–7; *LL* 9 Apr. 1914. I am grateful to Clare Collins for drawing my attention to the close friendship between Isabella Ford and the Glasiers.

[34]F. Brockway, *Socialism Over Sixty Years: The Life of Jowett of Bradford* (Geo. Allen & Unwin, 1946), p. 61.

that 'I have, alas! to speak at a Women's Liberal meeting on 27th & I will bring this in if I don't get so terrified (as I generally do) as to forget anything but Mrs Byles' & Mrs Connon's faces gazing at me.'[35]

Writing was a less stressful way for Isabella to express her ideas. She was able to display her talents to the full in a column, 'Up and Down the World', which appeared monthly between 1898 and 1899 in the ILP paper *Leeds Forward*. Her writings in the column ranged freely over a wide variety of questions of relevance to women in the different social classes – the state regulation of prostitution, the struggle for the vote, work conditions, and the role of women in revolutionary movements. Drawing examples from all over the world, Isabella tried to make her readers aware of the international dimensions of the women's movement. Clearly enjoying this attempt at regular journalism, she made sure that all her stories had a humorous twist, with Mark Twain a favourite source of amusing quotations.[36]

Her main purpose was not just to entertain her readers. She also wanted to show that women made a positive contribution to public affairs throughout the world and had a wider range of abilities than was usually assumed. A typical story was one in which she attacked the Board of Trade for refusing to give women a certificate of competence to manage a vessel. It concerned a New York ship that had been missing for over six months; the crew, including the captain, were helpless from scurvy, and when the ship was found 'the captain's wife was steering the vessel. She also prepared the food for the stricken men, which the rescuing boat brought on board for them and nursed them all safely through their sickness. She must be a tolerably competent woman.' Running through all her pieces was the theme that 'everywhere women have greater cause to cry for vengeance than men have, and that is why even for a peaceful revolution such as trade unionism or socialism, the presence and influence of women is absolutely essential'.[37]

Isabella also made use of material from other countries. Some came from friends living abroad, who sent Isabella items to use, but much of it was based on her own wide reading and travel. In July 1898, for example, she visited Jersey to stay with friends and found that 'there is no smoke here for there are no manufactures, and no one seems poor & miserable'. Her friends had lived here since October, '& have only once seen a beggar! . . . They have different land laws from ours. My friends grow potatoes for the market and it seems such a pleasant way of earning your living – and so easy.' None the less, she was still appreciative of the strengths of her own country. Although she found everything very slow in England compared to

[35]Isabella Ford to Millicent Fawcett, undated but *c*.1898–9, Manchester Central Lib. Mrs Byles was a Bradford suffragist and wife of the Liberal editor of the *Bradford Observer*. Rhoda Connon was a leading member of the Leeds Women's Suffrage Society.
[36]*LF* Oct. 1898; see also Dec. 1898.
[37]Ibid., Dec. 1898.

the upheavals abroad, the latter brought 'bitterness and rage which put things back so much afterwards. Think how our speech and our thoughts are unfettered in England – as they are nowhere else.'[38]

December was spent, as always, in her London flat, and on this occasion she gave a lecture for the Humanitarian League on the 'Women's Movement in Relation to Humanitarianism.' Isabella had spoken under the auspices of the Humanitarian League on a number of occasions, but it was not until this time that she decided to take a more prominent part in its affairs by becoming a member of the executive committee. The secretary was Henry Salt, and many other members of Edward Carpenter's circle of friends were involved in the League's activities. Its stated objects were to 'humanise . . . the conditions of modern society' and to seek the 'avoidance of the infliction of unnecessary suffering on any sentient being'. Members took a special interest in prison reform, the rights of animals, and the ending of cruel sports.[39] The League was an example of the many 'moral' reform groups of the period which drew together men and women from varied political backgrounds, in particular feminists, socialists, and radical liberals.

Given their family background it is hardly surprising that Isabella and her brothers and sisters supported the League; Isabella was chairman of the Leeds branch of the RSPCA, while Bessie founded a cats' home and took a lifelong interest in decrepit horses. In 1899, their brother John Rawlinson resigned his post as chairman of the council of the Yorkshire College rather than sanction the proposal of the Medical School to obtain a licence for vivisection.[40]

As far as Isabella was concerned, the treatment of female workers could also be included in any list of inhumane practices. In her lecture to the League in December she drew a vivid contrast 'between the benign, polished and respected employer as he appears in London society, and the same man as he is known (too often) to his workpeople in the dismal coal-tracts of the North'. As usual she made her lecture come alive by giving a 'series of life sketches, drawn from actual experience', which highlighted the rudeness of the overseer, the system of fines, and the 'tyrannous abuse of power by which the morality of the girls is often undermined'. After her customary attack on philanthropists she concluded: 'those who would benefit women should act on the humanitarian principle of *preventing* injustice instead of the philanthropic principle of merely trying to *palliate* it'.[41] Although the lecture followed a familiar pattern, it did focus more strongly than usual on the importance of the vote for working women. Isabella suggested that, whatever its imperfections, the vote was at least a

[38]Isabella Ford to Alf Mattison, 22 July 1898, Alf Mattison's Letter Book.
[39]'The Humanitarian League's Work', *Humanitarian* (Nov. 1903), pp. 162–3.
[40]*Humanity*, III, 50 (April, 1899).
[41]'The Woman's Movement', ibid. (Jan. 1899), pp. 99–100.

recognition of equality, and most industrial evils arose from the fact that women were treated as inferiors. This change of emphasis in her analysis was as yet only slight, and she continued to argue that trade union organization represented the best way forward for female workers.

Isabella spent the early weeks of 1899 in London, leaving Agnes Close to carry the burden of organizing work in Leeds. Agnes arranged the weekly socials at the Women's Trade Union Club and spoke at organizing meetings with officials of the Amalgamated Union of Clothing Operatives (AUCO). When she came back home in April, however, Isabella helped out as much as she could, often speaking to several meetings in the same week. But the effort involved was great, and she complained to Alf Mattison: 'I shall refuse to go to Heaven if they have meetings there, for I am weary of them.'[42]

In June Isabella returned to London once again to take part in an International Congress of Women. She was now on the executive committee of the WTUL and was asked by the secretary, Gertrude Tuckwell, to attend a meeting at Lipton's tea factory on the League's behalf. The meeting had been called by Mr Barnham of the Workers' Union, who thought that there was discontent among female workers in the firm. Isabella, however, found 'no mutiny (as usual!!) only two girls who came to pay in their money·. . . they funnel and wrap 35,000 packets of tea a week . . . wages 7s. If they rise to 50,000 wages 12s. This very seldom occurs. When girls faint and they don't come round soon & have to be sent home, their wages are stopped during the fainting episode and also the wage of the girl sent to see the sick girl home, while she is taking her home.'

After hearing that Keir Hardie was interested in conditions at Lipton's, Isabella sent him these details. Cautious as usual about the accuracy of her information, she warned him that all her statements needed verifying. She was unable to do this herself, she said, since she did not intend to return to London until November; but, she reported, 'I don't trust Barnham and the two men I saw were, I thought, rather boastful & wide in their statements'.[43] Members of the Women's Industrial Council, including Clementina Black, were later to take up some of the grievances noted by Isabella, and in 1902 Lipton's agreed that women workers should be provided with wash-basins and an afternoon tea-break.[44]

When she returned to Yorkshire at the end of July, Isabella took part in the campaign that had already begun to organize Bradford women workers, who were among the lowest-paid weavers in Yorkshire. In the context of increasing foreign competition in the 1890s, employers in the wool and worsted trade sought to cut costs by speeding up the pace of machinery,

[42]Isabella Ford to Alf Mattison, n.d., 1898., Alf Mattison's Letter Book.
[43]Isabella Ford to Keir Hardie, 12 Aug. 1899, Francis Johnson Coll., LSE.
[44]E. Mappen, *Women at Work: The Women's Industrial Council, 1889–1914* (Hutchinson, 1985), pp. 19–20.

substituting female for male workers, and lowering prices. This placed a barrier in the way of effective organization by reducing wages and dividing the interests of men and women. Faced with a low trade union membership among both sexes, the leaders of the GUTW decided to make a concerted effort to recruit Bradford weavers. The campaign began with a meeting of trade-unionists on 21 June. It was given a boost in the following month when 250 female weavers from Brigella Mills went on strike in support of male overlookers who had been dismissed.

Isabella joined the 'crusade' on the 26 July, when she spoke with Edith Priestman at a conference called by the Bradford Trade Council. They were optimistic that difficulties could be overcome if only male trade-unionists would encourage their female relatives to join a union. Isabella thought that any man who wished to be sent as a delegate to the Trades Council ought to be asked if his female relatives were in a union. If this were not the case, he should not be chosen. She gave examples of women's wages from her recent visit to Lipton's and ended her speech with a plea that teachers should give children a more positive view of trade-unionism.[45]

The campaign continued throughout the next two months. On 10 August, Isabella joined Arthur and Edith Priestman at a meeting held in their own factory and urged weavers to join the union. This was followed up by a tea-party for Bradford socialists at Adel. Here Mrs Harrison, a very energetic trade-unionist from Brigella Mills, proposed that meetings should be held throughout the winter and suggested that trade union literature should be distributed in the mills. Isabella felt optimistic about this new movement, for 'all of us who are trade union officials know that the best work often comes from the non-official workers of a union'. Women workers usually used the excuse that they had never heard of trade unions, 'but after this winter is over no worker in Bradford can use this excuse any longer – they will have to invent another'.[46]

In private, Isabella expressed greater reservations about the progress of female trade-unionism and the movement for independent labour politics. She was particularly concerned in the early months of 1899 about the problems faced by the Leeds ILP. Although the engineers' lock-out of 1897–8 had led to an influx of new members into the ILP and helped to change the political outlook of the Leeds Trades Council, the local party suffered from internal difficulties. Joseph Burgess, the former secretary, had run up massive debts before leaving the city, and Bessie and Isabella appear to have been left to deal with them. In July 1899 they wrote to tell Edward Carpenter that they were unable to give more than a £1 to his Prisoners' Aid Society because 'we are steadily being drained to pay off appalling debts and muddles which Burgess has left behind . . . they are debts which benefit no

[45]YFT 4 Aug. 1899.
[46]I. O. Ford, 'Organisation in Bradford', WTUR (Oct. 1899), pp. 1516.

one & we hate paying them, but someone must in order to save the Cause from disgrace . . . one wouldn't mind if they were really *nice* debts . . . it is a little wearisome, all this continual impecunity & falling among the prophets.'[47] By August things looked brighter. Local members of the ILP came to Adel to enjoy a gala, and in a letter written to Hardie a week later Isabella said she felt more hopeful: now that Burgess had left the city, the Leeds ILP seemed to be 'moving along', and she thought that 'our debts and troubles have brought some of us closer together'.[48] A closer collaboration between the AUCO and the Tailoresses' Union also appeared more likely during the summer of 1899. Agnes Close had recently taken part in recruiting drives among tailoresses in Manchester and Leeds with Joseph Young, General Secretary of the AUCO, who was taking a greater interest in organizing female workers. Isabella welcomed this development. Now that she was involved in women's trade unionism and socialist politics at a national level she had less time to give to the Tailoresses' Union and she wrote with some relief to Millicent Fawcett that the 'cutters' union (men) are undertaking it & will work with it . . . & I shall renounce any practical responsibility I now have'.[49]

Trade union membership among women in the tailoring trade was even lower than in the Yorkshire wool and worsted industry.[50] Clothing was produced in factories, small and large workshops, and in the home; these varied production methods, coupled with poor working conditions, hampered trade union organization among both men and women. On the surface it seemed as though female workers in the clothing factories were better paid than many other women workers. They could average 14/- to 15/- for a week's wages, although in practice they were rarely able to take such sums home. Weekly wages were systematically reduced by deductions for thread, the use of dining facilities, and donations to worthy causes, as well as fines for lateness and damaged goods. Take-home pay was lowered still further by seasonal variations in demand. With earnings so low, female workers were reluctant to pay contributions to a union which seemed too weak to do anything for them.

Divisions in the labour force based on method of production, sex, skill, and ethnicity reduced the willingness of clothing workers to take collective action or to organize together. Male cutters in the factories, for instance, who had often served some form of apprenticeship in the bespoke sector, felt little solidarity with less-skilled tailoresses. Existing divisions in the

[47]Isabella Ford to Edward Carpenter, 24 July 1899, Carpenter Coll., Sheffield Ref. Lib.
[48]Isabella Ford to Keir Hardie, 12 Aug. 1899, Francis Johnson Coll.
[49]Isabella Ford to Millicent Fawcett, undated but *c.*1898–9, Manchester Central Lib.
[50]In 1899 the Leeds Tailoresses' Union had 50 members; the AUCO had 1,222 male and 63 female members. AUCO membership figures are the total for all branches. There were no female members in Leeds. For a detailed discussion of the Leeds ready-made tailoring trade, see J. Hannam, 'The Employment of Working-Class Women in Leeds, 1880–1914', Ph.D. thesis, University of Sheffield, 1985.

factories were then reinforced by management practices. Male workers enjoyed privileges which did not apply to women; in contrast to female workers they could use the dining facilities without paying a weekly charge and could leave the factory when there was no work to be done, whereas women were forced to stay inside in case late orders came in.

Separate organizations had developed to cater for the different groups within the labour force, but by the turn of the century only a minority of clothing workers in the factory sector were organized. The Tailoresses' Union was reduced to a small core of active members, while the men's union found it difficult to recruit members at a time of increased competition in the ready-made trade. In this context leaders of the AUCO sought to broaden the union's membership base and, after much debate, the annual conference of 1899 finally agreed to admit women. A similar decision had been taken two years earlier by the Amalgamated Society of Tailors, which catered for the bespoke section of the trade. In welcoming these developments the Women's Trade Union League claimed that it had always believed that 'a great part of the difficulties attending the organisation of tailoresses would vanish if both the men's unions were willing to admit women'.[51]

This proved to be an exceedingly optimistic point of view. A formal decision to admit female members did not automatically mean that a great deal of effort would be put into their organization, nor that the specific needs of female workers would be emphasized. The enthusiasm of union leaders for a broader membership policy was not always shared by rank-and-file male workers, and the Leeds branch refused at first to take in female members. This may be the reason why the plan to amalgamate the Leeds Tailoresses' Union and the AUCO in November 1899 was not carried out.

It had been assumed that Agnes Close would become an organizer for the women's section of the AUCO.[52] When plans for the amalgamation were shelved she remained as an independent female organizer, using the Women's Trade Union Club as a base. Working among both tailoresses and textile workers she acted as a collector for the GUTW and held a special meeting at the club once a week in order to attract textile workers into the union. She still represented the Tailoresses' Union on the Trades Council, taking an active part in its affairs, as well as turning up to give help and advice at any dispute affecting female workers.

Early in 1900 Agnes Close took part in a campaign led by the WTUL and male trade-unionists to change many of the proposals in the latest Bill to revise the Factory Acts. Both Agnes and Isabella helped local women to draft a letter of complaint to the home secretary about those clauses which gave greater flexibility to employers to use overtime. Isabella was worried

[51] *WTUR* (Dec. 1899), p. 6.
[52] *YFT* 20 Oct. 1899. Details of the negotiations appeared week by week.

about calling for any restriction in overtime which only applied to women, but showed her usual willingness to change her views once she had spoken to the tailoresses themselves. Women were so firmly established in the ready-made tailoring trade that they 'shrieked with laughter' when she 'faintly suggested that to apply for further legal restrictions on their work, such as abolition of all overtime – might endanger their economic position and let in men to do their work. "Men do our work, not they! It's not men's work, not men's pay. They cannot do without us".'[53]

In a covering note to the home secretary, which accompanied the letter from the tailoresses, Isabella was careful to point out that the issues being raised were those that women workers themselves found important. Tailoresses objected to overtime because they received no extra rate of pay, were extremely tired after a normal working day, and could not put in good work.[54] The London Trades Council and the WTUL also campaigned against the provisions of the Bill, and some modifications were eventually made.

Isabella not only supported movements which brought together male and female trade-unionists at home, but also sought co-operation between workers across national boundaries. In July, therefore, she once again attended the International Textile Workers' Congress, held this time in Berlin. The delegation from England was much smaller than in previous years. There were only three Yorkshire delegates – Isabella, Ben Turner, and Allen Gee – compared with the eight at Roubaix which may have reflected the difficulties that the union was facing in attracting members. For a time these problems seemed remote as Isabella listened to the speeches of European delegates, and she left the congress with the words of Herr Liebnecht, the father of the German revolutionary, 'ringing in her ears'. She later wrote that he 'spoke of the Brotherhood of the workers', saying that this alone 'can build a new and a great nation, a nation which will include all races and will spread through all countries'.[55]

Such inspiring speeches helped to revive Isabella's spirits as she returned home to face the seemingly impossible task of trying to persuade even a minority of working women in the West Riding to join trade unions. She was keen to arrange her usual August garden party for textile workers so that they could meet Gertrude Tuckwell, who was staying as a guest at the Grange. Torrential rain threatened to spoil the event, and Isabella telegraphed to Bradford, Leeds, and Farsley to cancel it. But not everyone received the message and twenty-seven mill workers from Bradford, including Julia Varley and Mrs Harrison, leader of the Brigella Mills dispute,

[53] I. O. Ford, 'Women Workers in the Wholesale Clothing Trade', *Englishwoman*, 2/6 (July 1909), p. 638.
[54] *WTUR* (July 1900), pp. 32–5.
[55] Isabella Ford's contribution to 'May Day Messages from British Women', *LL* 29 Apr. 1915.

made the long journey to Adel. They went to Leeds by train and from there they took the tram to Far Headingley; after 'a lovely country walk', they finally arrived at Adel to be met by Agnes Close, Tom Paylor, and textile workers from Leeds.

A description of the garden party written by a Bradford mill worker gives a glimpse of what took place at these events. When they arrived at Adel, the textile workers and their union officials enjoyed a 'sumptuous tea', and were then joined by Allen Gee and Ben Turner as they explored the grounds. Some went on the lake where Mr Broderick, president of the Bradford branch, 'made heroic efforts to propel a boat oar, but being more used to the picking stick and shuttle, the speed was not of the university scullers. A good lot of fun was had in that half hour all the same.' As rain clouds began to gather, they went inside the house to hear Gertrude Tuckwell and Isabella give advice about how to organize a recruiting campaign during the winter. After much singing they set off for Leeds, some to visit friends and some to be entertained by Agnes Close at the Women's Club. No one, we are told, arrived home before the small hours of the morning. The writer of the article concluded that 'it is to be hoped that more of these gatherings will be organized, as the intercourse of members will surely be for the good of the union, rubbing off corners and melting reserve among the girls who will get to know each other better and understand the individual difficulties of their fellow workers'.[56]

Gertrude Tuckwell returned in November to help the Bradford recruiting campaign, and in the same month, at the invitation of the GUTW, Mrs Marland Brodie of the WTUL completed a fortnight's organizing work in Leeds. She met female union members at the Women's Trade Union Club and spoke at numerous indoor public meetings in the local area, including one at the Hunslet Co-operative Guild where she talked to the mothers of the girls she hoped to reach. Isabella chaired two meetings at her own Mill Hill night-school, and the League organizer praised both Isabella and Agnes for working 'hard and willingly, as they always do'.[57]

Although a few extra members were enrolled after such organizing drives, it was difficult to retain the interest once the enthusiasm generated by a meeting or a strike was over. By 1900, female membership of the General Union of Textile Workers had slumped from a high point of 1,400 in 1896 to 414. The Leeds Tailoresses' Union faced similar difficulties, and by the turn of the century had only 50 members. This led to renewed efforts to complete negotiations to amalgamate with the AUCO which had been abandoned several months before. Union leaders came to a tentative agreement in June, although obstacles were still put in their way. The Leicester branch objected to members of the Tailoresses' Union joining the AUCO

[56]*YFT* 31 Aug. 1900.
[57]*WTUR* (Jan. 1901), p. 15.

unless they paid an entrance fee; opposition was only dropped when Joseph Young reminded the men that this was an amalgamation, and therefore the tailoresses, as union members already, should not have to pay again.

It was not only male members of the union who expressed objections to the amalgamation. Many of the committee members of the Tailoresses' Union were unhappy about the decision. Several years later Isabella recalled that 'the women were somewhat reluctant to be thus amalgamated, fearing that those of their interests which were not identical with the men's interests might be neglected. I shared their fears.'[58] Isabella always felt torn by this issue. She knew that the specific interests of women workers were often neglected in male-dominated unions, but she had to balance this against the weaknesses that came from a divided labour force and single-sex trade-unionism. In the end she chose to advocate mixed-sex organization as a way of strengthening workers against their employers, although she was conscious that this could bring losses as well as gains for working women.

The transition to a mixed-sex clothing union marked a turning point for both Agnes Close and Isabella; the lukewarm and often hostile response of the Leeds branch towards female workers made it impossible for Agnes, with her feminist beliefs, to make a career as a full-time organizer of the AUCO. For some months she continued to act as an independent organizer. Persistent ill-health and frustration at being isolated from the mainstream of union work, however, persuaded her to change the direction of her life, and in 1902 she emigrated to Canada. Isabella's life was also changed by the amalgamation. There was little place for a middle-class woman in a mixed-sex organization run by working-class men, many of whom were overtly hostile to the needs of women workers. When the union did start to recruit more female members after 1906, its organizers were drawn from the ranks of working women, a development that Isabella would have approved of. She continued to speak at meetings and during recruiting drives, but no longer took part in the painstaking day-by-day work of organization.

Any practical barriers to Isabella's trade union work coincided, however, with a change of emphasis in her own ideas about the best way to achieve improvements in women's work conditions. In 1900 she was asked by the *Women's Trade Union Review* to join other leading male and female trade-unionists in giving her views on the difficulties of organizing women. Looking back over ten years of hard work, in which only a handful of women in the Yorkshire clothing and textile trades had become permanent union members, she had to admit that she had found the struggle 'a most disheartening and painful one'. She did not blame women for this. From an early age they were taught by relatives, by the 'orthodox religious world', and by philanthropists to be submissive and to reject trade-unionism.

[58]*LWC* 16 Jan. 1914.

Society encouraged selfish indifference in women; they were encouraged to put their own homes before anything else and, excluded from the parliamentary franchise, they were ignored as human beings. The only possible solution, in her view, was to change both the attitudes of society towards women and also the female worker's own perception of her industrial worth. 'It sometimes seems to me as if we had the whole world to fight; certainly every form of conventional thought must be fought, particularly amongst the workers themselves. Real trade unionism for women means a moral and industrial revolution, and many people dread a revolution. They prefer stagnation, particularly for women.'[59]

Isabella was beginning to think that only women's suffrage would provide the context in which such a change in attitudes could be achieved. She had always argued that both trade union organization and the vote were necessary to improve women's industrial position. The disappointments of her work among tailoresses and textile workers now led her to shift the emphasis of her own activities towards political action. In this respect it is interesting to compare pamphlets that she wrote at the beginning and end of the decade. In *Women's Wages*, published in 1893, she was optimistic about the possibilities of organizing women: 'when we observe the efforts now being made by men Trade Unionists to make women join their unions on the same terms with men; when we see that the idea is stirring in some minds that for the same work a woman is entitled to receive the same pay that a man receives; when we see all this, then we know that a better day is coming for women.'[60] By the early 1900s, when it was obvious that these high hopes had not been fulfilled, there was a subtle change in her analysis. In the pamphlet *Industrial Women and how to Help Them*, published in 1901, she continued to criticize philanthropists and called for a 'well organised rebellion' generated from below by working women themselves. This time, however, she put greater emphasis on the need to gain women's suffrage before any real changes could occur. The vote would encourage women to exercise the responsibilities of citizenship and would give them the legal power to improve their industrial conditions, whereas at the moment their lives were affected by laws in which they had no say. The crux of her argument lay in the relationship between the vote and trade-unionism.

> Certainly trade unions will never flourish amongst women, until on election days the female union voice can make itself heard alongside of the male trade union voice, and some legal result of trade unionism can come to women, won by their own efforts. It has always been so with men; and men and women are wonderfully alike. . . . That the improved status a vote would give these women would be a large factor in raising their wages there cannot be the smallest doubt. In the

[59] *WTUR* (Jan. 1900), pp.12–13.
[60] I. O. Ford, *Women's Wages* (Humanitarian League, 1893), p. 16.

language of the girls themselves about it: They don't dare put on a man same as they do on us; not they! 'Of course not,' said a man trade unionist; 'you see men have a vote.'[61]

Isabella had learnt a great deal from her experiences as a trade union organizer; she had developed her talents as a speaker and as a writer, become an acknowledged expert on the conditions of women's industrial work, and had gained skills as a negotiator and social investigator. Her greater confidence is suggested by the style of her pamphlet; speculating freely over a range of issues, she presented her arguments in a flowing style and allowed herself to depart from the safety of detailed facts and figures. After the turn of the century, however, she no longer used her talents in trade union work. Instead, she directed more of her energies towards political agitation. Having come to believe that women's suffrage and the achievement of socialism held out the greatest hope for a change in working women's industrial lives, she was now convinced that she had the ability to influence such developments at a national level.

[61]Id., *Industrial Women and How to Help Them* (Humanitarian League, 1901), p. 10.

5

Working Women and the Suffrage, 1901–1904

Political equality is an essential corollary to economic equality.

In the early 1900s Isabella played an increasingly important role in the affairs of the Independent Labour Party. Elected to the National Administrative Council (NAC) in 1903, she spent the next four years as a propagandist for socialism and women's suffrage at a national as well as at a local level. Convinced that neither women nor workers would achieve emancipation unless their causes were linked, she joined with other female socialists in trying to persuade the ILP and the wider labour movement to take the interests of women seriously. She also added her voice to all those who thought that the labour movement should take up women's suffrage for the sake of the woman worker. Her decision to concentrate on political work was not simply a result of the difficulties she had experienced as a trade union organizer. It must also be seen in the context of a more general revival of interest in women's suffrage towards the end of the nineteenth century.

One impetus for this came from the Boer War; the government's claim that it was fighting to secure political rights for the Uitlanders, a group of British *émigré* workers in the Transvaal, encouraged women to draw an analogy with their own exclusion from the parliamentary franchise. A further boost was given to the suffrage campaign when female textile workers in the north of England began to call for the vote. In both cases women from all social classes came together to demand the right to be heard and to take part in decision-making. This ensured that the movement for women's rights in the pre-war years would be more broadly based than before, with a greater prominence being given to the needs of working-class women, both as workers and as mothers.[1]

Although they differed in their attitudes towards the Boer War, feminists took advantage of the occasion to raise the question of women's rights.

---

[1] A. Phillips, *Divided Loyalties: Dilemmas of Sex and Class* (Virago, 1987), pp. 87–98.

Isabella opposed the war from the beginning. She had a deep-seated Quaker revulsion against the use of violence to solve disputes and also supported the ILP argument that this particular war was an abuse of imperial power. Joining her friend Alf Mattison on the Leeds branch of the South Africa Conciliation Committee – composed of anti-war ILP socialists and radical liberals – she addressed peace meetings all over the West Riding, often facing abuse from hostile crowds.

Women who opposed the war also began to link together feminism and peace, arguing that militarism could only be harmful to the interests of their sex. When the Women's Co-operative Guild organized a meeting in Leeds in December 1900 to protest against plans to introduce conscription, letters and messages came pouring in 'from women of all ranks of life, and this was fitting, for the evil, the possibility of which had brought us together, would affect both rich and poor'. Finding it impossible to confine themselves to opposing conscription, the female speakers turned the meeting into a more general indictment against the use of war to settle disputes and emphasized the special interest that women had in securing peace. Attention was drawn to the effects of war on the material conditions of women's lives, especially the rise in the price of food and other necessities. The suffering of women and children in South Africa was also considered. Isabella based her own speech on a letter that she had received from Olive Schreiner, who expressed the fear that 'to her and to many other colonists the worst legacy of this war would be their loss of love for England . . . how could it be otherwise when one saw, as she had done, farms set fire to, homesteads needlessly wrecked, and families, including of course the women and the little children, turned into the fields or streets, without food, extra clothing, or shelter?'. From the chair Mrs Courtney, wife of a Liberal MP and sister of Beatrice Webb, a leading member of the Fabian Society, spoke of the brutalizing effects of war on all participants: 'witness . . . the rejoicing over so many killed . . . the drunkeness, the shouting in our streets . . . and the loud expressions of vindictiveness'. Drawing attention to the relationship between war and notions of masculinity, Mrs Wilson, an ILP member from Halifax, criticized Boy's Brigades for teaching military drill, which 'familiarised our boys with war in their early and most impressionable years'.[2]

When they argued that women would tend to use their influence to secure peace, opponents of the war raised the question of voting rights; if women remained disenfranchised it would be impossible for them to have any effect on foreign policy. Even supporters of the war, including Millicent Fawcett and Agnes, used the publicity surrounding the political rights of the Uitlanders to demand that women at home should have the vote. At the same time, textile workers in the north of England also drew attention to women's suffrage by demanding that they too should have a voice in

[2] *Co-operative News*, 1 Dec. 1900.

politics. Working women had taken part in previous high points of the suffrage campaign; in the early 1880s Agnes Sunley from Leeds and Alice Scatcherd had taken a petition from door to door in working-class districts in Yorkshire and had obtained signatures from a large number of women workers. In 1893 Isabella and Millicent Fawcett collected over a quarter of a million signatures for a similar petition, circulated among women from all social classes. The North West was a particularly active area. However, the majority of female workers still showed considerable resistance to women's suffrage, and the campaign remained largely confined to middle-class women.

By the turn of the century, attitudes had begun to change. The movement for independent labour politics, which culminated in the formation of the Labour Representation Committee in 1900, raised interest in women's exclusion from the franchise. Female trade-unionists in the cotton industry found that they were being asked to pay a political levy to support prospective Labour candidates, including their own union leader, David Shackleton, without being able to vote themselves. This caused strong resentment and encouraged Esther Roper and Eva Gore Booth, members of the North of England Women's Suffrage Society, to launch a new petition to be signed by Lancashire workers. Recognizing that the growing interest of working women could add a new dimension to the suffrage campaign, they designed their petition to appeal to the specific interests of the female worker. It made connections, therefore, between political inequality and poor conditions of work, both in industry and the home. Suffrage workers, ILP socialists, and members of local branches of the Women's Co-operative Guild took round the petition; it was signed by over 30,000 textile workers before being presented to the House of Commons on 18 March 1901.[3]

News of the campaign soon crossed the Pennines; Isabella's friend Sarah Reddish, a former mill worker and now president of the Bolton Women's Co-operative Guild, had been one of the main organizers of the Lancashire petition. She decided to follow this up by launching a second petition among women textile workers in Cheshire and Yorkshire. In the Leeds area it was Isabella, Agnes Close, Tom Paylor, and Mrs Watson of the General Union of Textile Workers who knocked on doors or stood outside factory gates collecting signatures. By March 1902, 33,184 female textile workers in Yorkshire and 4,300 in Cheshire had signed; Agnes Close and Mrs Watson were among the working women who travelled to London to present the petition to a group of MPs.[4] Isabella went with them and found that, although the MPs spoke politely, 'the usual vagueness of expression employed on such occasions rather opened the women's eyes, . . . to a

[3]For a discussion of the campaign in Lancashire, see J. Liddington, *The Life and Times of a Respectable Rebel: Selina Cooper, 1864–1946* (Virago, 1984).
[4]*Yorkshire Factory Times (YFT)*, 14 Feb. 1902.

better understanding of the size of the battle which lies before them. Their backs began to stiffen a little.' In the evening Keir Hardie organized a public meeting in Chelsea where speeches were given by many of the women, including Agnes Close, Mrs Watson, and Sarah Reddish, whom Isabella described as the 'principal organizer of the work'.

In her account of the deputation and meeting, Isabella made a clear statement of why she saw the vote as so important. Denying that it was a purely political demand or one that was confined to middle-class women, she pointed out that the women's movement aimed to include all classes. If the Franchise Bills put forward were often limited in scope, this was only because of tactical reasons. From Mary Wollstonecraft onwards the women's movement had sought broad social reforms to benefit women, and that was why the question was 'so continually shelved and so intensely disliked by the House of Commons'. Aware that not all socialists took the women's movement seriously, Isabella criticized them for being short sighted: 'whenever a class is taught to accept as privileges what are really its rights, that class becomes demoralised and . . . retards the progress of the entire community'. It was no point complaining that women acted as blacklegs or undersold male workers. Those were the faults to which a class 'kept in a state of dependence, of political servitude, is prone'.[5] Women would only become fully responsible when they were able to take part in political life through the exercise of the vote.

The appearance of Isabella's article in the *Labour Leader*, a weekly paper owned and edited by Keir Hardie, the acknowledged leader of the ILP, provides just one indication of her more prominent role in party affairs. She now had more contact with the leaders of the ILP: in the first week of March she returned to London to take the chair at a meeting of the Metropolitan Council of the ILP when Keir Hardie spoke on the labour movement. Both Isabella and Bessie also began to give increased financial support to the party. In March they contributed £10 towards the £80 needed to cover Phillip Snowden's expenses in the Wakefield by-election and at the end of the year they donated a furthur £6 to the special effort fund.[6]

Just as Isabella was becoming more involved in national labour politics, the Leeds Central Socialist Club decided to honour the Ford sisters' contribution to the local labour movement. At a reception held in April, Bessie and Isabella were presented with an illustrated scroll, 'a work of art, done for love by a club member'. They were thanked for 'their unselfish work, not only for this institution, but for humanity in general . . . all trust Comrades Ford will live long to continue their strenuous efforts on behalf of a suffering community'. Friends they had worked with over many years –

[5] I. O. Ford, 'Women and the Franchise', *Labour Leader* (*LL*), 1 Mar. 1902.
[6] *LL* 15 Mar., 22 Mar., and 20 Dec. 1902.

Ben Turner, Walt Wood, Agnes Close, Tom Paylor – were all there to see the presentation and to enjoy the two sisters' 'invigorating speeches'.[7]

Despite the many long hours spent in local political and trade union work over the last twelve years, Isabella had somehow managed to continue writing fiction. Her second novel, _On the Threshold_, was published in 1895; it explored the dilemmas faced by the young middle-class women who enjoyed greater personal freedoms than their mothers but were still confined by social expectations and conventions. The two central female characters, Kitty and Lucretia, go to London, ostensibly to study art and music. Their main aim, however, is to escape 'well-bred respectability' and to find out about new ideas on love and marriage. In one passage Kitty says: 'You see, Lucretia, loving a person seems such a huge boundless thing; and when you talk of marrying, it seems to cramp it down, to fetter it. . . . women always have to settle – to settle down, just as if they were dregs.'[8]

In common with other 'new women' novelists of the 1890s,[9] Isabella used her first two books to express ideas about women's social role and the potential for change in personal relationships. In her third and final novel, _Mr Elliott,_ published at the end of 1901, she drew for the first time on her experiences as a trade union organizer. Dramatic action was provided by a strike, but the purpose of the book was to explore the psychology of Sam Elliott, a mill owner and self-made man, who had once been a factory worker himself. In the course of the novel he becomes increasingly selfish and neglectful of his wife, who never settles to her new role as a wealthy woman and misses her old friends from the mill. By the time of her death the couple have nothing in common; their rise to the ranks of the employing class has failed to bring personal happiness.

Most reviewers agreed that the novel provided a realistic description of life and work in a northern factory town. Some considered this a source of weakness, since it made the book too gloomy to enjoy. Others found the realism one of the book's strengths; the female reviewer in the _Women's Trade Union Review_ was particularly moved: 'Depression closes in on us while we read "Mr Elliott", and as we shut the book the sordidness and dreariness of the most debased life of our great northern factory towns seem to have entered into our souls'. None the less, she thought that 'some of the grace which characterised the previous slighter books is missing'.[10]

More unqualified praise came in a letter from a favourite nephew, Richard Ford Smith, whom Isabella visited regularly when she went to

---

[7] _YFT_ 4 Apr. 1902.
[8] _LL_ 16 Nov. 1895.
[9] For a discussion of the 'new woman' novelist, see L. Bland, 'The Married Woman, the "New Woman" and the Feminist Sexual Politics of the 1890s', in J. Rendall, ed,. _Equal or Different: Women's Politics, 1800–1914_ (Oxford: Blackwell, 1987).
[10] _Women's Trade Union Review_, Jan. 1902, p. 15. See also the collection of reviews in Isabella Ford's scrapbook, Leeds Archives.

London. It was addressed to him in the third person:

> His letter is delightful & so very understanding – I must write a line at once & thank him for it. All he says dear about the book is so exactly what I meant people to see in it that I feel quite set up with his letter, dear . . . I always feel he understands things in life Ford dear – he does – he isn't like other people . . . [11]

Isabella never found time again to write a full-length novel. After 1900, socialist and suffragist agitation came to absorb so much of her energy that she had to content herself in future with writing short stories. Most of these appeared in the *Labour Leader* between 1902 and 1906. 'Our Jane Annie', 'Mother and Daughter', and 'Maria on Strike' explored relationships between working-class women; the first two between mother and daughter, the third between women on strike. All the stories contained colloquial dialogue and were clearly based on experiences Isabella had gained in trade union work. In the third story she used the incident of the girl stealing a collecting box which had occurred during the Manningham Mills dispute in Bradford many years before. Inspiration for other stories came from diverse sources. 'In the Days of the Press Gang' was based on an old tale told to Isabella during one of her Whitby holidays, while 'The Children' was a translation from a German edition of Dostoevsky. [12] Although her novels had received favourable reviews, Isabella remained modest about her literary abilities. When she sent 'Our Jane Annie' to Keir Hardie she enclosed a stamped addressed envelope for return, 'as I am afraid it won't be of use to you'. [13]

Isabella's interest in literature was shared by many of her socialist contemporaries. In Leeds, Alfred Orage, a schoolteacher and member of the ILP, and Holbrook Jackson, a writer and Fabian, established an Arts Club to promote reform in art, manners, and culture. The membership fee of 10*s*.6*d*. was prohibitive for most working people; the club therefore attracted mainly white-collar workers, teachers, and middle-class intellectuals who had an interest in modernist aesthetics and socialist politics. The three Ford sisters all belonged to it; Emily, a vice-president of the Yorkshire Union of Artists, was enthusiastic about the modernist movement in art. Isabella, on the other hand, took a particular interest in drama, and one of her set speeches for the ILP was on Ibsen as a forerunner of socialist thought. [14] The Leeds Arts Club provided Isabella with a congenial environment in which to think and to develop her ideas in discussion with like-minded colleagues. It gave her a much-needed breathing space at a time when her life as a political agitator was becoming more and more hectic.

---

[11]Richard Ford Smith to Isabella Ford, 20 Oct. 1901, Correspondence Files, Fawcett Lib.
[12]*LL* 29 Nov. 1902; 4 April 1903; 27 May 1904; 15 Dec. 1905; 2 Mar. 1906.
[13]Isabella Ford to Keir Hardie, 10 Nov. 1902, Francis Johnson Coll., LSE.
[14]For a discussion of the Leeds Arts Club, see M. Gawthorpe, *Up Hill to Holloway* (Penobscot, Maine: Traversity Press, 1962), ch. 14.

The attempt to interest Yorkshire working women in the vote did not stop in March 1902 with the textile workers' petition. Later in the year the Women's Trade Union League gave support for a new petition to be circulated, this time among tailoresses in the West Riding. Once again Isabella, Bessie, Agnes Close, Walt Wood, and local leaders of the General Union of Textile Workers set about trying to collect signatures. The work was hampered, however, by a shortage of funds and by the departure of Agnes Close, who left for Canada in the autumn. Agnes was sorely missed; through her trade union work she had built up close contacts with tailoresses and had been an energetic petitioner, tirelessly calling on women in their own homes.

By January 1903 only 9,000 signatures had been collected.[15] It was with a sense of regret, therefore, that Isabella took time off from petitioning to travel to Newcastle, where she represented the ILP at the annual conference of the Labour Representation Committee.[16] As the only female delegate she might have felt isolated had it not been for the presence of old friends from Leeds, including Joseph Young of the Amalgamated Union of Clothing Operatives (AUCO). Although Isabella did not make a speech, her attendance at the conference shows that she was now taking a more important part in the affairs of the ILP. Isabella's first task after the Conference was to accompany the leaders of the GUTW to London to present the tailoresses' petition, which called for women to have the vote on the same terms as it is or may be given to men. Sympathetic MPs – Hardie, Burns, and Shackelton – met the deputation and agreed to submit the petition along with two others, signed by ILP members and Trade Councils, on the following Monday.[17] With the tailoresses' suffrage petition safely presented to Parliament, Isabella and Bessie went to Italy for a fortnight's holiday. They returned at the beginning of April in time for Isabella to attend the annual conference of the ILP as a delegate from Leeds. At the age of forty-seven she had at last made up her mind to stand for election to the NAC. Her success on the second ballot came at an opportune moment. The revival in the women's suffrage campaign, based as it was on the discontent of Lancashire working women, brought the 'woman question' to the forefront of political debate in the labour movement. This provided an ideal context for Isabella, as a co-leader of the party, to exert an influence on ILP policy. Her own propaganda was directed more and more towards the importance of the suffrage for working women. In putting forward her ideas, as a speaker and as a writer, she played an important part over the next three years in the growing campaign to convince the ILP to give wholehearted support to the women's cause.

[15] YFT 30 Jan. 1903.
[16] Labour Representation Committee, *Annual Report*, 1903.
[17] YFT 6 Mar. 1903.

Now that she was an official representative of the party, Isabella was invited to turn up to major labour and socialist events, where she became better known to other leaders of the ILP; on May Day, for example, she attended a rally organized by the Bradford ILP and Labour Church, and in the evening spoke alongside Keir Hardie on the need for independence in politics. In the following month she was in Castleford with other NAC members to support an ILP conference called for the mining districts of Yorkshire.[18] The crux of her message on all these occasions was that the interests of women and the interests of labour were inextricably linked and must be fought for together.

Isabella's new role on the NAC inevitably meant that she had less time to give to the West Riding labour movement. She missed Agnes Close, both as a friend and also as someone who could be relied on to carry out suffrage and trade union work in her absence. Mrs Watson, however, proved to be a willing replacement. A former weaver, she took over from Agnes as resident organizer at the Women's Trade Union Club and combined this role with that of collector for the GUTW. Despite her efforts, the Women's Trade Union Club, which for seven years had provided a focus for women's organization in Leeds, finally closed in June 1903. Many unions had used the facilities of the club for meetings, thereby helping to keep it solvent, but this source of revenue disappeared when the Leeds Trades Council at last raised the money for its own building.[19] The Women's Trade Union Club had been an attempt to create a separate space for women while at the same time keeping them in touch with the broader labour movement. When it closed, women were more fully absorbed into that movement, but at the price of their specific needs at the work-place often being ignored.

Mrs Watson continued her work as a union organizer and suffrage propagandist from smaller premises in Tong Road. Isabella helped out whenever she could; at the end of July she spoke with Ben Turner at a recruiting drive among female textile workers at Brighouse. A fortnight later she travelled to Morley with Mrs Watson to support Alice Scatcherd, who was trying to interest factory workers in women's suffrage. Isabella was now arguing that 'women must work first of all for the Parliamentary franchise. When they got that they would get everything else they wanted'.[20] It was difficult, however, to turn the initial interest shown by Yorkshire working women in the suffrage into a more sustained political commitment. The weakness of trade-unionism among female workers in Yorkshire meant that they lacked an organizational base from which to develop political confidence, while low pay and poor working conditions sapped their energies. This contrasted with the position in Lancashire,

[18]*LL* 6 June 1903.
[19]*YFT* 17 July 1903.
[20]*YFT* 23 Oct. 1903.

where higher-paid cotton workers used their industrial strength to push forward their political demands. As Christabel Pankhurst explained, 'women textile workers . . . are determined to have their enfranchisement made a trade union question. Already a ballot has been taken of the Bolton Weavers' Union, and the result is a majority of eight to one in favour of "making women's suffrage a trade union question in the same way that Labour representation is".'[21]

None the less, even the well-organized women workers in Lancashire were unable to win whole-hearted support for their demands, either from the Labour Representation Committee or from the trade union movement. The ILP was the most sympathetic group, and in public Isabella always praised its support for women's political equality. Privately, however, she admitted that when she joined Emmeline Pankhurst on the NAC she found its members 'no more than lukewarm on the subject of votes for women'. Among the leaders only Keir Hardie was strongly committed to women's suffrage, while key figures such as Phillip Snowden and John Bruce Glasier were actively hostile.[22]

The objections raised by opponents of the women's suffrage campaign were not necessarily the same; John Bruce Glasier, for example, saw no reason why women needed the vote when they could be represented by men, whereas Phillip Snowden disagreed not with the demand that women should have the vote but with the fact that it would still be a limited franchise. In a context in which voting rights depended on whether an individual householder paid a rent or mortgage, Snowden argued that it was likely that only upper-class women and a small number of middle-class women would be enfranchised. This could positively harm the Labour Party at elections; the majority of working-class women and many adult males would still be unable to vote, while Labour's political opponents would gain an increase in support. Snowden's solution was to call for a measure of adult suffrage which would enfranchise all men and women, regardless of their propertied status.[23]

Faced either with indifference or with outright hostility from the labour movement, Lancashire working women decided to set up their own group, the Lancashire, Cheshire, and Other Women Textile Workers' Representation Committee. Their aim was to field candidates in local and parliamentary elections who would be sympathetic to women's suffrage. This in turn inspired Emmeline Pankhurst, a member of the Manchester ILP, to form in October 1903 yet another group to exert pressure on the ILP to give more energetic support to women's suffrage, the Women's Social and Political Union (WSPU).

[21]LL 30 May 1903.
[22]E. S. Pankhurst, The Suffragette Movement [1931] (Virago, 1977), p. 167.
[23]See e.g. P. Snowden, 'The ILP and Women's Franchise', LL 16 Apr. 1904.

The excitement generated by these new developments encouraged women who were already members of the ILP to take an active role in the suffrage campaign and also attracted more young women into the party. Often self-supporting and employed in the expanding areas of clerical work and teaching, they were attracted by the ILP's ethical fervour and support for women's rights. Yorkshire had its share of female activists as well as Lancashire; Miss Muir from Bradford, Mary Gawthorpe from Leeds, and Ethel Annakin from Harrogate were all young schoolteachers who became popular ILP speakers in the early 1900s.

Ethel Annakin joined the Leeds ILP in 1903, shortly after taking up her first teaching post in the city. She made her debut as a speaker at the Keighley Labour Institute in September and was immediately described as a 'second Annie Besant'. One admiring writer in the *Labour Leader* claimed that 'to her good gifts of dark eyes, golden brown hair and rich colour, Nature has added a sweet singing voice and musical ability of no mean order . . . she has won the affectionate regard of all those who have come into intimate acquaintance with her by her warm enthusiasm for the cause.'[24] Isabella was immediately attracted to this young, talented recruit to socialism, and the two women developed a friendship that was close and longlasting.

In these early days, the WSPU was largely confined to Lancashire. Women in the Yorkshire ILP who wanted to show their commitment to the franchise campaign had to join more long-established suffrage groups. Ethel Annakin and Mary Gawthorpe both became members of the Leeds Women's Suffrage Society, founded by Isabella and Bessie and their sister-in-law, Helen Cordelia, in 1890. The Leeds Society was affiliated to the National Union of Women's Suffrage Societies (NUWSS), a predominantly middle-class and non-party political organization, formed in 1897 under the leadership of Millicent Fawcett. Up to now the leaders of the NUWSS had been unadventurous in their tactics; they sponsored Private Members' Bills, tried to gain the support of individual MPs, and organized petitions. Events in Lancashire, however, coupled with the influx of young members, gave the NUWSS a new vitality and led to the revival of many local societies.[25]

There was no rigid distinction as yet between suffrage groups. In November 1903 both Christabel Pankhurst from the WSPU and Isabella from the NUWSS spoke together at a public meeting in Sheffield presided over by Edward Carpenter. They tried to persuade working women to join the Sheffield Suffrage Society and agreed that women should demand the vote on the same terms as men. On the other hand it was clear, even at this early stage, that they had different views about the way in which women as

---

[24]*LL* 17 Mar. 1905.
[25]For a discussion of the development of NUWSS policies, see L. P. Hume, *The National Union of Women's Suffrage Societies, 1897–1914* (Garland Publishing, 1982).

a social group should pursue their political claims. Christabel was forthright in arguing that women should unite together to obtain the vote and that this should override all other loyalties: 'she urged women not to be divided, but to belong to one party, to join together on one question – the vote. She asked women to throw off "party", to stand together, and let their motto be – "He who is for us, for him are we".' Isabella was more cautious. She made a broad appeal to women to 'stand together for the sake of the children and for the sake of the nation'. Referring to New Zealand, where women had the vote, she claimed that 'poor women were treated with the same courtesy as those who were in a higher social scale. The woman question was a great national question – a man's question.'[26]

Christabel's views were later to lead her to reject socialist politics altogether, whereas Isabella remained a committed member of the ILP and never lost her belief that men and women should co-operate. Most ILP suffragists agreed with Isabella's argument that agitation for the vote could, and should, be combined with more general socialist propaganda. The suffrage campaign seemed to encourage women to come forward as ILP speakers; popular with labour audiences, they carried out propaganda on a range of issues, but took every opportunity to relate these general questions to the specific needs of women. During the last three months of 1903, for example, they became involved in the campaign, led by the ILP and the Women's Co-operative Guild, to resist government proposals to introduce a tariff on imported foods.

Meetings in favour of free trade were held throughout the north of England during the autumn. Isabella took her share of the speaking. On 21 and 22 October she made her first visit to Crook, where she spoke twice, on 'The Meaning of an ILP' and on 'The New Tariffs'. In the first week in November she attended a protest meeting against the tariffs at the Manchester Free Trade Hall which was aimed specifically at working women. The impressive group of female speakers, including Gertrude Tuckwell, Mrs Booth of the Women's Co-operative Guild, and Alison Garland, a writer on Hindu questions, argued that tariffs would increase the price of food. They believed that working women, who were unlikely to receive extra money from their husbands, would find it particularly difficult to make ends meet.[27] In December, Isabella supported Phillip Snowden when he visited Oldham as part of a whole series of meetings against the tariffs at which he was the principal speaker.

As a member of the NAC, Isabella received more invitations than ever before to speak to socialist groups. Even the death of her sister-in-law, Mrs Thomas Benson Ford, on 15 January 1904, did not interrupt Isabella's punishing schedule. Speaking mainly on the 'The Place of Women in the

[26]*LL* 14 Nov. 1903.
[27]*YFT* 13 Nov. 1903.

Labour Movement', she addressed one meeting after another in the last two weeks of January; on the 17th she was in North Salford, three days later she spoke at a meeting in Sheffield, and on the 22nd travelled to Stockton. From there she went to London, was back in Leeds for a meeting on the 28th, and on the last day of the month spoke in Hyde.[28]

Trying to arouse interest in, and support for, women's suffrage within the labour movement was no easy task; male workers felt threatened by the use of women as cheap labour and were not inclined to be sympathetic to any movement which challenged male superiority. In January 1904, for example, Isabella came into conflict with rank-and-file members of the Leeds branch of the AUCO who wanted to exclude women once again from the union. Their intention was to forward a resolution to that effect to the TUC, which was to meet in Leeds in September. This prompted Isabella to write a letter to the union journal, urging the branch not to take such a retrograde step. She was supported by Mary Macarthur, at that time a young WTUL organizer, who had come to Leeds to make preparations for the women's meetings to be held alongside the TUC. Mary Macarthur managed to persuade the Leeds AUCO to withdraw the resolution and acknowledged the help that she had been given by Isabella during her visit.[29]

Some of the problems that ILP suffragists faced in persuading the labour movement to take their cause seriously went deeper than the threat to men's position at the work-place or disagreements over the tactic of demanding a 'limited franchise'. Working men were suspicious of both the class background and of the values expressed by female socialists; a common fear was that middle-class women would try to reform their habits. Thus, although male leaders of the ILP, such as Hardie and Snowden, were strong advocates of temperance, it was women who were most identified with this movement. Ethel Annakin, for example, engaged in a long campaign against the consumption of alcoholic drinks in the Leeds ILP social club that was vehemently opposed by its male members.[30] Isabella's own views on temperance and general moral standards also aroused ambivalent feelings. These were expressed in a humorous sketch written as part of a series, 'Letters to Notables', for the *Labour Leader*. The author had feared that when Isabella joined the NAC it would become 'well-brushed, decorous, non smoking'. He had to concede, however, that nothing of the kind had happened. 'The Woman's Suffrage resolution has not taken the place of our Socialist declaration in our objects as a party, our members have not ceased wearing their unbecoming red ties . . . But I write awkwardly, for I approach with you with awe. There is an old faithful woman, from whose

[28] For a record of all her meetings see reports in the *LL* and *YFT*.
[29] *YFT*, 12 Feb. 1904 and *WTUR*, April (1904).
[30] *LL* 30 May, 13 June, 1 Aug., and 22 Aug. 1904.

4. Isabella Ford (*Woman Worker*, 1908). (*British Library, Newspaper Library, Colindale*)

cheeks the bloom of youth has gone, with whom I fell in love long, long ago.' The sketch ended with a rearrangement of Isabella's initials which once again drew attention to cultural differences. 'I never can write your initials – IOF – IO to me has been followed for over half a century by U! . . . Your initials upon your photograph on my mantlepiece (almost hidden behind tobacco boxes, pipes and other things less reputable) are a standing reproach to my sins, but wickedness was born in me – I am a bachelor – and it will be IOU and not IOF to the end of the chapter of yours humbly.'[31]

An incident involving Isabella in February 1904 provides a further illustration of the suspicions roused by her class background. After returning from a Women's Liberal Association conference in London, where she had moved a resolution on land nationalization, Isabella was alarmed to find a report in the *Leeds Mercury* which stated that she went to the conference as a member of the WLA. At her request the paper subsequently contradicted its statement, but she still sent a letter to the *Yorkshire Factory Times* to explain that she went as a guest and as a member of the ILP. 'I should not have thought it worthwhile to state this in your paper, only I find evil reports are sometimes easily, and I regret to say gladly, believed of "middle-class" women.'

Ben Turner was quick to spring to her defence: 'Some working men never give credit to a middle-class woman for good work and good intentions. . . . The sacrifices that the Misses Ford have made are surely enough to prove their bona fides, for they were fighting for Labour in Wilson's weavers' strike at Leeds, in the weavers' strike at Alverthorpe fifteen years ago; in fact had done a lot before some of their present day critics were ready for work.'[32] The incident is important for showing the strain that Isabella was under – criticized by members of her own class for her support for the labour movement, yet often under suspicion from labour men because of her middle-class origins.

These varied sources of tension between members of the labour movement and ILP suffragists formed part of the background to the annual conference of the Labour Representation Committee held in February 1904. Isabella attended once again as a delegate from the ILP, accompanied this time by Julia Varley, and became the first woman to speak at the conference. She seconded a resolution, proposed by Mr Wilkinson of the Burnley weavers, that Conference should agree 'with the principle of the franchise being extended to women on the same basis as that allowed to them for parochial purposes'. Most other women would have felt daunted by the prospect of addressing a room full of men, but Isabella was used to facing such audiences at International Textile Congresses and stood up confidently

[31]Teufelsdroch, 'Letters to Notables. ix Miss Isabella O. Ford', *LL* 30 Jan. 1904.
[32]*YFT* 11 Mar. 1904.

to speak. She 'commented upon the democratic basis up on which the resolution had been drawn, including as it did both married and single women. There was a feeling . . . that there ought to be a woman on the LRC Executive, but that would not be accomplished until the women workers pressed the matter on their different Executives.'[33] The resolution does not appear to have been voted on at this stage, and suffragists had to face another year before they could try again to get a formal commitment of support.

They had more success within the ILP. The annual conference of 1904 finally came out in support of a limited franchise, although many individual members remained unhappy with the decision. The lukewarm response from most sections of the labour movement began to discourage some ILP suffragists, especially members of the WSPU, from continuing their fight for women's suffrage from within the labour movement. It was in this context that Isabella made an all-out effort, both by speaking and writing, to convince suffragists, socialists, and trade-unionists that the women's cause and the labour cause must be seen as part of the same broad movement and that neither could be fully successful without the other.

[33]Labour Representation Committee, *Annual Report*, 1904, pp. 173–4.

6

Women and Socialism

Men as well as women suffer from the political slavery of women.

The new vigour of the suffrage campaign, rooted as it was in the discontent of working women in the north, created an atmosphere of intense excitement. Isabella could hardly contain her own enthusiasm now that the campaign was being taken seriously within the labour movement. Along with other ILP suffragists, she was inspired to even greater activity than before, addressing countless meetings all over the country on the importance of votes for women and on the need to keep the labour movement and the women's movement together. Platform propaganda work did not, however, detract her from thinking and writing; on the contrary, Isabella was so stimulated by her political work that she became even more prolific as an author.

Her writing reached a peak between 1903 and 1906, both in quantity and in quality. Articles and letters appeared regularly in the *Labour Leader*, varying from commentaries on recent political events to more discursive pieces which analysed women's social position. Years of experience as a trade union organizer and political propagandist had made Isabella far more confident about expressing her ideas, and this showed in the style and content of her writing. In articles written in the 1890s Isabella had provided a wealth of detailed information on the conditions of employment of the female industrial worker; her main purpose had been to demonstrate the importance of trade union organization for improving the economic and social position of the woman worker.

In the early 1900s she was less concerned to provide detailed case studies on women's work and was more interested in developing a theoretical framework to link sex equality and socialism. Isabella used her wide reading and knowledge of history to analyse the roots of women's oppression, but her ideas were not developed in a political vacuum. They grew out of the interaction between her reading, her practical experiences as a labour activist, and the contemporary political context. Her writings were designed to serve a political purpose: to convince a sceptical labour movement that women's suffrage and the interests of labour were inextricably linked. In putting forward her arguments, Isabella made use of concepts that were familiar both to suffragists and to ILP socialists; none the less, by drawing the two together, she managed to produce a new synthesis and made an important contribution to the contemporary debate on the 'woman question'.

It is worth spending some time on her writings. They can reveal the complexity of socialist and feminist ideas in the period and the points of similarity and dissimilarity between them, and can help us to understand why the suffrage became such an important issue for both groups. Too often it is assumed that women demanded the vote either because they sought equal rights with middle-class men or because they wished to exercise their maternal qualities in the public sphere. Isabella's articles and pamphlets, however, suggest that it is not always possible draw a rigid distinction between the two; she managed to mix both sets of arguments together, referring at one moment to equal rights and at another to women's special qualities. Her writings also make clear that the vote meant far more to suffragists than simply the formal right to participate in politics; for ILP members in particular it was a necessary first step to achieving economic independence for the working woman and was only part of a much broader set of demands which sought to transform all areas of the female worker's life.

Underlying all of Isabella's arguments was the assumption, shared by most of her contemporaries, that women had specific qualities; these were 'in part innate, owing to the share they have in the production of the race', and in part acquired, through their socialization in domestic roles.[1] She claimed, therefore, that if women had the vote they would use their political power in different ways to men – to help the poor and oppressed and to reform the home. Isabella was determined to challenge the view prevalent among many labour men that women were innately conservative and likely to oppose change. Using the examples of New Zealand, where women had the vote and yet where labour was also pushing ahead, Isabella noted that women had formed themselves into a national council 'which meets annually at the different towns to give expression to the wants of the organised women of the colony, and to plan work, both educational and *aggressive* (observe that refreshing word!), in the direction of humanitarian and political reform'.[2] She contrasted the lack of interest shown by the ILP in Tibet, Somaliland, and South Africa with the increasing international spirit of the women's movement which saved it from 'staleness and hopeless narrowness. . . . If we lifted our heads and our eyes oftener to the mountain tops, our Socialism would be a wiser and a better thing than it is; for the world is ours, not only Yorkshire, or even Scotland.'[3]

[1] I. O. Ford, *Women and Socialism* (ILP, 1904), p. 13.
[2] Id., 'What the Women are Doing', *Labour Leader* (*LL*), 27 Feb. 1904 (letter).
[3] *LL* 9 Apr. 1904.

These arguments contained important contradictions. If women's outlook was affected to some extent by their biological role, then it could be
seen as natural and unalterable. On the other hand, Isabella placed a far
greater emphasis on the way in which women's attitudes were shaped by
the society in which they lived and were therefore amenable to change.
Women often acted in conservative ways, but this was understandable.
They had been taught to put domestic concerns first and, without the vote,
could not be expected to take an interest in public affairs. A change in social
and political structures, however, would alter the way in which women
thought and behaved.

Using a historical perspective, Isabella tried to demonstrate that society's
expectations of women, and hence their own behaviour, changed over
time. Women themselves had played an important part in bringing about
these changes, often in the face of great opposition. In 'Woman As She Was
and Is', published in May 1904, Isabella argued that women's lives had
improved over the last fifty years. Quoting from tracts on women's
education written in the 1820s and 1830s, from Hannah More's advice on
how women ought to dress, and from the novels of Charlotte Brontë,
George Eliot, and Mrs Gaskell, Isabella showed how women's lives had
been restricted, colourless, and 'devoid of real living interest' for most of
the nineteenth century. By the 1880s and 1890s all this had begun to change;
women had access to higher education and the professions, while the advent
of the bicycle had encouraged a different attitude to physical fitness. When
she claimed that 'the idea that women are mere appendages to men's lives,
that they own no duty to themselves as human beings is now on its
deathbed, even though it may be long a-dying', Isabella was expressing the
new sense of optimism that pervaded the revived women's suffrage movement.

Turning the Christian view that women were 'the cause of all men's sins'
on its head, she reminded her readers that they owed their existence to Eve.
'For if Adam had been left to himself he would still, I imagine, be walking
round the garden of Eden, perpetually forming a domestic solo with Eve as
a mere running accompaniment. Whereas Eve, desiring something better
and less monotonous, defied the Almighty himself, and consequently
brought us into the world: Liberals, Tories and ILP – ers!' Isabella wanted
to convince Labour men that middle-class women would use their new
energies to help the cause of socialism and working women; after fighting
against terrible odds, often on behalf of the industrial woman, middle-class
women showed the 'same rebellious spirit' as Eve, who 'brought new
interests and vigour into the dull life of that well-conducted person, Adam,
and gave him some real work to do'.[5]

I. O. Ford, *Women and Socialism* (1906 edn), , pp. 9–10.
[5] Id., 'Woman As She Was and Is', *LL* 13 May 1904, p. 64.

The argument that women would use the vote to achieve social reforms was put forward by suffragists from all political parties; Isabella's more distinctive contribution to the debate lay in her emphasis on what the suffrage would mean to women workers. She found it impossible to separate political equality from economic equality. Praising an article on 'Wage-Earning Women' that had appeared in the *Labour Leader* in January 1904, she suggested that 'the claim for women's suffrage is, at bottom, the claim of the wage-earning woman for the opportunity to work out her economic emancipation on a footing of equality with wage-earning man'. The threat of a food tax made it particularly important for women to push their claim for the suffrage even more urgently than before, since the fiscal question would affect them more disastrously than men.

Context

All of Isabella's analysis rested on this one basic premiss that women workers must take an active part in any movement which aimed to improve their social and economic position:

> to work for female factory legislation before demanding full political power for the women workers, so that they themselves may work out their industrial salvation as men have done, is hindering the emancipation of women's labour more than it is helping it. Perpetually behaving to working women as if they were babies or half-witted persons, who do not know what they want, . . . would be irritating if it were not ridiculous, to those who are acquainted with the working woman as she really is – a wonderful compound of patience, fortitude and stolid endurance.[6]

Isabella had turned to political action after her efforts to persuade working women to join trade unions had failed. Her commitment to political equality for women was then reinforced by the emphasis of the ILP on achieving socialism through the constitutional means of participating in elections. Isabella wanted women to take a full, active part in this process, not just to be given rights and privileges once political change had already been achieved. On the contrary, women needed the vote so that they could struggle alongside men for socialism and have a say in shaping the new society, which was likely to be broader and stronger in consequence.

The crux of Isabella's argument was that women's suffrage and the emancipation of all working people had to go hand in hand. Having at first tentatively tried out her ideas in shorter pieces of work, she drew them together in the pamphlet *Women and Socialism* – her most sustained attempt so far to analyse the relationship between class and sex oppression. Proofs of the pamphlet were presented to the June meeting of the NAC, and it was given formal approval for publication as an ILP pamphlet in September 1904. It was the only official text produced by the ILP in this period which

[6] *LL* 16 Jan. 1904. The article by Gavroche, 'The Woman Wage Earner', was published on 9 Jan. 1904.

examined the 'woman question' from a much broader perspective than the current debate on the suffrage. It also represented a culmination of Isabella's efforts, both on a practical and a theoretical level, to grapple with the potential conflicts that could arise between class and gender politics and which were brought to the surface so clearly by the debate over women's suffrage.

Isabella based her pamphlet on the premiss that the women's movement and the labour movement had 'fallen and risen together, and the same events have affected each, more or less in the same manner'. Both suffered from the 'common evil' of economic dependence on the owners of property, which had grown steadily worse since the fifteenth century.[7] Sharing the fascination of many of her contemporaries with the Middle Ages, she followed William Morris in assuming that women and labour had enjoyed a higher political and economic status in medieval times. It was the development of a capitalist economy which had undermined their position and subjected them to simultaneous attacks; the most recent being the government's use of the law against trade unions and its overt hostility to the cause of women's suffrage.

Recognizing that the Labour Party was suspicious of the women's movement because of its middle-class character, and that members of the women's movement feared the development of socialism, Isabella's main objective was to show that these suspicions were groundless. With the prejudices of the Labour Party in mind she argued that once a middle-class woman became involved in public life she acquired 'a clearer understanding of the economic meaning of her cause, and of how her cause and that of the industrial woman are one'.[8] Middle-class women were beginning to demand the vote, not for themselves alone but so that they could improve the work and social conditions of working-class women. Moreover, she pointed out, working women would never take an interest in trade-unionism or labour politics until they were enfranchised.

Addressing herself to suffragists, Isabella claimed that the other two political parties could never give them what they wanted, 'since now both those parties represent the capitalist interest, an interest as opposed to their cause as it is to the Labour cause'. Wherever women had the vote – as in New Zealand – they had been largely responsible for the introduction of factory legislation, old age pensions, and other social reforms. Even though they might not realize it themselves, they were the 'friends of the Progressive Party'.[9] The pamphlet concluded by urging, once again, that the two groups should go forward together, since both were forces 'making for the reconstruction and regeneration of society'. They could 'benefit each

---

[7]I. O. Ford, *Women and Socialism* (1904 edn), pp. 3–4.
[8]Ibid., p. 7.
[9]Ibid., p. 10.

other enormously' by bringing different qualities. 'The Labour movement will keep the economic side in view, a side women are apt to overlook, and of which they frequently fail to understand the vast moral significance. Women will help to keep more clearly before our eyes, than is always possible now, those great ideals for which after all Labour Representation is but a means of accomplishment.'[10]

Isabella's most original contribution to the contemporary debate on the 'woman question' lay in her concern to fuse socialist and feminist politics. In her emphasis on equal rights, on women's special qualities and the power of the vote, she shared many of the objectives and concerns of the contemporary women's movement. She accepted, for example, that the vote would provide women with a weapon to challenge inequalities in their lives and therefore emphasized their need to gain access to formal political institutions. However, her socialist beliefs and unique understanding of the problems of working women brought a new dimension to her feminist ideas. This enabled her to depart from the liberal framework of argument which predominated in the suffrage movement. She rejected individualism in favour of collectivism and co-operation, and located the source of women's oppression in their subordinate economic position within industry and the home as well as in their political subjection.

Throughout the pamphlet, Isabella drew attention to the importance of family life and women's role within it. The home was the starting point from which men and women developed a sense of citizenship, but reforms were necessary to improve the conditions 'under which the poorest live'. Until these took place there would be no 'recognition or understanding of the real value of motherhood . . . The question of fatherhood too receives no consideration at all. And yet, what matters are of more importance to the growth of the race?'[11]

Isabella's own interest in these questions must be seen as part of a more general concern after the turn of the century with motherhood and the 'development of the race'. In a context of increasing military and economic competition with Germany, the rejection of a third of all recruits to the army during the Boer War on the grounds of ill health led to fears that the population would not be strong enough to maintain Britain's imperial position. This in turn focused attention on child health and the importance of good mothering.[12] Social Darwinists, who were interested in the struggle between nations, added scientific weight to this growing 'ideology of motherhood'. Karl Pearson, for example, rejected the view that women were inferior in the scale of evolution and argued instead that their role as mothers was of vital importance for the state because they had the future of

[10]Ibid., p. 13.
[11]Ibid., p. 10.
[12]A. Davin, 'Imperialism and Motherhood', *History Workshop Journal*, 5 (1978).

the race in their hands. His ideas were taken up by many feminists who were attracted by the recognition that he gave to the social value of women's place within the home.[13]

Labour women also began to focus on women's domestic role, albeit from a different perspective. Members of the Women's Co-operative Guild, for instance, were well aware of the difficulties that working-class women experienced during pregnancy, childbirth, and child-rearing, and began to call for reforms to improve health and housing conditions. These questions had been neglected for so long that women could only benefit from any such reforms. On the other hand, a focus on motherhood, whether from the perspective of the state or from the needs of the individual woman, reinforced the ideology of separate spheres which permeated both the women's movement and the labour movement. This ensured that neither movement mounted an effective challenge to the sex division of labour at home and in the work-place and undermined the aim of many suffragists to achieve economic independence for women.

Isabella's own views were complex; her knowledge of the conditions of working-class family life led her to reject the sentimental picture of motherhood so often found in socialist writings and speeches. She noted that the working-class home was 'often a back to back slum reeking with smells of cooking, washing, cleaning, and general living, full of unrest, noise and weariness – in no way a place in which a great and strong race can possibly be reared'.[14] Defending the married woman worker from the barrage of criticism so often meted out by middle-class reformers, Isabella pointed out that the wage-earning mother often had no male provider, or else family income was low. Working day and night to make ends meet, 'when can she ever rest? Suppose she did wilfully neglect her home and her children what right should we have to blame her? . . . Is motherhood always honourable and voluntary? When motherhood is regarded as honourable, and treated with reverence, and when homes are places pleasant to live in, we shall have reason to revile the married woman.'[15]

On the other hand, Isabella accepted that 'trained motherhood' was vital for the well-being of the community. She found Pearson's arguments particularly persuasive, both because he asserted the positive value of women's special qualities and because he linked the oppression of women and labour. Her pamphlet began with a quotation from Pearson that 'there has never been a Labour Question without a Woman's Question also'. She used his assertion that 'the status of woman and the status of labour are intimately associated with the manner in which property is held and wealth

---

[13]For a discussion of Pearson, see L. Bland, 'Marriage Laid Bare: Middle-Class Women and Marital Sex c.1880–1914', in J. Lewis, ed. *Labour and Love: Women's Experience of Home and Family* (Blackwell, 1986).

[14]I. O. Ford, *Women and Socialism* (1904 edn), p. 9.

[15]Id., 'In Praise of Married Women' *LL* 2 Sept. 1904.

inherited', as the basis from which to develop her own arguments. In her conclusion, which celebrated feminine values, she again used a quote from Pearson:

> There is one ray of hope . . . that the past subjection of women . . . has . . . so chastened woman, so trained her to think of others rather than of herself, that after all it may have acted more as a blessing rather than a curse to the world? May it not bring her to the problems of the future with a purer aim and a keener insight than is possible for a man? She may see more clearly than he the real points at issue . . . and . . . may be able to submit her liberty to the restraints demanded by social welfare, and to the conditions needed for race permanence.[16]

Isabella never quite managed, therefore, to deal satisfactorily with women's economic dependence within the home. She may have been critical of the conditions suffered by working-class mothers, but did not question that women should take a major responsibility for child care. In addressing the needs of working women, she advocated trade union organization as a solution to economic dependence. However, in the case of married women who did not work for wages she fell back on the panacea of the vote, arguing that political freedom would result in a more equal companionship between the sexes within the home. From this basis of equality they would be able to take action together to achieve socialism.

Her long-standing refusal to draw a boundary between personal and political life led Isabella to argue that the vote would have a direct effect on the relationship between the sexes within marriage. Women's view of themselves would change from the inside; treated as full human beings they would have greater confidence in their economic worth and would recognize their value to society. This in turn would affect political behaviour. Isabella wrote approvingly of those suffragists who 'believe that to continue the moral injustice of placing disabilities on sex prevents the growth of the world's vision and thereby stops all progress. They believe that the spirit of injustice if nourished in the innermost relationship of life, – the relationship between man and woman, – will, and does, spread into all the wider relationships between citizens and between nations.'[17] It was for this reason that the interests of women and the interests of labour had to be seen as one and the same thing, for 'men as well as women suffer economically from the political slavery of women'.[18]

Women and Socialism was published at a key moment, when tensions between gender and class politics were running high. Isabella's intention, therefore, was to play down potential conflicts of interest between working-class men and women and between middle-class women and the labour movement. This task was made easier by her view of what socialism meant

[16]Id., *Women and Socialism* (1904 edn), pp. 13–14.
[17]Ibid., p. 12.
[18]Letter in *LL* 16 Jan. 1904.

and how it could be achieved. Along with most ILP leaders, she denied the importance of sex hatred and class war, believing that men and women from all social classes would be drawn to work for socialism once they realized that it implied a higher form of civilization.[19] On the one hand she argued that all women suffered from a common oppression because they were low paid and economically dependent. On the other, Isabella also thought that working men and women both suffered from the injustices of capitalism and should work together for social change. She analysed women's oppression, therefore, in terms of their exclusion from the owner-ship of property and the antagonism that they experienced from the state, rather than in terms of male power over women.

In a revised edition of the pamphlet, written two years later, Isabella spent a little more time on women's oppression within the family. She again argued that the relationship between the sexes in the home was 'the core, the centre around which society grows, for the family, the home, is the very heart of the nation.' If parents were to teach their children how to 'build our state out of this moral regeneration which Socialism calls for' they had to understand 'justice' equally in their own lives. 'As things are now, neither understands it, – (the man as occupying the more ignoble position, that of the oppressor, even less perhaps than the woman) – for they stand in a false position of inequality towards each other, and that falseness spreads, as a fungus spreads its evil growth, into their relationship with others. Hence we have the world as we now see it; founded not on justice, not on freedom, but on a make-belief of both.' She still framed her solution, however, in political terms. 'Socialism goes straight to the home, to the heart of the world, in its cry for freedom. Free the home, let the woman no longer be in political subjection, and free the worker, it says.'[20]

Women and Socialism was the culmination of Isabella's attempts to find a framework in which to link class and sex oppression. Arising directly from her political practice, as a socialist and a suffragist, it reflected, and tried to deal with, the tensions between women's needs and broader labour interests which were highlighted by the suffrage campaign. Isabella never wrote such a sustained piece of work again – perhaps because of the increasing demands on her time as a speaker or perhaps because, for her, to go beyond these ideas would have posed a major challenge to her whole conceptual frame-work. The arguments expressed in her pamphlet provided a basis for all her later articles and informed her political actions until the end of her life.

When Isabella's pamphlet was first published in 1904 it was well received by the ILP. One commentator, writing in the *Labour Leader*, was impressed by the way in which she saw women's emancipation as part of 'the great world movement' for socialism, and thought that her pamphlet said 'all that

[19]*Leeds Weekly Citizen*, 30 May 1913.
[20]I. O. Ford, *Women and Socialism* (ILP, 1906), p. 3.

it is necessary to say on this phase of the subject'. He agreed that there was a strong bond of sympathy between women, which led middle-class women to help their poorer sisters, and concluded that this had 'lifted the woman question into the arena of practical politics'. It had brought the women's movement 'on all fours with the general Labour claim'.[21] This did not necessarily represent the views of most Labour Party members and trade-unionists, who still remained wary of the suffrage movement. Adult suffragists within the ILP itself were also critical of the pamphlet; H. Jennie Baker, for example, denied that the Labour Party was prejudiced against the women's movement just because of its middle-class character, since this ignored the objection that a limited franchise would not give working women the vote, and why should they be 'content to stand aside to be represented at the polling booth by their "superior" sisters'.[22]

Although the ILP Conference of 1904 had come out in favour of a limited franchise, many members continued to be unhappy with the decision. Differences of opinion were expressed throughout the year in the pages of the *Labour Leader*. Controversy reached a peak of intensity in November when a Private Member's Bill, providing that 'no person shall be prevented on grounds merely of sex from exercising the vote', was introduced in the House of Commons. This prompted a flood of letters to the paper and illustrated the very tentative nature of the link between the labour and suffrage cause.

[21] *LL* 16 Sept. 1904.
[22] *LL* 7 Oct. 1904.

7

Co-leader of the ILP, 1903–1907

> The connections between the women's movement and the socialist movement seem closer than ever.

The ILP debate over women's suffrage in the autumn of 1904 centred on the issue of a limited versus an adult franchise. Adult suffragists, including Phillip Snowden and Ada Nield Chew, a full-time organizer for the Women's Trade Union League, opposed a limited franchise on the grounds that only middle-class women would be included. Not only would this strengthen the Labour Party's political opponents, it would also do nothing for working women. The only consistent policy for a socialist party, therefore, was to call for an extension of the franchise to all adult men and women.

Limited suffragists accepted that their demands would not enfranchise all women – although they questioned the extent to which working-class women would be excluded. For them it was the principle that mattered. Once it had been conceded that some women were capable of exercising the vote, it would be easier to extend political rights to a wider group. In a joint letter in support of the Suffrage Bill, Isabella and Emmeline Pankhurst also made the point that a demand for adult suffrage did not necessarily mean that women would be included. They argued that ILP supporters of the Suffrage Bill 'raise this clear issue, namely, that sex must not be a disqualification for political rights, because they know that if this is not done the claims of women to the vote will in the near future be again set aside, as they always have been in the past, when extensions of the franchise were being given to men'.[1]

The debate over women's suffrage was not, however, simply about political rights and questions of tactics. It was often the outward expression of a more fundamental difference in approach towards gender and class politics. By highlighting the specific inequalities suffered by women, which placed them in a subordinate position to men at the workplace and in the

[1] *Labour Leader (LL)*, 18 Nov. 1904.

home, suffragists questioned the emphasis of socialists on the shared class
interests of working men and women. William Anderson, a prominent
member of the ILP who was to marry the trade union leader Mary
Macarthur, was explicit in raising such issues in his contribution to the
suffrage debate. He feared that any attempt to focus on women's common
oppression as a sex would undermine labour unity and divert attention
from the more important question of class exploitation: 'It is inconsistent
for a Socialist party to lend its support to a movement which is deliberately
attempting to distract the attention of women workers from the wrongs of
their class to the wrongs of their sex.' He claimed that many suffragists
were uninterested in trade unions except as a vehicle to forward their one
aim, and that Lancashire cotton workers were being 'taught that all their
woes may be traced to their voteless condition, and they are kept blind to
the fact that there is no sex in industry, and that lack of organization is the
primary cause of bad conditions'.[2]

Isabella took a completely opposite point of view. Her years as a trade
union organizer had convinced her that female industrial workers did suffer
from specific forms of discrimination simply because they were women – in
particular, low pay. They therefore needed a political voice so that they
could fight for economic independence. These differing views were increasingly difficult to reconcile as suffragists became more insistent that
their cause should be given higher priority. This was eventually to lead to a
split between limited suffragists and the labour movement. For a further
two years, however, propaganda for women's suffrage and socialism continued to be combined – a general trend that was reflected in Isabella's own
activities.

Isabella was always ready to undertake public propaganda work for a
limited franchise. During one of her visits to London in December she
agreed to take Sylvia Pankhurst's place in a debate against the adult
suffragist Margaret Bondfield, an organizer for the Shop Assistants' Union.
The two protagonists could not have been more different. According to
Sylvia, 'Miss Bondfield appeared in pink, dark and dark-eyed, with a deep,
throaty voice many found beautiful. She was very charming and vivacious,
and eager to score all the points that her youth and prettiness would win for
her against the plain, middle-aged woman, with red face and turban hat
crushed down upon her straight hair, whose nature yet seemed to me . . .
kindlier and more profound than that of her younger antagonist.'[3] Margaret
Bondfield was a practised speaker but so was Isabella, and the latter
managed to survive her opponent's shafts unscathed.

As the Labour Party's annual conference drew closer ILP suffragists
stepped up their campaign to gain support for a limited franchise. On 21

[2]Ibid.
[3]E. S. Pankhurst, *The Suffragette Movement* [1931] (Virago, 1977), pp. 177–8.

January 1905 Isabella spoke to the Leeds Arts Club on the subject of 'Women and the State'. Referring to the way in which women's rights had been eroded since medieval times, she argued that they needed to claim these again, 'not so much as women, but as human beings . . . women were almost the most important half of humanity, because they had the upbringing of the race in their hands'. She travelled to Glasgow next day and continued with the theme that older societies had given an 'honourable place to women' when she addressed the Clarion Society on 'Civilisation, Old and New'.[4]

At the end of the month Isabella attended a large public meeting on women's suffrage, sponsored by the Women Textile Workers' Representation Committee, the Manchester and Salford Women's Trades Council, the WSPU, and the General Union of Textile Workers. The meeting was held in Liverpool, one day before the start of the Labour Representation Committee (LRC) Conference, and was a last attempt to persuade delegates to support a limited franchise. Isabella was surrounded by the familiar faces of Allen Gee, Sarah Reddish, Emmeline Pankhurst, Keir Hardie and Phillip Snowden as she rose to speak in her 'best humorous–serious vein'. She claimed that women did 'not want to use dynamite. They were accustomed to move slowly in this country. Their lords and masters did so, and they were content to follow in the slow, sure – and large! – footsteps of the men.'[5] The meeting was well attended, and hopes were high among supporters of women's suffrage that they could achieve a victory at the conference.

The motion to support a limited franchise for women was proposed by J. Husband of the engineering union and seconded by Selina Cooper, a Lancashire working woman who was rapidly becoming well known for her suffrage activities. During the course of the debate the motion was amended in favour of adult suffrage, and once again limited suffragists had to go home disappointed. The decision was to add to the unease already felt by some ILP suffragists about continuing to work within the labour movement, but for the time being they still carried out both socialist and suffrage propaganda. The day after the suffrage debate in Liverpool, Isabella went back to Leeds to address the South Leeds Socialist Union on labour representation. In the first fortnight of February she spoke twice on one day for the Attercliffe ILP, taking as her topic 'Is Socialism a Religious or a Political Movement?', travelled to London for a meeting to protest against the Bloody Sunday massacre in Russia, and then spoke to the Bolton Labour Church on 'Women's Votes'.

Isabella did manage to take a break from propaganda work in March when she attended the wedding of Ethel Annakin and the chairman of the

[4]LL 27 Jan. 1905.
[5]LL 3 Feb. 1905.

NAC, Phillip Snowden, who was twice the age of his young bride. It was a measure of their close friendship that Bessie and Isabella were the only guests of the bride, apart from her sister, at the quiet wedding held in Otley registry office. Accustomed to simple Quaker weddings, Isabella particularly enjoyed the ceremony because it was not 'entirely drowned and obliterated in carpets, and rice, and clergy, and flowers and clothes'. She was impressed by its solemnity and simplicity, and commented that the faces of the two principal actors 'shone with a happy cheerfulness you do not often see on the faces of the worried, nervous looking persons led up to the altar by crowds of gorgeously clad relatives. As we ate our lunch in the hotel, and as we walked back to the station in the brilliant sunshine, we all felt we had assisted at something true and excellent, and full of hope.'[6]

Phillip Snowden had come to know Isabella well as a fellow member of the NAC and spoke of the Ford sisters as 'noble characters' whose 'close friendship with my wife and myself over a long period is one of our sweetest memories'.[7] All four had a broad view of the meaning of socialism and shared similar attitudes towards peace, temperance, and women's rights. Phillip Snowden's appearance at the women's suffrage meeting before the Liverpool Conference was the first public acknowledgment that he too now supported a limited franchise. Sylvia Pankhurst claimed that this change had been 'effected by the witchery of the genial old Isabella Ford',[8] although it is more likely that it was the combined pressure of Isabella and his future wife that had brought about Snowden's conversion.

Contemporaries all agreed that Isabella played a vital role in maintaining the commitment of the ILP to women's suffrage; in his history of the socialist movement, Joseph Clayton, secretary of the Leeds ILP in the 1890s and a strong supporter of women's suffrage, listed Isabella among other women who were 'co-leaders' of the party. They 'gave it a tendency to look upon women's suffrage as a reform of vital need, and the equal co-operation of men and women in politics not an ideal but an everyday business'. Millicent Fawcett made a similar claim: 'I do not think anyone will ever fully know all that she did in framing the mental attitude and outlook of the founders of the Independent Labour Party.'[9] After the ILP Annual Conference of 1905, Isabella's role became even more important; she was the only woman elected to the NAC, just when there at last seemed to be some positive developments in the women's suffrage campaign.

After considerable lobbying, Emmeline Pankhurst and Keir Hardie managed to persuade the MP Bamford Slack to introduce a Private Members' Bill to enfranchise women. On 12 May Isabella joined 300 women, including

[6]*LL* 17 Mar. 1905.
[7]P. Snowden, *An Autobiography*, vol. i (Nicholson & Watson, 1934), p. 78.
[8]Pankhurst, *Suffragette Movement*, p. 203.
[9]J. Clayton, *The Rise and Decline of Socialism in Great Britain, 1854–1924* (Faber & Gwyer, 1926), pp. 83–4; M. Fawcett, 'Isabella Ormston Ford', *Woman's Leader*, 25 July 1924.

charwomen, widows, and members of the Women's Co-operative Guild, who gathered in the lobby of the House of Commons when the Bill was debated. Their anger grew as the Bill was talked out, but Isabella remained optimistic, buoyed by the conviction that in the heart of each of the women there, 'the seed of discontent and revolution is now too deeply implanted for us to fear for the future. The future is ours.'[10] The defeat of the Bill was to stiffen the resolve of the WSPU to find more effective tactics to put pressure on the government. For the time being, however, there was no chance of the suffrage being won, and Isabella turned her attention to more general labour issues.

In July Isabella joined many old friends at the International Textile Workers' Congress in Milan, where she was one of only two female delegates. In her reports of the congress she asked, 'when will the Lancashire women become something more than silent members of their union, and send one of their own sex to these Congresses?' She deplored the chauvinism of the English delegates. They contributed most to the international funds and therefore insisted that the secretary should be English and also a Lancashire man, despite the fact that other nations preferred Ben Turner. 'It is a pity English delegates cannot understand any but their own tongue. If they could they would learn to appreciate the intelligence and education and the courteous manners of our foreign fellow textile workers and they would not be so apt to think that an Englishman is God's noblest work.'[11] Despite the blistering heat of Milan, Isabella took the opportunity to visit local mills. She never lost her interest in learning first-hand about the experiences of working people, but found that 'it was not easy, under the eyes of ubiquitous managers and "bosses" to discover the real truth about wages and conditions of work'.[12]

On her return home, Isabella became involved in a long struggle on behalf of mining families in the Yorkshire village of Hemsworth. The miners had been evicted for nonpayment of rent, and the Board of Guardians refused to give them food for their children. Members of the ILP, including Isabella and Ethel Snowden, organized practical relief for the miners in the form of food and clothing parcels and also took the opportunity to push home their political message. At one meeting in late October, Isabella, Keir Hardie, and Mary Macarthur stood on a wagonnette in the pouring rain to urge a crowded meeting in Hemsworth to learn a lesson from the evictions and to return a Labour MP at the next election.[13]

It was in this same month that more exciting events began to take place in the suffrage campaign. When Sir Edward Grey appeared at the Manchester Free Trade Hall to appeal for a Liberal government to be returned at the

[10]I. O. Ford, 'Women and the Legislators', *LL* 19 May 1905.
[11]Id., 'At Milan: Inside the Congress', *LL* 7 July 1905.
[12]Id., 'The Textile Congress at Milan', *Women's Trade Union Review* (Oct. 1905), pp. 11–12.
[13]*LL* 20 Oct. 1905.

next election, he was interrupted by Christabel Pankhurst and Annie Kenney, members of the Manchester WSPU and ILP. They waved flags and asked if he would be prepared to support votes for women. The two women were promptly arrested, and their subsequent imprisonment led to a storm of protest from women's suffrage groups and from the ILP. Isabella interrupted her visit to the National Union of Women's Suffrage Societies' annual convention in Hull in order to attend a protest meeting in Manchester organized by the Central ILP. All the speakers, including Keir Hardie, Isabella, and members of the WSPU agreed that the women's actions had been constitutional and that their arrest was a breach of the right of free speech.

Even the older, more staid NUWSS was not left untouched by the atmosphere of excitement, and Isabella sensed a new mood of defiance at the NUWSS convention. She found a greater willingness to unite on one common demand for the franchise and to make support for women's suffrage a test question before helping candidates at elections, whereas 'in the old days it used to be received with hesitation'. Esther Roper's account of the arrest of the Manchester women was well received, although Isabella felt that the Tories were more inclined to 'admire women of spirit' than the Liberals, who 'looked upon the incident with austere disapproval'. Carried away herself by the euphoria of the moment, she concluded that 'the newer and more revolutionary ideas and methods are gradually supplanting the older and more subservient ones, for women are beginning to realize what freedom really means; that it means, as one speaker pointed out, the right to work, the right to give the State what it so much needs, women's work, women's help.'[14]

Millicent Fawcett voiced similar ideas in a letter written two months later. She failed to see why asking a 'political question at a political meeting can rightly be described as a disturbance. . . . We have conducted ourselves with perfect propriety in our middle-class way, and have got nothing for our pains. A new element has come upon the scene – working women . . . Their way is not our way; it is possible it may be a better way than ours.'[15] Always eager to see the NUWSS take more positive action and to support working women, Isabella was 'delighted' with this letter, claiming that it would do 'so much good it has so cheered me up – I feel so grateful to you for your name carries such tremendous weight of course & it is such a beautiful & convincing letter . . . We have ordered two dozen copies Bessie & I to send to weak kneed persons.'[16] Many individual members of the ILP approved of the new tactics of the WSPU and were tempted to adopt militant methods themselves. Walt Wood, for example, put a question

[14]I. O. Ford, 'Women's Suffrage Convention', ibid., 27 Oct. 1905.
[15]LL 19 Jan. 1906; printed in other newspapers before this date.
[16]Isabella Ford to Millicent Fawcett, 14 Jan. 1906, Suffrage MSS, Manchester Central Lib.

about votes for women to Asquith at a meeting in Morley. There were howls from the crowd and he had a fight with stewards who tried to throw him out. 'Mrs Wood was also pulled down, but, as Walt adds proudly, "Not before she had broken her umbrella over three of their heads".'[17]

The excitement surrounding such actions awakened an interest in women's suffrage and led to an influx of new members at a local level into the older suffrage societies. It was the arrest of Christabel Pankhurst and Annie Kenney that persuaded Mary Gawthorpe, vice-president of the Leeds ILP, to became involved in the women's suffrage campaign. With her usual daring she attended all the election meetings in Leeds to ask candidates whether they supported votes from women. She also wrote an article on the subject for the *Yorkshire Post*. This brought her to the attention of Isabella who was impressed to hear how this 'little teacher' had gone to the meetings, with 'her young man' to protect her, and had managed at last to extract a promise from Herbert Gladstone that he would vote for women's suffrage.[18] In her capacity as organizing secretary of the Leeds Women's Suffrage Society, Isabella persuaded Mary to join the executive committee, and for almost a year the two women worked closely together to further the cause of women's suffrage and socialism in the West Riding.

The long-awaited general election was finally called in December 1905, and Isabella rushed off to Manchester to attend a special conference of the ILP, convened to decide its election policy. It was agreed that candidates who pledged to vote for women's suffrage and labour interests should be supported by ILP members in constituencies where no one was standing for the Labour Party. Isabella and Bessie were well pleased with the decision and contributed £1 each to the election funds. On her return home Isabella found that in the excitement generated by the election, the Leeds WSS was being inundated with requests for speakers from a variety of labour groups, including the ILP, the Women's Co-operative Guild, and trade union branches. She wrote to Mary Gawthorpe in January 1906 asking her to 'fix something for Miss Rowlette', an NUWSS member who lived in Leeds. 'She is so good on w. suff: and you have her for no charge. A cottage meeting is better than nothing. How about teachers?' Mary had little difficulty in arranging a full programme for Miss Rowlette, as well as speaking tirelessly herself.[19] Isabella spent most of her time campaigning for Phillip Snowden in Blackburn. She was pleased to report to Millicent Fawcett that he 'told the men with determined emphasis that in every respect women were their intellectual equals. The women cheered – & the men were silent – it was a huge meeting of Lancashire weavers.' The election may have drawn attention to women's suffrage, but Isabella re-

[17]*LL* 9 Feb. 1906.
[18]Isabella Ford to Millicent Fawcett, 14 Jan. 1906, Suffrage MSS.
[19]M. Gawthorpe, *Up Hill to Holloway* (Prebscot, Maine: Traversity Press, 1962), p. 209.

ported that even in Lancashire, female workers had mixed reactions to the cause. After she and Phillip Snowden had held street meetings at the dinner hour for factory people, she wrote: 'I am sorry to say the girls are most tiresome – they broke up one of mine & reviled me so, for speaking of their having votes. But again, the older ones are wild with enthusiasm.'[20]

The election resulted in a massive overall victory for the Liberal Party. The Labour Party could also congratulate itself on the return of twenty-nine MPs – a substantial group, including Hardie and Snowden. Isabella found it 'wonderful' that so many friends were being returned and told Millicent Fawcett that 'labour men meeting me in the street, beam and say "women's getting on you see, we shall see you in Parliament soon!" Oh!!' When Phillip Snowden told the women he was going to work for them 'they cried, & waved, & crowded round him – it was most touching'.[21] The results gave renewed hope to suffragists, in particular Liberal members of the National Union, that their cause would soon be won. Leaders of the WSPU, however, were more sceptical.

When Christabel Pankhurst addressed a large suffrage meeting in Leeds early in February she expressed the fear that the National Liberal Federation had made promises to women just to keep their services for electioneering purposes; her doubts seemed justified when, a few days later, the prime minister, Henry Campbell-Bannerman, refused to see a suffrage deputation. Christabel was also having doubts about the attitude of the Labour Party. After returning home from Leeds she wrote to ask Mary Gawthorpe to contact ILP MPs to find out what Labour members intended to do for women now they had been elected. 'From what I have heard it is quite necessary to keep an eye on them . . . JKH is the one who really wants to help. The further one goes the plainer one sees that men (even Labour men) think more of their own interests than of ours.'[22]

Isabella shared some of these worries. None the less, she always tried to give her Labour Party colleagues the benefit of the doubt. On 13 February, at a meeting in London between suffragists and sympathetic MPs, she was delighted to find that nearly fifty MPs had turned up, compared with only a dozen or so on previous occasions. She thought this represented an 'immense change' and rejoiced that 'numbers of women outside the Socialist Party are realising that this change is due to the Labour movement'. Those present agreed to get the support of MPs for a suffrage petition to be presented to the prime minister, and Isabella felt that 'for the first time women's enfranchisement is considered as now coming within the sphere of practical politics'.[23]

[20]Isabella Ford to Millicent Fawcett, 14 Jan. 1906, Suffrage MSS.
[21]Isabella Ford to Millicent Fawcett, 18 Jan. 1906, ibid.
[22]Gawthorpe, *Up Hill to Holloway*, p. 210.
[23]I. O. Ford, 'Women's Votes: Conferences of MPs', *LL* 23 Feb. 1906.

Although Isabella's and Christabel's views about the Labour Party were diverging, they had not yet reached the point of becoming irreconcileable. Isabella allowed herself, therefore, to be persuaded by Keir Hardie to lend money to the Pankhursts to pay for the hire of the Caxton Hall for a suffrage meeting on 16 February. Isabella was still in London and attended the meeting, after first walking in a procession with working women from the East End. She then went to the House of Commons with small contingents of women to lobby MPs. After twenty had been admitted the rest were refused entry, which appeared to be a new regulation. Isabella was 'sad and disgusted' with the treatment they received and stood outside in the rain with a large number of women and 'some Labour men comrades'. She felt that the women who had taken part were now more resolved than ever to fight for their rights.[24]

Isabella was re-elected to the NAC in April and chosen, with Emmeline Pankhurst, to represent the ILP at the Labour Party's next annual conference, to be held in Belfast. But relations between the ILP and the WSPU, and between the different suffrage groups, were becoming more strained. These differences were largely over the question of militant methods. On 25 April, when Keir Hardie was introducing a resolution in the House of Commons in favour of the enfranchisement of women, his speech was interrupted by WSPU members in the public gallery. As the women were thrown out they met a hostile reception from Ethel Snowden and other non-militant suffragists, who believed that they had wrecked all chance of gaining the support of the House; Isabella also later recalled that it was over this incident that she and Mrs Pankhurst 'parted company in the ILP'.[25]

However, representatives from both the WSPU and the NUWSS went together to see Henry Campbell-Bannerman when he at last agreed to receive a women's suffrage deputation. Isabella took part in the historic meeting, which took place on 19 May. After putting their case to the prime minister, members of the deputation went on to a rally in Exeter Hall. One thousand women listened enthusiastically to Hardie and Charles Maclaren MP urging them to be impatient and to 'all act together in one united course of action'. Isabella concluded that 'the day of patience is over now, one feels, even with the quieter, staider sets of women . . . Truly it was a wonderful day.'[26]

Any unity between the suffrage groups was only temporary. The determination of WSPU members to disrupt the meetings of even sympathetic MPs was directly contrary to the political strategy developed by the NUWSS over many years, and threatened to push the two groups further

[24]A. Rosen, *Rise Up Women!* (Routledge & Kegan Paul, 1974), p. 58.
[25]Isabella Ford to Millicent Fawcett, 10 Aug. n.d. (post-WWI) Correspondence Files, Fawcett Lib.
[26]I. O. Ford, 'Exeter Hall and Trafalgar Square', *LL* 25 May 1906.

apart. These different approaches caused tensions for individuals at a local level, regardless of which group they belonged to. When she was invited to tea at Adel early in June, Mary Gawthorpe found herself subject to an 'unexpected attack' from Isabella and Ethel Snowden. They criticized her for writing a letter in support of WSPU militancy to the *Yorkshire Post* without first gaining permission. Mary felt completely naïve faced with two women who were politically experienced and in touch with national events: 'Isabella was the questioner, but from that day I observed a new Ethel who had now made the acquaintance of the House of Commons as the wife of the newly-elected member for Blackburn. In London, a few days previously, she and Isabella Ford had witnessed and taken part in that great deputation together. They were fully aware of the powerful currents unknown to me then setting in to separate suffrage workers into rival camps.'[27] Isabella's own views were not as clear cut as this implies. John Bruce Glasier, who visited Adel Grange at the end of June, found that she was torn between her older suffrage friends and the newer, more militant women.[28]

For the time being, Isabella and Mary continued to work together as members of the ILP and Leeds WSS. 'All fire and quick response, a flash of energy, of sympathy, of comprehension', Mary shared Isabella's strong sense of humour and with her 'fog and frost' voice, was a popular and entertaining speaker.[29] The two women combined labour and suffrage work, speaking to a variety of groups during the early summer. They spent the first fortnight of June in Leeds, addressing 'camp stool' meetings – meetings which were held in the open air and were so called because camp stools could be hired for a penny.[30] Speaking to the New Wortley Labour Party on the 10th, they argued that men and women should co-operate together. They then addressed meetings of tailoresses and printers' operatives, where they urged women workers to join their respective unions. At the end of this rush of meetings Isabella and Mary travelled to the first annual conference of the Women's Labour League, held in Leicester on 21 June.

The League was the first attempt to establish a separate organization for women under the auspices of the Labour Party. Margaret MacDonald and Mary Middleton, both the wives of Labour Party leaders, were largely responsible for this new initiative. They had managed to persuade the party to give official support to their scheme by arguing that it would encourage women to take an interest in Labour politics. Isabella felt ambivalent about

[27]Gawthorpe, *Up Hill to Holloway*, pp. 215–16.

[28]John Bruce Glasier to Lizzie Glasier, 6 July 1906, Glasier papers, Liverpool. I am grateful to Clare Collins for this reference.

[29]H. Swanwick, *I Have Been Young* (Victor Gollancz, 1935), p. 192.

[30]Gawthorpe, *Up Hill to Holloway*, pp. 221–2.

separate organizations for women within mixed-sex political groups. She had been very critical when 'The Women's Outlook', written under the pseudonym Iona by Katharine Bruce Glasier, appeared as a regular feature in the *Labour Leader*. Isabella was dismayed; she 'thought that the day had gone by for the separate treatment of men and women's interests, and that the *Leader* at least would be free from that kind of thing', a stand in which she was supported by Ethel Snowden.[31]

When the question of the Women's Labour League (WLL) was raised before the ILP's annual conference in April, Isabella again expressed doubts, although she accepted that the women's group recently formed by the East Leeds LRC had been successful in recruiting more female members.[32] It was with considerable reservations, therefore, that Isabella attended the Leicester conference. Her main interest was in the League's attitude towards women's suffrage. Given the Labour Party's refusal to make a commitment to a limited franchise, this proved to be the most controversial issue of the conference. The WLL's main objective was stated simply as 'to work for independent Labour representation in connection with the Labour Party'. Mrs Pethwick Lawrence moved an amendment, seconded by Isabella, to widen the aims to include a commitment to seek 'full rights of citizenship for all women and men, and to work for the immediate removal of sex disability'. This was lost by twenty-eight votes to eighteen.

In order to salvage something from the debate, Isabella moved that the objectives should include the words 'and to obtain direct Labour representation of Women in Parliament and on all local bodies'.[33] The resolution was successful; it did not commit the League to support for a limited franchise and was therefore far less controversial. Once the conference was over, Isabella no longer took any active role in the affairs of the League. Her commitment to a limited franchise was so strong that she was not prepared to spend time on an organization which did not share her views. The League's lukewarm response on women's suffrage was indicative of a far more general attitude to any issue which threatened to disrupt labour unity. The main aim of the League was to involve more women in election campaigns on behalf of the Labour Party, and the specific interests of women tended to take second place. This represented a vital difference of approach to that of Isabella and many other ILP suffragists; for them, no progress could be made in labour politics unless women were enfranchised and could work alongside men for socialism. Women's suffrage, therefore, was a priority.

Immediately after the conference, Isabella continued with her general political propaganda for the ILP. She spent a week on a speaking tour of

[31]*LL* 2 Mar. 1906.
[32]*LL* 27 Apr. 1906.
[33]First Annual Conference of the Women's Labour League, *Report*, p. 4.

South Wales and the Bristol area; topics for her talks included 'Socialism is Practical Christianity', 'Socialism and the Home', and 'Women's Suffrage'. She was feeling so overworked that she had to decline Ramsay Mac-Donald's request to act as an interpreter at the International Socialist Congress to be held in London in July. 'Interpreting workmen's speeches on their wages . . . is very different from translating Jaures & such! & I don't feel I can do it at all . . . Also I have two tiresome lectures in Cambridge & Croydon on Wednesday p.m. and Thursday. How about Adolph Smith??'[34]

As Isabella rushed from meeting to meeting, she was unaware of the crisis which was about to break apart the fragile alliance which she had worked so hard to maintain between women's suffrage and the labour movement. The immediate occasion was provided by a by-election in Cockermouth. Frustrated by their failure to make any headway with the Liberal government and disenchanted by the Labour Party's attitude to women's suffrage, Christabel Pankhurst and Annie Kenney went into the constituency determined to make an impact. They not only carried out propaganda against the Liberal candidate, but also opposed Robert Smillie of the ILP, who appeared to be ambivalent about women's suffrage.

Their actions led to a storm of protest within the ILP, with many branches calling for the two women to be expelled from the party. Isabella, however, supported their right to remain. In a letter to the secretary of the ILP, both she and Margaret McMillan, a fellow member of the NAC, expressed concern that Smillie had not been required to make his views on women's suffrage clear before he was adopted as a candidate. Anyone who hesitated on this they said, could not be a 'sincere socialist', and went on to demand that all candidates make their policy on women's suffrage clear: 'in order to prevent the Party losing the support of such of us, during election times, we should very much like this course to be adopted'.[35] After Christabel Pankhurst and Annie Kenney had agreed not to repeat their tactics, the Manchester Central ILP voted against the resolution to expel them. It was argued that they had 'simply endeavoured to carry out the immediate extension of the franchise to women, which is included in the official programme of the party as one of its objects'.

The immediate crisis was overcome. On the other hand, the actions of WSPU members at Cockermouth had brought into the open questions of political loyalties and tactics which still had to be resolved. The most controversial issue was not the use of militant methods, but whether they should be directed against labour candidates. As the women's suffrage

[34]Isabella Ford to James Ramsay MacDonald, 15 July 1906, LP GC 6/235, Labour Party Archives.
[35]Isabella Ford and Margaret McMillan to Francis Johnson, 28 Oct. 1906, Francis Johnson Coll., LSE.
[36]LL 7 Sept. 1906.

campaign intensified over the next few months, labour women found themselves facing uncomfortable political choices. The Pankhursts began to call on women to put the struggle for the vote before anything else, even if that meant acting against the Labour Party. They had moved the head-quarters of the WSPU to London, away from their base among working women in the north, and urged other ILP women to join them in concen-trating on suffrage propaganda. Among those who responded was Mary Gawthorpe; she had gone down to Cockermouth to work for Robert Smillie, putting labour first and suffrage second, but emerged from the by-election a 'full-time militant'.[37]

Isabella also faced a dilemma about her political loyalties. Mary Gawth-orpe later recalled that she 'was at this time divided, as to policy, between allegiance to the . . . Parliamentary Labour Party on the one hand, and the imperative need for dynamic action on the other, to reinforce her NUWSS self, now impatient of delays and informed by the knowledge of years'.[38] Isabella put off making any decision, however, and continued to urge both suffragists and socialists to go forward together. At the same time, she became more and more insistent that women's suffrage must be a precondi-tion for any other social change. Thus, drawing attention to the new constitution that had just been proposed for the Transvaal, Isabella noted that women had been omitted. They would be handed over 'into the power of every mine owner, every ignorant official (it is generally the middle-class ne'er-do-well who is sent to South Africa by his irate parents), every male creature of proper age'. She hoped that Labour women would protest about this, and reminded them of the centrality of the women's cause for labour's objectives: 'there can be no economic freedom for any country where women are not politically free equally with men. Our cause underlies every Labour question. We are the sweated and industrially most oppressed section of the whole world and until political power be given us we shall continue to keep back the wheels of real progress.'[39]

Believing that the battle for the vote was at an acute stage Isabella decided to revise *Women and Socialism* for republication, so that 'the absolute expediency for the welfare of the State, as well as the justice of granting the vote to women, should be made perfectly clear'. Hoping to persuade women to carry on the suffrage fight from within the labour movement, she tried to demonstrate even more forcefully than before that only social-ism could bring about the kind of changes that they hoped to see. She wrote a new section to explain the meaning of socialism: '[it] demands more than that we should merely import Socialistic institutions into our midst, such as free meals for children . . . and consider that they will regenerate society

[37]*Book of the Suffragette Prisoners*, Questionnaire by the Suffragette Club, pp. 4–5.
[38]Gawthorpe, *Up Hill to Holloway*, p. 216.
[39]I. O. Ford, 'Women and the Transvaal Constitution', *LL* 10 Aug. 1906, p. 181.

and turn us all into Socialists. It insists on a moral regeneration of society of the most complete and searching kind.' The Labour Party's success in the last election was responsible for the distinctly optimistic tone of the revised pamphlet. 'At the present moment the connections between the women's movement and the Socialist movement seem closer than ever . . . Now, in Parliament, the Labour Party has definitely and decidedly espoused the cause of women's enfranchisement, and the two causes are, therefore, in the House of Commons at least, distinctly joined together.'[40]

Isabella must have known that support for women's suffrage among Labour MPs was nowhere near as strong as she implied. At the end of the year, therefore, she once again made a plea for unity between the cause of women and labour. Using a historical example to add weight to her argument, she published a letter in the *Labour Leader* which had been written by Jeanne Deroine and Pauline Roland from their prison cell in Paris in June 1851, when the 'darkness of reaction' had 'obscured the sun of 1848'. Writing in support of the American Women's Suffrage Convention, they regretted that the French Assembly had told the women that they must wait. In doing so, they said, it had 'kept silence in regard to the right of one half of humanity . . . No mention was made of the right of woman in a constitution framed in the name of Liberty, Equality and Fraternity.' Deroine and Roland wrote of their conviction that 'only by the power of association based on solidarity – by the union of the working classes of both sexes to organize labour – can be acquired . . . the civil and political equality of women and the social right for all'. These stirring words exactly mirrored Isabella's own views, moving her to comment that they could have been 'written yesterday instead of fifty-five years ago'. In her final comment on the Deroine–Roland letter, Isabella once again showed an understanding of the subtle ways in which women experienced oppression. She had always recognized that prevailing definitions of femininity were internalized by women, leading them to modify their behaviour and attitudes, and now she explored the effects of language: she supposed that in France, 'it is the use of that unfortunate masculine word, "fraternity" which excludes women. Women are evidently not brothers. English socialists must, therefore, find a new word which will include us.'[41]

Isabella's confidence in the possibility of maintaining unity between the suffrage and labour movements, and among suffragists themselves, appeared to be justified when the NUWSS and the ILP both expressed support for the eleven WSPU members who were imprisoned after demonstrating at the opening session of the House of Commons in October. In an

[40]Id., *Women and Socialism* (1906 edn), pp. 2, 8.
[41]*LL* 2 Nov. 1906. Jeanne Deroine was a socialist, leading trade-unionist, and the first woman to stand for election to the National Assembly in 1849. She was an admirer of Fourier, Cabet, and Blanqui. See G. Malmgreen, 'Anne Knight and the Radical Subculture', *Quaker History*, 71 (Fall 1982).

impressive display of solidarity, the ILP produced a manifesto to 'congratulate the brave women', many of whom were ILP members, which was signed by Isabella, Margaret McMillan, and dozens of rank-and-file women from the branches. On the prisoners' release Millicent Fawcett hosted a banquet in their honour on behalf of the National Union. She spoke warmly of 'the gay courage, the endurance, the self sacrifice' of the arrested women, while Isabella seconded 'vigorously . . . in the name of the women workers of the North'.[42]

After the new year dawned, differences of opinion over political tactics and the most effective methods of agitation increasingly posed a threat to this outward show of unity. The assertion by WSPU members that women's suffrage should take precedence over all other issues, their actions at the Cockermouth by-election, and the escalation of militancy intensified the fear and hostility already felt within the Labour Party towards a cause which put the solidarity of sex above class loyalty. Disagreements over political priorities and loyalties came to a head at the Labour Party's annual conference at Belfast in February 1907. The usual resolution was put forward calling for the immediate enfranchisement of women on the same terms as men. Speaking eloquently in favour of the resolution, Selina Cooper, a working-class suffragist from Lancashire, argued that it would give the vote to many working women and had a greater chance of success than an adult suffrage measure. Keir Hardie followed with an emotive speech which concluded that 'so long as women are held to be inferior to men they cannot expect the comradeship in the great Labour movement which we all desire to see'.[43]

The majority of delegates, however, gave overwhelming support to an amendment calling for adult suffrage, and once again the supporters of women's suffrage were left bitterly disappointed. Hardie threatened to resign if the decision meant that his actions in the House of Commons would be limited, a stand that Isabella thought was 'magnificent'. 'It is not only we women who are indebted to him,' she claimed. 'I consider all the Socialists, both men and women, must thank him from their hearts for his recognition of the fact that it is only from a real democracy that a real Socialism can spring, and that we can have no such democracy and therefore no such Socialism until we have our women as well as our men . . . free.'[44]

In contrast, the ILP's annual conference held two months later in Derby decisively reaffirmed support for a limited franchise. There was a tense atmosphere in the hall, however, as delegates debated a resolution which condemned the electoral tactics of the WSPU as 'detrimental to the Party'.

[42] *Manifesto to the Women's Social and Political Union* (ILP, 1906); *LL* 14 Dec. 1906.

[43] J. Liddington, *The Life and Times of a Respectable Rebel: Selina Cooper, 1864–1946* (Virago, 1984), pp. 175–7.

[44] *LL* 8 Feb. 1907.

It went on to assert that loyalty to the constitution and policy of the party was an 'essential condition of membership'. Convalescing from an illness in Switzerland, Isabella was unable to attend the conference. None the less, she still joined other leading women, including Ethel Snowden in writing a letter which pledged that they would never go down to 'any constituency or take part in elections unless we are going to help the Labour Party'.[45]In an emotional speech Mrs Pankhurst dissasociated herself from the letter. which was read out by Margaret McMillan, but the conciliatory message had won the day and the resolution was withdrawn.

In practical terms this made little difference to Emmeline and Christabel Pankhurst. They had already decided that the best way to achieve women's suffrage was to gain the support of wealthy and powerful women in London. Soon after the conference they resigned from the ILP, severing all ties between the WSPU and the labour movement at a national level. Prominent ILP women found it difficult, therefore, to remain on terms of close personal friendship with WSPU leaders. According to Mary Gawthorpe, for example, she and Isabella never corresponded again once Mary was fully militant.[46] At a local level, however, the situation was more fluid, with many women continuing to belong both to the ILP and the WSPU.

Leading ILP suffragists who did not wish to follow the WSPU in cutting their links with the labour movement were still affected by the split that had taken place. The negative attitude of the Labour Party towards the women's cause and the growing momentum of the suffrage campaign forced them to reconsider their political loyalties. Isabella was not alone, therefore, in making her decision to give priority to the struggle for the vote; in February 1907 she stood successfully for election to the executive committee of the National Union of Women's Suffrage Societies. The new direction taken in her political work was then confirmed in April when she made up her mind not to seek re-election to the National Administrative Council of the ILP, 'for we who are in the Women's Suffrage Party have all agreed to put our cause before everything else and to fight for it first'.[47] This was a logical position for all those who had come to believe that political equality was a necessary first step towards the achievement of socialism and that it was the only way to ensure that women's needs would be recognized in the new society. Isabella expressed the views of many of her colleagues when she wrote that 'it is not until woman, strong and free, stands beside man, helping him to reach this better life, and not as now holding him back from it, that we shall begin in real earnest to walk towards the full light of day'.[48]

---

[45]Ibid., 5 Apr. 1907. Among the signatories were Mrs. Cobden Sanderson, Charlotte Despard, and Ethel Snowden.
[46]Gawthorpe, *Up Hill to Holloway*, p. 226.
[47]I. O. Ford, 'Why Women Should Be Socialists', *LL* 1 May 1913, p. 10.
[48]Id., *Women and Socialism* (1906 edn), p. 14.

8

The Long Red Scarf, 1907–1911

> We intend, as soon as we have votes, to turn everything upside down.

For a short period after 1907, women fought their battle for the vote alone, outside the labour movement. Isabella joined them in this fight. No longer a leader of the ILP, she felt free to commit herself heart and soul to the campaign for women's suffrage. She had left the NAC, however, with great regret and never gave up her membership of the party. In deciding to use the NUWSS as the base for her suffrage work, rather than the ILP, Isabella did not give up hope that the labour movement and the women's movement could be reconciled. During the next four years she worked towards that end, and in her propaganda for the vote never lost sight of the fact that it was just one part of a broader struggle for socialism and the emancipation of working women.

Isabella's political activities were curtailed by illness during the first part of the year and she spent four months in Switzerland to recuperate. Returning to England in June, she threw herself with renewed energy into the struggle for the vote which was beginning to gather momentum. The campaign was spear-headed by three groups; the Women's Social and Political Union, the Women's Freedom League, and the National Union of Women's Suffrage Societies. They all put forward the same demand – votes for women on the same terms as men – but were divided over political tactics and in their attitudes towards militancy. Many younger ILP suffragists were attracted by the militant methods of the WSPU; the disruption of meetings, clashes with police and subsequent arrests were exhilirating and transformed the lives of those who took part. The political strategy of the WSPU, however, posed difficultes for those who remained in the ILP. Emmeline and Christabel Pankhurst not only attacked all government candidates, regardless of their views on women's suffrage, but also became increasingly hostile to the Labour Party. This was reflected in their theory of sex oppression; Christabel moved further and further away from a socialist analysis as she came to see 'the domination of women by men as more fundamental' than class differences.[1]

The Pankhursts' attitude towards labour politics and their autocratic leadership prompted Teresa Billington Grieg and Charlotte Despard to break away from the WSPU in October 1907 to form the Women's Freedom League. Members of the League continued to attack all government candidates and to use direct action to achieve their aims. On the other hand they were more sympathetic to the labour movement and used different militant methods, including tax resistance and peaceful picketing. Isabella sympathized with the militants' enthusiasm for taking action, although she could not bring herself to join them. Moderate by temperament, with a deep-rooted belief in constitutionalism and non-violence, she was far more at home in the NUWSS. Moreover, the democratic basis of the organization and its strategy of supporting any candidates who were sympathetic to women's suffrage was compatible with her continued membership of the ILP.

Disagreements between the suffrage groups should not be exaggerated; relations were more strained in some periods than in others, and the rifts between the leadership of the suffrage groups, and between the WSPU and the labour movement at a national level, were not necessarily duplicated among the rank and file in the provinces. In Leeds, for example, Lily Escritt, Maud Dightam, Marie Foster, and many others were members simultaneously of the WSPU, the WLL, and the ILP. They collaborated with the local labour movement and were interested in wider questions than the vote. By confronting the power of the state through their militant methods, local members of the WSPU could also link with the direct action of industrial workers in the pre-war years.

In many respects the NUWSS, with its predominantly upper middle-class and Liberal membership, had fewer attractions for rank-and-file labour women than the WSPU. On the other hand the NUWSS was not left untouched by the new vigour of the militants; the executive committee started to develop new tactics and sought ways to make it a more effective, popularly based organization. When leading ILP suffragists became more active within the NUWSS, they too helped to change its staid, establishment image. A new constitution was adopted in 1907, making the national council into a policy making body with more control over the branches. The NUWSS was still committed to gaining the support of individual MPs for a women's suffrage measure, but there was a shift in emphasis away from lobbying at the House of Commons towards more grass-roots constituency work, including greater intervention in local elections. Processions,

[1]E. Sarah, 'Christabel Pankhurst: Reclaiming Her Power', in D. Spender, ed., *Feminist Theorists* (Women's Press, 1983), pp. 272–3.

rallies, and large public meetings were also held to draw more women into suffrage activity.

Isabella was particularly enthusiastic about building up popular support in the provinces. At executive committee meetings she tried to ensure that fellow members did not remain too London-centred; on 3 July 1907, for example, she moved that a telegram be sent to all the candidates standing in the Colne Valley by-election to ascertain their views on women's suffrage. Victor Grayson, standing as an independent socialist, gave the strongest reply, and on Isabella's suggestion it was agreed that NUWSS workers could be sent to help him. She also proposed that any letters publicizing suffrage demonstrations should be sent to the provincial as well as the London press, and at a later meeting argued that local branches should be expected to take twelve copies of the *Women's Franchise* each week so that their members could keep in touch with events.[2]

The three Ford sisters put a great deal of energy into the campaign in their own local area and virtually ran the the Leeds Suffrage Society; Bessie held the office of treasurer and Emily and Isabella were vice-presidents. Now that she was an executive member of the NUWSS Isabella no longer had the time to be organizing secretary of the local society, and that demanding job was taken over by an ILP suffragist, Mary Foster. The Leeds Society had committee rooms in the centre of the city, but Adel Grange was also used for garden parties, fund-raising events, and meetings.

Emily, Bessie, and Isabella had not worked so closely together for the same cause since the labour unrest of 1889; in the intervening years Emily had been busy painting altar panels in churches and had not been as active in the labour movement as her two sisters. The battle for the suffrage brought her fully back into the world of political agitation; she was not only a lively speaker, often entertaining audiences with her 'Yorkshire sketches', but also used her artistic talents to help the cause. She designed the membership cards for the Leeds Society and was vice-chairman of the Artists' Suffrage League, dividing her time between Adel Grange and her studio in London, which was described as 'a meeting ground for artists, suffragists, people who *did* things'.[3]

Isabella's own visits to London became more frequent now that she had to attend NUWSS executive committee meetings. She usually took the opportunity afforded by these visits to speak to local groups. In December 1907 she was asked to chair an important public debate between Margaret Bondfield, the adult suffragist, and Teresa Billington Greig, supporter of a limited franchise, which must have reminded her of her own debate with

[2]For a discussion of changes in NUWSS organization and tactics, see L. P. Hume, *The National Union of Women's Suffrage Societies, 1897–1914* (Garland Publishing, 1982), ch. 2; also NUWSS Executive Committee Minutes, 9 Apr. 1908, NUWSS Papers, Fawcett Lib.

[3]Dora Meeson Coates, quoted in L. Tickner, *The Spectacle of Women: Imagery of the Suffrage Campaign, 1907–1914* (Chatto & Windus, 1988).

Margaret Bonfield two years before. Isabella made it clear to the audience that she took her role as chairman seriously, for the 'object of the Chairman is simply to announce what is going to happen and to be absolutely impartial'. She urged that 'those who are prejudiced on one side ought especially to listen to the arguments of the other side', adding, 'I speak with feeling because I am a very prejudiced person myself, and therefore I endeavour to listen always with patience and respect to the arguments of my opponents, and I expect you to do the same.'[4]

Her own patience was sorely tried when confronted with the complacent attitudes of many middle-class members of the NUWSS. At the quarterly council meeting held on 29 January 1908, she urged delegates to take vigorous action to gain the vote, for 'I have not eternal youth and therefore cannot be patient.' Every day, argued Isabella, working women faced threats to their economic position from factory legislation, and for them the vote was a matter of urgency. Ethel Snowden spoke in support of this view; it was 'criminal' to wait for the vote when 'working women needed it so badly'.[5]

Isabella, Ethel Snowden, and other ILP suffragists did not abandon their socialist beliefs when they decided to work full-time for women's suffrage. On the contrary, they took their political ideas into the NUWSS and worked hard to make its well-to-do middle-class members more aware of the needs of working-class women. The day after the quarterly council meeting, Isabella took part in an NUWSS deputation to Herbert Asquith, the home secretary, where she again emphasized the relevance of the vote for working women. When Asquith complained that he had yet to hear of any widespread demand for the vote among women themselves, Isabella retorted that, if he would come with her to meetings of working women, 'she could show him that there were thousands of women who keenly desired the vote'. Asquith was unconvinced and replied, 'in his most forbidding air, "The prospect does not greatly attract me".'[6]

Commenting on this meeting in a letter to Millicent Fawcett written many years later, Isabella wrote that she could remember her, 'internal fury', and how 'Miss A [squith] sat behind him & heard him insult us'. 'I had told him he never met women at his meetings, only men, & so he couldn't possibly know what women thought & so on.' Asquith had asked Millicent Fawcett if she could guarantee good behaviour on the part of the deputation, and Isabella recalled Millicent's reply with delight: '"I know all these ladies personally & can answer for them, but I don't know *that* lady"

---

[4]*Verbatim Report of Debate on Dec. 3 1907. Sex Equality (Teresa Billington Greig) versus Adult Suffrage (Margaret G. Bondfield)* (Manchester, 1908), pp. 3–4.

[5]NUWSS, Minutes of Quarterly Council Meeting, 29 Jan. 1908. NUWSS Papers.

[6]M. G. Fawcett, *The Women's Victory and After: Personal Reminiscences, 1911–1918* (Sidgwick & Jackson, 1920), p. 18.

& you pointed to Miss Asquith to our great joy! for your words implied Miss A might break out into violence.'[7]

Both women were disappointed with Asquith's response to the deputation, but Isabella had greater hopes of support from the Labour Party. On 20 February 1908 she chaired a meeting at which NUWSS members tried to persuade Labour Party officers to press the government to give full facilities to a Women's Suffrage Bill. The Labour Party remained suspicious, however, of the political implications of a limited franchise, and once again the women were unsuccessful. Even the ILP appeared to be lukewarm on the subject of women's suffrage now that the most prominent suffragists no longer took a leading part in its affairs. The *Labour Leader*, which was edited by the adult suffragist John Bruce Glasier, gave little publicity to the women's struggle for the vote, and Isabella wrote in to urge the ILP to help women more than it did.[8] Keir Hardie's long absence on a foreign tour had contributed to the lack of interest shown within the ILP towards women's suffrage, and it was with some relief that Isabella joined ILP leaders at the Albert Hall in April to welcome him back. Wearing a long red scarf to emphasize the links between her socialist and feminist beliefs and as 'an emblem of the revolt of the women', she spoke 'feelingly of the loyal support that he had rendered to the women's cause'.[9]

These setbacks and disappointments did not prevent Isabella, Ethel Snowden, and Selina Cooper from spending a great deal of time trying to bring the NUWSS closer to the labour movement. Selina Cooper was now a full-time organizer for the NUWSS, and Isabella often worked closely with her. When she was unable to join Selina in a propaganda campaign in 1907, Isabella wrote to offer her apologies and expressed an unusual degree of emotion: 'I cannot come alas & alas . . . & I *would* so like to be campaigning with you again – please don't be so disagreable as to sign yourself "respectfully" to *me* – or I must do it too & I feel "affectionately" & not respectfully . . . for I like you dear Mrs Cooper. Please try and like me.'[10] Despite these overtures the two women do not appear to have become close friends. They shared very similar political views, but it may have been Selina's natural reserve and the difference in their class backgrounds that stopped them from developing a real intimacy.

Isabella was having some success in persuading the NUWSS to look favourably on the Labour Party; in April she managed to get permission from the executive committee for the Leeds Society to campaign on behalf of her old friend Ben Turner, who was standing as a Labour candidate in the Dewsbury by-election. In the middle of the month she rushed back to the

---

[7]Isabella Ford to Millicent Fawcett, Autumn 1919 and 10 Aug. n.d. (post-WWI), Correspondence Files, Fawcett Lib.

[8]*LL* 6 Mar. 1908.

[9]*LL* 10 Apr. 1908.

[10]Isabella Ford to Selina Cooper c.1907, Nelson Public Lib.

West Riding to take part in Turner's campaign, but though she 'spoke bravely' on his behalf he failed to get elected.[11] Turner had been a supporter of women's suffrage long before it had become such an important political issue. He received no help from the 'militants', however, who were there to spread anti-government propaganda.

Until 1908 the 'constitutionalist' and 'militant' wings of the suffrage movement still managed to co-operate, and joint membership of the different groups was common. Isabella was willing, for example, to give publicity to the two separate processions, organized by the NUWSS and the WSPU respectively, which were to be held in London on 13 and 21 June. Her letter to the *Labour Leader* urged ILP women to attend both demonstrations if they possibly could. Describing the planned NUWSS procession, she claimed that 'the Artists' League are working most beautiful banners for the various societies. Our Leeds Women's Suffrage Society has a banner in blue and gold, with the Leeds arms and the words "Leeds for Liberty" . . . Every banner will be gorgeous and beautiful in colour and design.' She hoped that some delegates to the International Women's Suffrage Alliance Congress in Amsterdam would come over for the procession, because 'it would be a refreshing sight – and a most terrifying one I suppose, for Mr. Asquith – if the women Members of Parliament for Finland could be present. I would like here to remind women that the Upper Chamber in Finland has been already abolished, largely, I am told, through the action of the women's vote.'[12]

The demonstration on 13 June lived up to expectations with at least 10,000 women, representing forty-two organizations, taking part. Bessie was elated by the experience of marching in procession with so many other women. In a letter to Kate Salt she contrasted her humdrum work as treasurer of the Leeds Society, which made her lose sight of all the meaning and beauty of the cause, with the feelings she experienced in London: 'Those women's faces are beautiful – it was quite glorious to see them, they seemed to shine . . . no, nothing can push it back, women are stirring and rising up everywhere, it's like a great flood.'[13]

Isabella felt a similar sense of excitement as she made her way next day by boat to Amsterdam to attend the congress of the International Women's Suffrage Alliance. Women came to the conference from all over Europe and the United States to give each other mutual support in their struggle for the suffrage. Isabella was one of three delegates chosen by the NUWSS to give the official report from Great Britain. In her opening statement she emphasized that working men were now more enthusiastic about women's suffrage, both because of the NUWSS's work at by-elections and because

[11]*LL* 24 Apr. 1908.
[12]Ibid.
[13]Bessie Ford to Kate Salt, 15 June 1908, Carpenter Coll., Sheffield Ref. Lib.

they knew how hard the lives of working women could be. She urged the Conference to 'have faith in the people and they will respond to your faith through their innate goodness'. It was not an easy conference for Isabella. Representatives from more militant groups were determined to give a different perspective on events. Dora Montefiore, a socialist member of the WFL, objected to the statement in the official British report that 'the Labour Party had endorsed the women's claim'. All reference to Labour support was subsequently omitted from the final report.[14]

Reporting on the conference for the *Labour Leader*, Isabella deliberately emphasized the links between the women's movement and socialism:

> The women there were such noble people, so full of enthusiasm, so eager and so able . . . All references to Socialism were cheered except when the German Social Democrats were mentioned, and then the German women shook their heads. For the Social Democrats with them have never helped women. How glad they were to hear of our ILP, and how proud I was to tell of its work and true Socialist spirit.

She was elated by the display of international solidarity: 'it was a wonderful evening, and as I left the room and went away through the gardens in the sweet night air to my train, I kept thinking, "now is the day of woman's freedom, of woman's awakening and the day, therefore, of the coming of a full and complete Socialism at hand" . . . and my heart was full within me.'[15]

Fluent as she was in French and German, Isabella felt at ease with women from other countries and took a positive pleasure in the feeling of sisterhood that she experienced at these international congresses. For her, the meaning of the congress was that 'never again must the women of one country feel that they have to stand alone in any of their struggles for liberty', for henceforth they 'would stand together, and fight together, for freedom, anywhere, and everywhere, for both men and women'.[16] The last phrase, 'for both men and women', was a significant one. It was because she believed that political equality would transform the behaviour of both sexes that Isabella saw the vote as so important. Only when they were politically free would men and women co-operate, 'helping and teaching one another as equals and friends, instead of as now often living alongside one another as strangers, sometimes even as enemies'.[17]

In Isabella's eyes, sisterhood was not a replacement for comradeship between the sexes, but rather a complement to it. On the other hand, she clearly valued the closeness with other women that developed out of their struggle for a common cause. The suffrage campaign strengthened and deepened some of her existing friendships, in particular with Millicent

[14]International Women's Suffrage Alliance, 4th Annual Conference, *Report*, pp. 24, 31.
[15]I. O. Ford, 'Women's International Congress', *LL* 26 June 1908.
[16]Ibid.
[17]Ford, *Women and Socialism* (1906 edn), p. 14.

Fawcett. In the 1890s, Isabella's letters were addressed to 'Dear Mrs Faw-cett'. After 1906, however, she used the more intimate and affectionate term of 'Dear or dearest Millie'. The campaign for the vote also brought new friendships with women such as Helena Swanwick who shared Isabella's democratic approach and her interest in the needs of female workers.

Although the suffrage movement brought women together from varied backgrounds to fight for a common cause, divisions between them became more apparent after March 1908 when Asquith was appointed prime minister. His opposition to women's suffrage was well known, and WSPU members began to increase the scale of their militancy; they stepped up their attacks on individual MPs and engaged in serious skirmishes with the police – actions which the leaders of the NUWSS felt unable to condone. The executive committee refused, for example, to publish an article by Keir Hardie because he appeared to support militancy. As usual, Isabella found herself in the role of conciliator. She wrote to Francis Johnson, secretary of the ILP, on 10 August to explain that the reason her colleagues would not print the article 'as I wanted them to do', was because in one sentence he upheld militant tactics. She tried to get round the problem by suggesting that Hardie should offer the article to the Women's Freedom League 'and we shall buy it from them & we shall buy it from anyone who prints it but we cannot print it ourselves'.[18]

The letter suggests that Isabella was more sympathetic to the militants than many other executive members of the National Union. She considered that most militant actions were still constitutional in character, and that any violence was usually provoked by the authorities; in one letter she drew attention to the way in which women could no longer go near the House of Commons, as they had every right to do, because 'police are all around, lying in wait to arrest them'. Unwilling herself to take part in acts of violence, she could understand why women who had no other way to express their views would resort to such methods. Many years earlier she had pointed out how women who were desperate from watching their children die of starvation had been at the forefront of riots in Milan. Her conclusions from this had been clear. 'If a revolution occurred in England I should consider I had a perfectly legal right to use the only force allowed me i.e. physical force. A vote I am not allowed, therefore I may use my hands. Of course, moral right is not in the question at all.'[19]

Isabella's tolerance and understanding of the militants was not shared by all constitutionalists, and the rift between the societies was growing wider all the time. From the autumn of 1908 until the end of the following year, suffragists from all groups made repeated attempts to persuade the govern-ment to sponsor a Women's Suffrage Bill, or to give facilities for a Private

[18]Isabella Ford to Francis Johnson, 10 Aug. 1908, Francis Johnson Coll., LSE.
[19]LL 6 Mar. 1908; Leeds Forward, June 1898.

Member's Bill. The failure of all their efforts meant that frustration increased; militancy escalated as WSPU members rushed the House of Commons and began to throw stones at property. Millicent Fawcett considered these to be criminal acts. By 1909, therefore, the NUWSS had become openly critical of the militants, and joint membership between the groups was increasingly uncommon.

At the congress of the International Women's Suffrage Alliance held in London in June 1909, Isabella expressed her frustration at such disunity, for 'suffragists were mostly women of strong character and individuality' and therefore 'the forging of them into one purpose was a difficult thing'.[20] She took heart, however, from her belief that the 'great mass of women are making and moving on truly democratic lines', and was convinced that it was for this reason that the 'richer classes and employing classes dislike and dread our movement. They have an uncomfortable feeling that we intend, as soon as we have votes, to turn everything upside down . . . ' Isabella never wavered from the view that feminist and socialist politics were both needed to bring about such an upheaval. In her article for the *Labour Leader* she claimed that socialism had 'watered and quickened the roots of our movement', but 'until women are freed and awakened from their long slumber, and so can effectively help men, we shall never have a socialism worth the name . . . Till women are free men can never be free. Till our victory is won the battles of the Labour Party cannot be won, except in part only, as they are now.' For the first time Isabella spoke openly about what it had cost her in personal terms to give priority to women's suffrage. The Labour Party's failure to firmly support the women's cause 'arouses within some of us a great sadness to feel that we cannot, till our battle is gained, fight for our party. Our hearts, as of old, are with it, but if we would work our *best* for it we must first win our own struggle.' The non-party stand of the NUWSS added at times to the tensions Isabella experienced. If all candidates in an election were supporters of women's suffrage only general propaganda work was undertaken. On one such occasion, a by-election in Croydon, Isabella refused to go and help with this general work: 'I knew I could not have borne to be there and not be on Frank Smith's platform. I longed for him to win with all my heart, but our creed is "non-party", for no party is absolutely ours.'[21]

This dilemma would only be resolved when the Labour Party decided to give more positive commitment to women's suffrage. ILP suffragists within the NUWSS continued to work, therefore, towards bringing both movements together. Through her writings, speeches and work on the executive committee Isabella aimed to make National Union members more aware of the needs of working women. All her suffrage speeches

---

[20]*Common Cause (CC)*, 17 Mar. 1910.
[21]I. O. Ford, 'The Lessons of the Women's International Conference', *LL* 2 July 1909.

referred to the work conditions and home lives of female workers, and middle-class audiences were 'struck with the masterly and forcible way' with which she handled the material.[22]

Isabella also tried to ensure that the NUWSS became more popularly based and did not neglect the provinces. Whenever time permitted, she worked hard to build up support for women's suffrage in her own local region. In the first few months of 1909 she worked closely with Mary Fielden, a full-time organizer for the NUWSS, who had recently been allocated to the West Riding. A variety of methods were used to publicize women's suffrage, including public meetings, mock debates, garden parties, and petitioning, but progress was dishearteningly slow. In June, therefore, Isabella and Mary Fielden decided to organize a caravan tour of the area in an inventive attempt to arouse more widespread publicity.

During the first few days of the tour, visiting Whitby, Kirkby Moorside, Pickering, and Helmsley, Isabella and Mary did most of the speaking. In Helmsley, Isabella reported how 'some delightful visitors at the inn there took us in to supper after hearing our speeches – the supper included the most delicious cream – and next morning photographed us and escorted us some half mile on our way. The cows in the field at Helmsley where our van was placed (free of charge!) were delighted with us, and rubbed themselves against our wheels all night in spite of our remonstrances.' The two women were joined at Helmsley by Ray Costelloe, later to become well known as Ray Strachey, author of *The Cause*, the first standard history of the women's suffrage movement. When the caravan reached Harrogate the speakers were entertained by Mrs Ryley, the proprietor of the Clarendon Hotel, who would not allow them to pay for anything. The maids also refused the usual tips, and Isabella was so moved by their generosity that she wrote to the *Common Cause* to urge other suffragists to stay at the hotel if they visited the town: 'I feel that all we Women Suffragists . . . should stand by one another. The camaraderie in our movement is, I think, one of its finest features . . . '

The tour continued to the end of July, with Mary Fielden accompanying it all the way and other speakers giving more intermittent assistance. Not all middle-class women could face the rigours of vanning, which included the possibility of hostile crowds, and the propaganda work was hampered by a shortage of helpers. There were many problems, Isabella complained.

The Thirsk route was impossible, owing to steep hills. Two people in a van cannot easily manage the work. Of Miss Fielden's energy, care, and unselfish kindness and economy I cannot speak too highly, but she needs helpers. Nice as vanning is it is extremely tiring when you have to earn your living as you go along and to make all arrangements for horses, men etc. It is too hard work for only two people, if daily travelling is necessary. All the way along through

[22]Speech at Plymouth, *CC* 20 May 1909.

beautiful old villages we distributed leaflets and did house to house visiting, so that we were constantly on the go, constantly talking and arguing. We found Miss Costelloe invaluable, a very excellent collector (and cook).[23]

Isabella and Ray Costelloe spoke at the last meetings of the caravan tour in Keswick and Workington on 22 and 23 July.

By the 27th Isabella was back in Leeds to attend a garden party to raise funds for the local Leeds Women's Suffrage Society. The weather was so bad that everything had to be taken indoors, but in the afternoon a large crowd assembled in the dining room to hear a speech from Ethel Snowden, who had just returned from a lecture tour of America. She argued that if women had the vote, 'the industrial conditions of this country would be improved, for the government would have to realise that they must give equality to their servants of both sexes.' The talk was followed by a light-hearted mock debate between a suffragist and an anti-suffragist – a favourite activity at local meetings. Isabella agreed to take the part of the anti-suffragist, Miss Ford Cromer, and gave her usual witty performance. In a tongue in cheek account of the proceedings Mary Fielden described how Isabella, 'with particular delicacy drew attention to that most touching and pathetic line of Mr Austen Chamberlain – "Men are men and women are women!" It was, however, to be regretted that she was apparently unable to remember her opponent's name, a misfortune from which, I believe, some anti-suffrage great ladies suffer.' At the close of the debate the resolution favouring women's suffrage was carried, 'Miss Ford-Cromer's *two hands* being the only dissentient ones'.[24]

Although such meetings were largely confined to middle-class women, the Leeds society also tried to build up support among working-class male voters, in particular in West Leeds, the constituency of the home secretary, Herbert Gladstone. A working man, Mr Hennessey, was engaged to help. He managed to hold fifty-six meetings in July and August in working men's clubs, Liberal clubs, and public parks, and was able to send Gladstone forty-seven resolutions in favour of women's suffrage, largely signed by voters. Isabella reported that Hennessey had recruited 335 men as members of the Leeds Society 'by selling them our new red bages, which are much liked'.[25]

In the middle of August, Isabella's suffrage work was brought to an abrupt end when she contracted diptheria. Enquiries about her health, accompanied by good wishes, flooded into the Grange; one editorial in the *Common Cause* referred to the 'many hundreds of us' who 'will be wishing we could "do something" for her. All the love and loyalty she has roused in

[23]I. O. Ford, 'The Yorkshire Caravan', *CC* 17 June 1909; letter re. Clarendon Hotel, ibid., 5 Aug. 1909.
[24]*CC* 5 Aug. 1909.
[25]*CC* 24 Sept. 1909.

us must surely have some effect in fighting, with spiritual weapons, a carnal disease.'[26] Perhaps these good wishes helped, for after four weeks Isabella was sitting up in her room, and by November she felt well enough to take an interest once more in political events. But it would be some time before she was able to resume her normal busy life. Writing to the *Labour Leader* to inform ILP secretaries that she would not be able to lecture until after Easter so they could save their time and postage stamps, she joined into a controversy involving her friend Ethel Snowden. Ethel had been growing more and more disillusioned by what she saw as the ILP's lukewarm support for the suffrage campaign. Matters came to a head in October when she discovered that two members of the NAC, Fred Jowett (the chairman) and Mary Macarthur, were active members of an adult suffrage society, and she decided to resign from the party. In responding to her friend's resignation Isabella regretted that her illness had prevented her from keeping in touch with the suffrage movement in the ILP, but was 'astonished' to find that the chairman was an adult suffragist. She warned that if a limited suffrage was no longer ILP policy, 'many of us will be compelled to leave the party for which we care so much'. Isabella's illness did not prevent her from giving an astute assessment of the current political situation. It was far less optimistic than her usual public statements: 'from our knowledge of the Liberals *as a party* . . . we are convinced neither this Government nor a Tory Government will admit women to a full suffrage as yet'. As always, she emphasized that direct practical experience was the only way to develop an informed political opinion. 'Of course, if anyone's knowledge of the full-fledged MP is confined to tea parties on the terrace and pleasant dinners and "at homes", that person will quite believe in the possibility of attaining womanhood suffrage very soon. Those who have interviewed members, lobbyed them, written to them, asked questions at their meetings . . . know better.'[27]

Sceptical about whether any Labour MPs, except for Hardie and Snowden, would refuse to vote for a suffrage measure which did not include women, Isabella was careful none the less not to take any precipitate action. Once reassured that the ILP was still committed to a limited franchise for women, as a preliminary step towards adult suffrage, she remained a member of the party. The incident did not harm her friendship with Ethel Snowden, but it did reveal the difference in their personalities. Volatile, quick-tempered, and uncompromising, Ethel gained a reputation for being difficult and was often in conflict with her colleagues. By contrast, Isabella's approach tended to be conciliatory; in a short biographical sketch written in 1908, J. J. Mallon, secretary of the Anti-Sweating League, which fought to secure minimum wage legislation, found her 'broad and well

[26]*CC* 12 Aug. 1909.
[27]*LL* 5 Nov. 1909.

balanced, and even for Suffrage . . . refuses to be a fanatic. She swims in the main stream: she belongs to the centre . . . Her deepest interest is in life, not movements.' Her sense of humour also made her easy to get on with, 'and, blessed gift, [she] can look quizzically upon her own frenzy. Sweet humour puts a twinkle in her eye and on her lips a laugh, at herself maybe, with no bitterness. She has urbanity and a knowledge of men, and no expectation of the impossible . . . '[28]

It was the last quality that accounts, perhaps, for Isabella's political shrewdness. Her assessment of where the women's cause stood in the autumn of 1909 appeared to be well founded. By the end of the year, all efforts to make headway with a women's suffrage measure in Parliament had failed. The attention of the Liberal Party had been diverted towards other concerns, notably the rejection of Lloyd George's 'People's Budget' by the House of Lords. An escalation in WSPU militancy had also alienated many previously sympathetic MPs and driven a further wedge between the militants and the NUWSS. When the government declared that there would be a general election in January 1910, however, suffragist hopes revived once again. Asquith's announcement that he intended to introduce a Franchise Reform Bill in the new Parliament, which could be amended to include women, was a further reason for optimism.

The general election certainly gave the Leeds Suffrage Society a new lease of life. Isabella's illness and Mary Foster's resignation as organizing secretary had hampered the work of the society, which had only a few active members. With the approach of the election an extra effort was made to gain public support. Numerous public meetings were held throughout the city, although speakers often had to face hostile crowds. When Emily chaired a meeting outside the ironworks there was 'some violence against the women' from 'drunken hooligans'. On the other hand, 4,000 people signed a suffrage petition, displayed on a huge placard in front of the Society's New Briggate shop, and Hennessey managed to enrol 365 male supporters from the West Ward into a Women's Suffrage Band. With her usual enthusiasm, Isabella recounted how this group had voted according to their suffrage sympathies rather than in line with their usual political views.[29] She was prevented by her illness from taking a full part in the campaign – a contrast with previous elections, when she and Bessie had thrown off their middle-class reserve to walk as 'sandwich men' with a 'woman suffrage poster in front and a woman suffrage sentiment on the back'. Although some people laughed, 'many working men encouraged them and took their hats off them'.[30]

The Liberal government was returned with a greatly reduced majority

[28]J. J. Mallon, 'Isabella Ford', *Woman Worker*, 7 Aug. 1908.
[29]*CC* 13 Jan., 27 Jan., 14 Apr. 1910.
[30]International Women's Suffrage Alliance 4th Annual Conference, *Report* p. 31.

and now had to rely on the support of the Irish Nationalists to stay in office. The changed balance of parliamentary forces encouraged H. N. Brailsford, a Liberal MP, to launch a new initiative on women's suffrage. He managed to gain support from members of all parties for a Conciliation Bill, which would have enfranchised about a million female occupiers or householders. Although the provisions of the Bill were kept deliberately narrow to appeal to a wide range of MPs, the NUWSS decided to back the measure on the grounds that it would establish the principle of women's right to vote.

Over the next two years, the NUWSS concentrated its efforts on trying to gain support for the Bill. Already a much stronger organization, with a larger number of permanent staff and a steadily increasing membership, it used its extra resources to step up propaganda work at by-elections, to organize large demonstrations, and to generate interest in women's suffrage at a grass-roots level. It was also during this period that socialist members of the Union intensified their pressure to make it more responsive to the needs of working women and laid the groundwork for an alliance with the Labour Party which finally took place in 1912.

Isabella took a full part in this propaganda work. It was not until March 1910, however, at a meeting of the national council, that she was well enough to appear on a public platform. The delegates gave her a 'warm reception', but she was not yet strong enough to speak and had to thank them in a letter. Explaining that she still found speaking in public rather beyond her powers, she wrote 'I thank everyone from my heart, and it was delightful to me beyond words to find myself once more amongst my fellow workers in the cause we all love so dearly.'[31] She was also welcomed back by the Leeds Society in April, at a sale of work held in the grounds of Adel Grange. As long ago as December Isabella had appealed to readers of the *Common Cause* to contribute second-hand books for the sale: 'No sermons are wanted. Sixpenny paperbacks will be acceptable, anything readable and saleable.' She wrote again in February to explain that the sale had been deferred until April because of election work: 'I wish the railway companies would run a trip train to Leeds on that day – the books are worth it!' When it finally took place, the sale was opened by Councillor Margaret Ashton from Manchester on the first day, and on the second by Dr Marion Phillips, a leader of the Women's Labour League. The sum of £67 was raised for local funds.[32]

As her health improved, Isabella returned to more active work and soon embarked on a heavy schedule of speaking engagements to gain support for the Conciliation Bill. In June she travelled to London to take part in an NUWSS deputation to Asquith, but it had few positive results. In the following month she returned to London once more to join in a suffrage

[31]*CC* 24 Mar. 1910.
[32]*CC* 2 Dec. 1909; 10 Feb., 21 Apr., 5 May 1910.

demonstration designed to coincide with the Bill's second reading. The marchers gathered in Trafalgar Square to hear some of the NUWSS's best-known speakers. Isabella shared a platform with Margaret Robertson and Helena Swanwick, Manchester women who shared her support for the labour movement. They spoke on an appropriate theme: democratic objections to women's suffrage.

After two days of debate, the Conciliation Bill passed its second reading. A substantial minority of MPs, however, had voted in opposition and therefore the government refused to give further facilities. Undaunted, suffragists continued to keep up the pace of public meetings and pinned their hopes on the autumn session of Parliament. Isabella was so busy in August that she was unable to accept an invitation from Philippa Strachey to speak at a meeting in Trafalgar Square. Her letter of apology was almost breathless with excitement: 'All these provincial meetings! How the country is awakening.'[33] This punishing schedule of meetings continued throughout the autumn, reaching a peak in October and November, just before the second general election of 1910.

The meetings were varied in character, but Isabella took them all in her stride, moving easily from sedate drawing-room meetings, attended by less than fifty well-to-do women, to more rowdy public gatherings in draughty halls or in the open air. The years of propaganda for trade-unionism and socialism had given her plenty of experience in dealing with hostile crowds; she used this to good effect at a public meeting in Keswick on 7 October when the Anti-Suffrage League 'turned up in force' to ask awkward questions. Isabella had travelled to Keswick to help Millicent Fawcett and Helena Swanwick host a reception for members of the provincial council. After a brief return to Leeds she spent the last week of the month on a speaking tour of the north-east, visiting Filey, Bridlington, and Driffield.

Isabella devoted November to work in her home territory, again speaking to a wide variety of groups. On the 2nd she crossed the Pennines to speak at a public meeting in Salford with Margaret Ashton and on the 11th moved a resolution in favour of the Conciliation Bill at a meeting in a Congregational Schoolroom in Leeds; five days later she explained the provisions of the Bill to the Burley Women's Labour League. On the afternoon of the 22nd Isabella joined Mary Fielden to address a drawing-room meeting in Batley and then stayed on to take part in a public meeting held in the evening at the town hall. On the following day she spoke with Mary Fielden in Morley. Isabella returned to Leeds on the 24th so that she could address a gathering of Leeds University women in the afternoon and a public meeting in the evening, where again she was supported by Mary Fielden.[34]

[33] Isabella Ford to Philippa Strachey, Aug. 1910, Correspondence File, Fawcett Lib.
[34] Isabella's meetings were reported regularly in the CC.

5. The deputation from the National Union to the prime minister, 21 June 1910. Isabella Ford is on the far left (*Common Cause*). (*British Library, Newspaper Library, Colindale*)

When Isabella came on to the platform, audiences would have seen a middle-aged woman of unprepossessing appearance. She had none of the fashionable glamour of the Pankhursts; with her plain clothes and flat hat, she reminded Hungarian feminist Rosika Schwimmer, of a 'caricature of an English spinster'.[35] Appearance mattered little, however, when Isabella began to speak, for her wit, humour, and depth of knowledge about her subject soon captured the attention of her audience. Described as the 'raciest' speaker in the NUWSS she spoke 'with equal success to an audience of 5,000 working men or 25 clergymen – they laugh and weep as she chooses, and they all love her'.[36] Isabella usually went about her work with 'humour and gladness', but meetings could also leave her drained and physically weary. Once, bracing herself to speak, she confided to Helena Swanwick: 'They will expect me to be funny and it is not always easy.'[37] The weariness had become worse since her attack of diptheria, and in 1911 Isabella decided not to stand for re-election to the executive committee of the NUWSS. With less strength to offer, she felt that the suffrage campaign in the West Riding should have first call on her time.

Provincial societies were beginning to form regional federations in order to co-ordinate their activities. Isabella took the initiative to convene a meeting of suffrage groups in Yorkshire in March 1911 which led to the establishment of the West Riding Federation of Women's Suffrage Societies. Only five groups affiliated at the first meeting, but the number steadily increased to eleven by May and to eighteen early in 1912. As chairman of the federation, Isabella played a key role in its early growth. She gave considerable financial support, paying a month's expenses for the local NUWSS organizers, and it was thought that 'without her donations the work of the Federation must have ceased'.[38]

She also helped to develop new tactics, encouraging local societies to seek the support of town councils, trade union branches, and trades councils for the Conciliation Bill. She was one of five women from all political parties who formed a deputation to the Leeds City Council on 1 March 1911. They were sympathetically received, and by the end of the year resolutions in favour of the Bill had been passed by the councils of Barnsley, Bradford, Huddersfield, Dewsbury, Sheffield, Leeds, and Isabella's own parish council, Adel-cum-Eccup. Of even greater significance were the growing signs of support from the labour movement. Resolutions in favour of the Bill were passed by trades councils and local union branches, including the Amalgamated Union of Clothing Operatives, the General Union of Textile Workers, and the Gas Workers' Union, all of which had been closely

[35]R. Schwimmer, 'Women's Age of Innocence', typescript, R. Schwimmer-Lloyd Coll., New York Public Lib., p. 109.
[36]'Miners and Suffragists in Scarborough', CC 3 Oct. 1913.
[37]'Isabella O. Ford: In Memoriam', Women's Leader, 1 Aug. 1924.
[38]West Riding Federation, 1st Annual Report, May 1912.

associated with Isabella when she was a trade union organizer. There were never enough speakers to go round, and 'frequent and tiring calls' were made on Isabella and two other Leeds suffragists, Mrs Parrish and Mary Foster. In March Isabella spoke in Goole, Stalybridge, Pendleton, and Wakefield, as well as taking part in numerous events organized by the Leeds Society, which now had 300 members. The only condition that she attached to the use of her services as a speaker was, significantly, that she required long notice.[39]

All of this propaganda was directed towards support for a new Conciliation Bill which had been drawn up after the second general election of 1910. Although the Liberal Party had gained enough seats to form a government, Asquith still depended on the support of either the Labour Party or the Irish Nationalists to remain in power. When the Conciliation Bill was debated in the House of Commons on May 1911, there was a substantial majority in favour. The Liberal government refused, however, to give more time to the Bill that session, for members of the cabinet were preoccupied with reforming the House of Lords. None the less, suffragists were encouraged by Asquith's promise that time would be given to the bill in the next session; militant actions were suspended for the time being, and both the militants and the constitutionalists decided to march together in a procession on 17 June 1911.

Isabella urged NUWSS members to 'be there in tens of thousands . . . Let us forget all that divides the two great societies, and let us think only of the cause which unites us.' She wanted the local societies to send as many members as possible so that the Union's share of the procession would be 'most splendid' and would impress the 'colonial potentates' and other dignitaries who would be in London to attend King George's coronation.[40] The procession attracted large numbers, and as the women walked through brilliant sunshine with their colourful banners they 'filled the Embankment along its whole length from Blackfriars to Westminster'.[41] On her own initiative, Emily had offered to make shield-shaped banners in NUWSS colours, displaying the names of town councils which had passed resolutions in favour of the Conciliation Bill. They were 'so made as to show no possible relation to the WSPU'.[42]

The size of the demonstration, coupled with Asquith's promise, revived the hopes of all women's suffrage campaigners. For the first time in many years, therefore, Isabella felt able to take a long rest in August, away from political agitation. As so often before, she went to Switzerland, where the clean air of the mountains always seemed to renew her strength. She much

[39]Ibid.
[40]*CC* 27 Apr. 1911.
[41]R. Fulford, *Votes for Women* (Faber & Faber, 1958), p. 208.
[42]Emily Ford to Philippa Strachey, 7 July 1911; Philippa Strachey to Emily Ford, 9 June 1911, Correspondence Files, Fawcett Lib.

preferred climbing in the mountains to staying in her hotel; in a description of one of these expeditions she caricatured those fashionable English tourists 'who spent their days in gossip and embroidery, and their evenings in dancing in ball dresses – in a hot room with tightly-closed windows, while outside the moon was lighting up the Matterhorn'. When everyone was still asleep Isabella went out early in the morning, 'before the sun was up', with her regular Swiss guide, Polycarpe. 'Down the hillside we tramped over dewy grass slopes and slippery rocks, pausing for a moment at a spring of cold, clear water dripping out of a mossy hole, where Polycarpe carefully filled his flask . . . Round blue crevasses and over ice hillocks we climbed, and up the rocky mountainside opposite.' From the top of a small mountain they could see into Italy. 'Italy, how the very word stirs one's bones. It stands for wonders and beauties indescribable; for Garibaldi and his thousand, and all that makes history great.'[43]

The trip to Switzerland in 1911 was unusual; Isabella was accompanied by two working women who had saved up for years to go with her. On her return she wrote enthusiastically about the holiday to Edward Carpenter – 'We have had such a good summer. I took two working women for a week to Lucerne – a Polytechnic tour . . . and I never had a nicer time – they were "that happy" as they expressed it . . . we enjoyed every minute, every second of our time.' This period of relaxation continued into September when Isabella accompanied Bessie to Seascale in Cumberland. 'Here it is beautiful – sea & sky & mountains no people, except very cheerful children with spades.' She had been reading Olive Schreiner's book, *Woman and Labour*, but was not very impressed. As she told Edward Carpenter, 'I am so very, very tired of Woman with a big W! that I wasn't a good judge – but I thought it was rather stale.'[44]

This comment is surprising, for Olive Schreiner's book is widely acclaimed as 'the most influential piece of feminist writing of its time'.[45] Isabella made no further references to the book. She may have been dissatisfied, however, by her friend's attempt to make sweeping generalizations about women as a group, when her own writings sought to differentiate between them on the basis of class, occupation, and marital status. For Isabella, a detailed analysis of the work and home lives of women, located in a specific historical context, was a necessary condition for understanding the complex ways in which women experienced oppression and for developing strategies for change.

Although it was many years since she had been involved in trade union organizing work, Isabella kept herself informed about the conditions of

---

[43]I. O. Ford, 'A Day with the Mountains', *LL* 24 June 1910; see also id., 'Life in a Swiss Village', *LL* 13 July 1906.

[44]Isabella Ford to Edward Carpenter, 17 Sept. 1911, Carpenter Coll.

[45]L. Stanley, 'Olive Schreiner: New Women, Free Women, All Women', in Spender, ed., *Feminist Theorists*, p. 239.

women's employment and continued to write on the subject. In 1909 she produced an article on women workers in the wholesale clothing trade, which gave a detailed account of wages, fines, deductions, and the attitudes of tailoresses themselves towards their employment. In contrast to Schreiner's view that women were likely to become more parasitic as their work in the home was reduced by labour-saving devices, she argued that more and more women in Leeds were entering the tailoring trade: 'the home life of the nation is, therefore, changing because the economic position of women is changing. They are becoming the wage earners of the nation in increasing numbers.' Her conclusion emphasized the positive contribution that working women could make to the life of the whole community if they had the vote. 'The wife fighting for bread for her sick husband and children is often a most impressive person . . . would not, therefore, her opinion about how to deal with the change in woman's home life be of immense value to the nation and the more so since she dislikes and resents this change exceedingly?'[46]

Younger suffragists were particularly impressed by these arguments; impatient with the NUWSS's sedate, drawing-room image, Maude Royden, Catharine Marshall, and others were attracted by Isabella's sympathetic understanding of the needs of working women and by her socialist ideas. As an unmarried woman with no children of her own, Isabella took on the role of a loving relative to her young friends. She signed letters to Catharine Marshall as 'your affectionate aunt'. Rosika Schwimmer recalled Isabella as 'one of the most lovable women I ever met. Courageous and warm-hearted, with a fine mind and broad human understanding . . . she was like an intelligent mother to us younger women. And how she could laugh.'[47]

Maude Royden, in particular, was influenced by Isabella's ideas when writing her own pamphlet *Votes and Wages*, published by the NUWSS in 1911. She used Emily's poster of a factory girl for the front cover and thanked Isabella in the preface for 'her help and advice in compiling this pamphlet.' Isabella had read it before it went to press, she said, and her approval was 'a guarantee in itself that the case is not overstated, nor the conditions described overdrawn'.[48] Maude Royden relied heavily on Isabella's arguments in making a case that the vote would affect women's economic position. She pointed out, for example, that women's wages were lowered because they were restricted to a narrow range of jobs and that this resulted partly from protective legislation in which they had no say. While emphasizing the importance of the vote, Maude Royden did not

[46]I. O. Ford, 'Women Workers in the Wholesale Clothing Trade', *Englishwoman*, 2/6 (July 1909), p. 644.
[47]R. Schwimmer, 'Age of Innocence' p. 109.
[48]M. Royden, *Votes and Wages* (NUWSS, 1911), Preface.

6. Propaganda postcard protesting against the Factory Acts. By Emily Ford, dated 1908. (*Mary Evans Picture Library*)

neglect the necessity for trade-unionism, arguing that male workers had always used both political power and industrial strength to achieve improvements in work conditions.

The growing interest shown by suffragists after 1910 in the needs of women workers helped to lay the basis for a closer relationship between the NUWSS and the labour movement. This was already apparent at a local level, where many ILP and trade union branches had pledged support for women's suffrage. In 1912 these informal links were recognized at a national level when the NUWSS and the Labour Party formed an alliance for electoral purposes. Initially intended as a matter of tactics only, the alliance was to transform the character of the suffrage campaign over the next two years. It broadened the basis of NUWSS membership, brought suffragists into closer contact with labour politics and concerns, and changed the terms in which the suffrage debate was conducted.

9

Labour–Suffrage Alliance, 1912–1914

I feel like bursting with joy over it at times.

Two events provided the immediate background to the closer relationship between the National Union of Women's Suffrage Societies and the Labour Party: the defeat of the Conciliation Bill in March 1912 and Asquith's decision to introduce an Adult Suffrage Bill which, he claimed, could be amended to include women. The failure of several sympathetic MPs to vote for the Conciliation Bill confirmed the misgivings already felt by NUWSS leaders about the effectiveness of their existing policies and they began to look for a new political strategy. Earlier in the year the Labour Party's annual conference had taken a significant step towards support for women's suffrage; it was agreed that no future franchise reform would be acceptable if women were excluded. This finally convinced the NUWSS to change political tactics; instead of seeking the support of individual MPs, backing would now be given to the one party which had come out in favour of votes for women.

Although H. N. Brailsford played a key role in promoting the alliance between the two groups,[1] it was the work undertaken by men and women of the ILP over many years which had made the Labour Party and the NUWSS more receptive to the idea of working together. Late in 1911, ILP officers launched a Political Equality Campaign with a leaflet circulated to all branches. It called for a 'striking crusade on behalf of political justice and freedom alike for men and women . . . We do not take up this question as a matter of party politics, but as a matter of human right.'[2] Under the new editorship of the young Fenner Brockway, a supporter of women's suffrage, the *Labour Leader* also took a more positive stand and helped to lead the campaign for the vote over the next two years.

The new policy of co-operation with the Labour Party was inaugurated

[1]Brailsford's role is emphasized in L. P. Hume, *The National Union of Women's Suffrage Societies, 1897–1914* (Garland Publishing, 1982), p. 147.

[2]J. Liddington, *The Life and Times of a Respectable Rebel: Selina Cooper, 1864–1946* (Virago, 1984), pp. 223–4.

at a special meeting of the NUWSS national council in mid-May. Millicent Fawcett made clear that her support was given for tactical reasons and on suffrage grounds alone. She argued strongly that the alliance did not imply support for socialism or for Labour's wider programme. Such a narrow definition was not shared by ILP members of the NUWSS. They welcomed the new strategy wholeheartedly and hoped that women's suffrage would now be integrated more fully into the broader movement for 'progressive' social reforms. Support for this policy was not confined to socialist women alone, and an increasing number of suffragists were attracted to labour politics as a result of their work for the 'alliance'.[3]

It was assumed that an increase in the number of Labour MPs would put the Liberal Party under pressure to do something for women. An Election Fighting Fund (EFF) was therefore established to raise money to help the Labour Party fight elections. Thirteen committee members were drawn from the NUWSS, including Isabella, Ethel Snowden, Margaret Ashton, and other women with labour connections, and they were joined by sympathizers such as H. N. Brailsford and Margaret McMillan.[4] Millicent Fawcett chaired the committee, but it was younger suffragists, such as Catharine Marshall, the secretary, and Margaret Robertson, the chief organizer, who energetically carried out the day-to-day work.

Now in her late fifties, Isabella seemed to gain new energy from the alliance. Her own view was that the strategy of support for a definite party was likely to have far more effect than the 'Keep the Liberals Out' policy. It was 'attacking men with proper weapons and in a really manly fashion and not with the old fashioned methods of fists and disorder . . . It is sometimes such a comfort to be manly as well as womanly!'[5] Eager to strengthen the alliance, Isabella wrote an article for the *Labour Leader* in which she used the example of her own life to try to persuade women to become socialists, arguing as usual that only socialism would bring freedom and equality to both sexes.[6]

Beneath the surface, however, the Labour–suffrage alliance was fraught with tension. Many National Union members with liberal sympathies were unhappy with the new policy; they feared alienating former Liberal supporters and were often appalled at the idea of having close links with socialists. The alliance could hardly have worked, therefore, if there had not been women at all levels of the union who were determined to make it a success. As early as 6 June, some members of the executive committee raised the problem of what stand the NUWSS should take in elections

[3]S. Holton, 'Feminism and Democracy: The Women's Suffrage Movement in Britain, with particular reference to the National Union of Women's Suffrage Societies, 1897–1918', Ph. D. thesis, Stirling University, 1980, ch. 8.

[4]NUWSS, *Annual Report*, 1912, pp. 25–6.

[5]I. O. Ford, 'A Personal Testimony', *Common Cause (CC)*, 19 Sept. 1912, p. 409.

[6]Id., 'Why Women Should Be Socialists', *Labour Leader*, 1 May 1913, p. 10.

where all the candidates supported women's suffrage. Isabella spoke in favour of a resolution which pledged the union to support Labour candidates unless they opposed an old friend of the cause, in which case only general propaganda would be carried out.

The resolution was successful, and immediately after the meeting Isabella returned to Holmfirth in Yorkshire to help in the first by-election held under the new policy. NUWSS women entered into the campaign with great energy. With two motor cars at their disposal they were able to speak in all the small villages which made up this scattered constituency. ILP women, including Isabella, Mrs Annot Robinson, and Ada Nield Chew, now a full-time organizer for the NUWSS, were the main speakers, but all the suffragists made important contributions: 'The Labour Party never lacks workers, but its volunteers can rarely give time during the day. Suffragists of all parties are doing their share of clerical work. Suffragists who are personally inclined to the labour view are peculiarly valuable as canvassers and speakers.'[7] Although the Labour candidate, Mr Lunn, did not win, the suffragists could congratulate themselves on his increased share of the poll.

After taking a month's break in Switzerland in August,[8] Isabella returned to England to make a twofold contribution to the suffrage campaign. As a propagandist she went from one meeting to another, explaining the new policy and seeking support for the various women's suffrage amendments to Asquith's Adult Suffrage Bill. As a supporter of the alliance she made every effort to reassure NUWSS members that the Labour Party would not let them down. She reminded suffragists that the ILP had been committed to women's equality from the beginning. In consequence, she pointed out, its female members 'are not made of submissive, doormat material, and consequently the relationship between them and their mankind is of a more wholesome and cordial nature than is always usual between men and women'. Labour men, although by no means angels, were unlikely to let women down because they understood the suffragists' cause 'from the inside'. 'Their understanding of us is not founded on mere second-hand knowledge gained through reading . . . for it is their women who are affected by bad economic conditions in a way that other women are not.'[9]

The Labour–suffrage alliance was always in danger from apathy or hostility within its own ranks. Members of the EFF-committee were particularly nervous, therefore, about any additional threats from outside. Their fears grew in the summer and autumn of 1912 when an increase in WSPU militancy threatened to undermine Labour Party support. Attacks on property and on individual MPs were added to the usual WSPU tactics

[7]CC 20 June 1912.
[8]CC 1 Aug. 1912.
[9]Ford, 'A Personal Testimony', p. 408.

of marching on Parliament and disrupting meetings. Isabella was still unwilling to condemn their actions too harshly in public. She reminded a suffrage meeting in Harrogate in September that 'although we disassociate ourselves from the militants, there are many different religions by which we may get into Heaven, and probably many different ways by which we may win our way into the House of Commons – if we may regard that as a Heaven!'[10]

On the other hand Isabella was worried about the influence of militants on ILP branches. She was appalled to find out in December that the WSPU hoped to gain the support of ILP members for a march of working–class women on the House of Commons. She believed that this was a blatant attempt to manipulate working women, who would not realize that the march could end in violence and that such actions were illegal. After a long discussion in the EFF committee, Isabella agreed to write to the press in a private capacity to warn working women of the dangers they faced. The march was eventually called off because so few ILP branches responded to the appeal, and Annot Robinson claimed that this was largely due to the pleas of herself and Isabella.[11]

Of even greater concern to EFF supporters was the commitment of individual Labour MPs, in particular Ramsay MacDonald. The third reading of the Adult Suffrage Bill was due to take place early in 1913, and EFF members had to work hard to ensure that if the women's suffrage amendments failed, Labour MPs would keep to their pledge to vote against the bill. By the end of 1912 they had managed to establish a close relationship with the ILP leadership, who agreed to explore ways in which 'the National Union could influence the selection of candidates'.[12] Isabella played an important part in negotiations with the ILP; she had returned to the executive committee of the NUWSS in 1912, and with her labour connections was uniquely placed to carry out the role of conciliator between the two movements. After long years of political experience her opinions commanded respect, while her personality was particularly suited to smoothing over difficulties.

In December Isabella had a meeting with the ILP treasurer, T. D. Benson, to arrange for funds to be transferred from the NUWSS to ILP candidates in selected constituencies. In return Benson assured her that ILP members would stand firm on the third reading, although he expressed concern that a number of trade-unionists, especially the miners, might seek to weaken the Labour Party's stand on women's suffrage at the next annual conference. As a result of Isabella's report on this meeting, the NUWSS

[10]*CC* 17 Oct. 1912.
[11]Minutes of Election Fighting Fund Committee, 20 Dec. 1912, NUWSS papers, Fawcett Lib.
[12]Holton, 'Feminism and Democracy', p. 248.

executive resolved to inaugurate a special campaign among trade-unionists in January and to approach Mary Macarthur and Arthur Henderson for assistance.[13]

As the time for the third reading approached, an all-out effort was made to strengthen the resolve of Labour MPs. Isabella played an important part in this. In a letter published in December 1912 in the *Daily Citizen*, the official organ of the Labour Party, she tried to convince labour colleagues that suffragists now realized that 'the unjust position of the industrial woman is at the very root of our demand for political enfranchisement. She is the person who needs help most.' Although the proposed measures were unsatisfactory, 'to refuse anything because it is not the whole would be suicidal. Men obtained their freedom in instalments, so it is probable we shall receive ours in like manner.' Isabella warned that the bill would not stand a chance unless everything was done in a legal manner. If a large group of people came to the House of Commons it would end in a riot and arrests: 'MPs are, as we know, very sensitive about women rioting, though they regard men's riots, of course, with a sympathetic mind.' There were plenty of more constitutional ways to bring pressure on MPs. Deputations from constituents, 'memorials, personal letters, post-cards, resolutions from meetings are all effective ways of fighting'.[14] The letter reached a wide audience. Reprinted in the *Common Cause*, it also formed the basis of a further letter to the *Labour Leader*. In this Isabella appealed to working women to help the campaign, for their active support was of supreme importance at 'this most critical moment'. They must know that 'political equality with men is . . . the only hope for the working woman, the only possible way of obtaining equal pay for equal work for both men and women'.[15]

The campaign to strengthen the Labour–suffrage alliance reached a peak at the end of January with the *Labour Leader*'s special suffrage supplement, edited by Helena Swanwick. The editorial, in claiming that suffragists and labour members were united in their belief that 'in freedom, mutual trust and comradeship of the sexes lies the hope of progress and social regeneration', was a vindication of the arguments developed by Isabella throughout twenty years of writing and political agitation. A member of the committee which organized the supplement, she also joined Hardie, Snowden, Mrs Annot Robinson, and other friends in contributing an article. In this she concentrated on a familiar theme – the important role that women had always played in the ILP, not just as canvassers, but also as members of the NAC, where 'they are consulted, they are listened to, just as much as men'. Women had always helped the labour movement in industrial disputes, and

[13]Minutes of EFF Committee, 20 Dec. 1912., NUWSS papers.
[14]*Daily Citizen*, 27 Dec. 1912.
[15]*LL* 2 Jan. 1913, p. 9.

now the Labour Party needed their help at the ballot box, 'a more civilized method of warfare'. She concluded with the warning that if men betrayed women over the Franchise Bill, they would betray socialism and 'those who bear the heaviest burden in the labour world'.[16]

All this pressure paid off: the Labour Party's annual conference in 1913 re-affirmed support for women's suffrage in even stronger terms than before. But Labour MPs were never put to the test in Parliament; before the third reading of the Adult Suffrage Bill could take place, the Speaker ruled that the women's suffrage amendments were out of order and the bill was withdrawn. In this context, the NUWSS changed political strategy once again. Millicent Fawcett argued that they must now concentrate on gaining a government-sponsored Women's Suffrage Bill after the next general election. This made it even more important for the NUWSS to ensure the election of Labour candidates at by-elections, and the two groups were brought closer together.

The NUWSS now showed a greater interest in the needs of working-class women; the *Common Cause* devoted more space to articles on social and economic questions of special concern to female workers which expressed a greater sympathy for the married woman worker and a more positive attitude towards trade-unionism. Ada Nield Chew went one step further in a series of articles in which she questioned the view that women were eminently suited to child care, although her attack on the sexual division of labour remained a minority position. Isabella was critical of the sentimental picture so often drawn of motherhood and home life among the poor and never wanted to see women's horizons limited by domesticity. Tongue in cheek, she quoted the example of a woman 'who, I am sure, was more devoted to her door step and keeping it clean than she was to her husband and children'. She assumed that when women had the vote they would take an interest in public affairs and then 'devotion to household matters' would 'sink to its proper place'.[17] None the less, she did not challenge the importance of women's role as child carers and thought that girls should receive training for the task.

Always open to new ideas in the past, Isabella now seemed unwilling to move beyond more 'traditional' suffragist arguments and concerns. In articles written in 1913 and 1914 she returned to the theme of women's work conditions, giving details of the problems female workers faced and suggesting that practices such as fining would only be abolished if women had the vote.[18] Isabella did not become involved, however, in debates about

---

[16]Ibid., *Special Supplement on Women's Suffrage*, 9 Jan. 1913, p. 1; I. O. Ford, 'Women in the Labour Movement', ibid., p. 7.

[17]I. O. Ford, 'Why Women Should Be Socialists', p. 10.

[18]Id., 'Factory Girls and Gambling', *CC* 15 Aug. 1913; id., 'A Deputation and Its Answer', *CC* 25 Apr. 1913.

women's sexuality, their control over reproduction, and economic assistance for mothers – controversial issues which were widely discussed in the labour and suffrage movements in the immediate pre-war years. The reason for this may have been one of generation; younger suffragists were less likely to feel constrained by an older moral code and were bound to be influenced by the contemporary focus on the economic independence of mothers.

Even when she dealt with the more unusual topic of Girl Guides, Isabella's ideas were essentially familiar ones. She had become involved with the organization in Leeds and aimed to show that it did not have military overtones. On the contrary, guiding had positive benefits for working-class girls; it provided an 'ethical code' and showed them that there was an alternative to the 'rivalry, dissension, blacklegism' fostered by a competitive industrial society. Working-class girls from 'miserable homes' were introduced for the first time to a whole range of activities – drilling, first-aid instruction, gardening, swimming – which transformed their 'joyless girlhoods' spent 'in helping widowed mothers to support their small brothers and sisters'. Isabella could see only advantages in 'anything which takes working girls out of their homes, and which teaches them to walk about somewhere else than in gaudy, dreary streets'. In the 1890s, Isabella had used similar arguments in support of trade-unionism. She now hoped that guiding, like trade union organization, would lead to a 'teaching of comradeship'.[19]

In preparation for the next general election, NUWSS members took part in an intense propaganda campaign during the course of 1913 to build up support among trade union and labour groups. The union appointed more working-class organizers, and they were in great demand to work among trade-unionists in industrial areas. Isabella took a full share in this campaign, in particular in the provinces. After speaking to several meetings of factory workers in the Reading area in March,[20] she travelled to Manchester at the end of the month to take part in a rally organized by local branches of both the ILP and NUWSS. Speaking alongside Hardie, Margaret Ashton, and Mrs Annot Robinson, she must have had a sense of *déja vu*: she had attended many similar meetings in the early 1900s, when the WSPU was almost indistinguishable from the ILP, and the new alliance with the Labour Party had now brought the movement almost full circle.

Isabella always felt happiest, however, speaking to labour and suffrage groups in her own home area. To mark her fifty-eight birthday in May, and to honour her contribution to the campaign, the Leeds Women's Suffrage Society presented her with a cheque for £75 to use in propaganda work and a badge for herself. Returning thanks, Isabella claimed that 'although she often spoke in different parts of the country, her heart was always in the

[19]Id., 'On Girl Guides', *CC* 5 Sept. 1913.
[20]Ibid., 21 Mar. 1913.

West Riding . . . the best outcome of their propaganda was that people were realising what the movement meant – that it stood not only for the vote, which was a mere symbol, but for the march of civilization . . . The times were with them, and that was something to be thankful for'.[21]

Her feeling of optimism was reinforced by two events which followed closely on each other. The first was the IWSA congress in Budapest; the determination of women to achieve the suffrage and to work for peace in a Europe that seemed poised for war made this, for Isabella, the best conference that she had ever attended. The second was the Pilgrimage, organized by the NUWSS in July as a spectacular propaganda exercise. Starting from different places, women from all over the country walked in separate processions to converge on London for a mass demonstration. Isabella, Bessie, and other members of the Leeds Women's Suffrage Society waited in Roundhay Park to greet the marchers when they reached Leeds. Large meetings were held as the Pilgrimage passed through the West Riding, and it was reported that the prominence of women's work in the area and the friendliness of the men's unions 'secured a sympathetic hearing'.[22]

The membership of NUWSS groups, however, was not large. The Leeds Society had 341 members, an increase of only five on the year before, although the leaders were described as 'zealous and influential'.[23] In Dewsbury the hostility of the Liberal press and outbursts of militancy had reduced sympathy for the cause, while in other towns middle-class women were put off by the involvement of some NUWSS activists in labour politics.[24] On the other hand, the local labour movement showed a greater willingness to support women's suffrage; labour papers devoted more space to the issue and resolutions in favour of the vote were passed by trade union branches and trades councils. The Leeds Trades Council, for example, gave its support in October 1912, after agreeing that Isabella should address the meeting on women's suffrage.[25] Labour groups showed so much interest that the West Riding Federation could not find enough speakers; this prompted Isabella to offer to take a speakers' class every Wednesday afternoon to give women more confidence.

The widespread strikes of the period 1910 to 1914 at last led to an increase in the number of female trade-unionists in the West Riding textile and clothing trades. Many of them became involved in labour politics and took an interest in the vote. They may not have been attracted to the NUWSS, which still had a largely upper-middle-class membership, but they did raise the issue of women's suffrage in their trade union branches and political groups. Emily Tate and Bertha Quinn, for example, both

[21]*Leeds Weekly Citizen (LWC)*, 30 May 1913.
[22]*CC* 18 July 1913.
[23]*CC* 4 and 11 July 1913.
[24]West Riding Federation, *Annual Report*, 1913.
[25]Minutes of Leeds Trades Council, 30 Oct. 1912, Leeds Archives.

full-time organizers for the Leeds branch of the Amalgamated Union of Clothing Operatives, carried out propaganda for women's suffrage within the labour movement. On one occasion Bertha Quinn, acting on behalf of the AUCO, moved a resolution at the Leeds Trades Council to protest against the Cat and Mouse Bill, a Bill which gave the Government power to rearrest hunger strikers given temporary discharge from prison in order to recover their health. She told the story of how she had had great pleasure in 'throwing a boot at Mr Redmond', a supporter of the bill, when he visited Leeds, and her resolution was passed 'with enthusiasm'.[26]

Support for women's political equality did not mean an end to the conflicts raised by the 'woman question' in the local labour movement. Difficulties still arose over the question of political loyalties. A number of working-class women in the West Riding were attracted by the militancy of the WSPU; in Leeds, most members of the East and North East Women's Labour League also belonged both to the North East branch of the ILP and to the WSPU. Conflicts arising from their joint membership came to a head in November 1913. They went along with other suffragettes to heckle Phillip Snowden when he spoke at a meeting in Leeds against militarism, and their action split the local WLL.

Jeannie Arnott, secretary of the Leeds Central WLL and wife of a Labour councillor, was swift to condemn the hecklers. She argued that members of the WLL were expected to support Labour MPs and could not, therefore, also be members of the WSPU. Maud Dightam, secretary of the East and North East WLL and wife of the vice-president of the Leeds Labour Representation Committee, defended her actions on the grounds that the Labour Party had fallen away from its ideals in refusing to grant sexual equality. The debate dragged on for many weeks in the local press and was not finally brought to an end until the outbreak of war.[27]

Other conflicts arose over the sexual division of labour at the work-place. Labour Party members and trade-unionists alike accepted the principle that men should earn a 'family wage' which would enable their wives to give a full-time commitment to the home. It was assumed that men and women, as members of the same family, agreed with this objective and had a common interest in fighting capitalist exploitation. The Labour Party's support for women's suffrage, therefore, was couched in terms of the importance of women using the qualities they had developed in the domestic sphere for the benefit of the whole community – an argument that was also central to the NUWSS.[28]

Support for women's political equality thus did not imply a challenge to their subordinate position in the work-place and in the family. In the 1890s,

[26]*LWC* 1 Aug. 1913. The Cat and Mouse Act was passed 25 March 1913.
[27]*LWC* 21 Nov., 5 and 26 Dec. 1913; 9 Jan. 1914.
[28]See e.g. speech of James O'Grady MP, *LWC* 31 Jan. 1913.

arguments over married women's employment in the West Riding textile trade had demonstrated that women's work was viewed as marginal. In the pre-war years, industrial unrest once again drew attention to women's unequal role in production and posed a challenge to the view that the interests of male and female workers were the same. When the AUCO tried to increase minimum rates of pay for both sexes in the Leeds tailoring trade, their different interests were brought to the surface. The minimum rate for women was raised from 4d to 5d, but the union accepted that employers would be complying with the agreement as long as 70 per cent of their female workers received the new minimum. It was generally believed that the percentage clause had been accepted to safeguard the minimum rates already agreed for male workers, and there was widespread discontent among women in the trade. A furious exchange of letters ensued in the press. The aguments raised recalled the different approach to class and gender politics in the earlier dispute over a limited versus an adult franchise.

One tailoress, writing under the name of 'Justice', argued that men should have gone on strike to get a better rate for female workers. She claimed that women were at a double disadvantage because of their sex and class, with men, ready 'to exploit women of their own class'. Union organizers, both male and female, were quick to refute these allegations. For Bernard Sullivan, a member of the negotiating committee, 'there is no sex war in the economic field, but there is a class war which demands the whole of the energy and activity of the workers, irrespective of sex or creed, in one camp, if they wished to attain a fuller and higher life'. Emily Tate also claimed that 'all the bitterness and hatred in me is reserved for the men – aye, and the women too – of the master class, who have oppressed my class for centuries'.[29]

The controversy was so heated that it prompted Isabella to join in. She reminded the AUCO that it was the Tailoresses' Strike of 1889 that had first inspired the men to organize. Although she supported mixed-sex trade-unionism, she was aware that women's interests could be neglected. They were rarely consulted, and yet the percentage question 'affects women, and should be decided by women'. Her letter showed once again why the struggle for the vote had become so central in her life.

> It is a matter of deep regret to me that, owing to the long struggle for the vote (the only weapon of real, effective and permanent use), I am unable to work for Trade Unionism for women as I have done formerly. Men's unions will never be really strong until women's unions are strong; and women's unions will always be weak and powerless until women are voters.[30]

Isabella was confident that the conflict between the sexes at the work-place

---

[29]*LWC* 12 and 26 Dec. 1913; 9 Jan. 1914.
[30]*LWC* 16 Jan. 1914.

would be overcome once women had the vote. Male workers were only antagonistic to women because they were used as cheap labour; political equality would raise women's expectations, improve their trade union organization, and lead to equal pay. Maude Royden echoed these views. 'If the terrible competition for cheapness ceased, men and women would find their way eventually to those industries to which each was best suited, and sex-antagonism in the industrial world would utterly disappear.'[31]

The fact that men and women were working together for the suffrage seemed far more important, therefore, than the conflicts between them at the work-place, and helps to explain Isabella's mood of optimism and excitement. Writing in reply to a letter from Edward Carpenter in August 1913 she found that it was a great comfort to hear from old friends in such 'turbulent days . . . Oh this dreadful vote battle! I am sure we shall win it at once in the new Parliament'. Labour meetings were 'so splendid that I feel comradeship, the real thing, is growing fast, just because of this battle. I never felt anything like it sometimes & its growing amongst our sort of women . . . I feel like bursting with joy over it at times.'[32]

Her optimism seemed justified when even the Miners' Union, long an opponent of women's suffrage, decided to support the women's cause at the annual conference held in Scarborough in October 1913. The NUWSS had spent several months in preparing the ground, despatching Selina Cooper to gain support in mining communities in the West Riding. Her efforts culminated in a women's suffrage meeting on the eve of the conference. It was appropriate that Isabella was chosen for the delicate task of chairing the meeting, where Muriel Matters spoke for the NUWSS. Suffragists had to gain the support of Robert Smillie, the miners' leader, and Isabella wrote in jubilant mood to Millicent Fawcett immediately after the meeting: 'I spoke to several of the men and they agreed that the thing was done since Smillie, who had never consented to sit on a women's suffrage platform before, came and made so good a stand. He was much impressed by Miss Matter's speech. It was first rate.'[33]

Isabella's final major commitment of the year was the Keighley by-election of November, where she spoke in the bitter cold with Selina Cooper to one of the largest meetings held during the election; after some early disorderly scenes the meeting took place in a pleasant atmosphere. The NUWSS had decided to carry out only general propaganda on this occasion, since labour organization in the constituency was weak and the Liberal candidate was a well-known suffragist.[34] But this decision revealed

[31] M. Royden, *Votes and Wages* (NUWSS, 4th edn, 1914), p.30.
[32] Isabella Ford to Edward Carpenter, 25 Aug. 1913, Carpenter Coll., Sheffield Ref. Lib.
[33] Isabella Ford to Millicent Fawcett, 14 Oct. 1913, Correspondence Files, Fawcett Lib.
[34] *CC* 14 Nov. 1913.

7. Isabella Ford (*left*) and Muriel Matters (*right*), (*Common Cause*, 1913). (*British Library, Newspaper Library, Colindale*)

once again the serious splits within the NUWSS on election policy; a number of ILP suffragists believed that the labour candidate should have been supported; they also accused some NUWSS members of campaigning for the Liberal candidate rather than carrying out general suffrage propaganda.

In spite of such disagreements, NUWSS leaders could look on their political strategy as a successful one. The Labour Party had not won any more seats, but its share of the vote at by-elections had increased, usually at the expense of the Liberal candidate. Labour MPS had gained greater confidence from the widespread industrial militancy of the pre-war years, the rise in the number of trade-unionists, and the increase in support for Labour candidates at municipal elections, all of which encouraged them to take a more independent stand in Parliament. In this context their alliance with the suffragists seemed particularly threatening to the Liberal government, and Asquith began to show more willingness to consider the women's claim.

After six years of continuous work for the suffrage cause, ILP suffragists also found that their emphasis on the relationship between the labour and suffrage cause was more widely accepted in the NUWSS as a whole. Union members increasingly regarded the vote 'not as a sex question but as a democratic one' and linked the suffrage to issues of class.[35] In the course of making her own contribution to these changes, Isabella had gained a reputation as the 'best-loved personality' in the NUWSS. A short biography, written in the *Common Cause* just before the Scarborough Conference, claimed that 'it makes no difference whether one likes her opinions or not; one cannot help loving her . . . The other day one member of the N. U. was commending a friend to the good offices of another friend: "You will like her. She is a great admirer of I. O. Ford's, and really loves her," "Oh, if I have to like everyone who loves Isabella – !" was the despairing reply.'[36]

Although disappointments had been frequent, Isabella's enthusiasm for the cause never wavered and she remained convinced that success was possible. Her optimism had been strengthened by the closer relationship between the NUWSS and the Labour Party. At the beginning of 1914 she not only looked forward to a general election later in the year, but also took time to reflect on what had gone before; the causes that she had supported and the friendships that had been strengthened. When Millicent Fawcett's brother died in February, Isabella wrote in the warmest of terms to invite Millicent and her sister Agnes to Adel: 'A brother is such a precious person – & we feel deeply for you – . . . sometimes, looking back over past years,

---

[35]Speech by Margaret Robertson, quoted in L. Garner, *Stepping Stones to Women's Liberty: Feminist Ideas in the Women's Suffrage Movement, 1900–1918* (Heinemann, 1984), p. 19.
[36]'Miners and Suffragists', ibid., 3 Oct. 1913.

it comes over me with such a rush how much, how very much, I owe to you & to Agnes – more than you can ever know – but I know & bless you over & over again.'[37]

Time for reflection was limited, however, as the NUWSS stepped up its propaganda campaign even further in the early months of 1914. Once again, there was such a demand for speakers in the Leeds area that the Leeds Suffrage Society could barely keep up. Approaching her sixtieth year, Isabella embarked on a punishing schedule of meetings that would have exhausted even a younger woman. In February she spoke at least three times a week in the Leeds area and in March travelled up and down the country, addressing meetings as far apart as Bournemouth and Rotherham.

The memories must have come flooding back as she appeared once again at 'key' labour events. For the first time in many years she went to the ILP's annual conference in April to celebrate its coming of age, and heard Katherine Bruce Glasier praise the contribution made by Bessie and herself to the feeling of comradeship between men and women in the West Riding ILP. As one of the founding members it was particularly fitting that Isabella should have been there, at a time when the ILP was helping to lead the women's suffrage campaign. In the following month she was back in Leeds to speak on women's suffrage at the May Day rally, an event that she rarely missed. In June she accompanied Ben Turner and Allen Gee to the International Textile Workers' congress at Blackpool and, as so many times before, made a speech deploring the fact that she was the only female delegate from England.[38]

The congress only took Isabella away from suffrage campaigning for a week. When she returned to London in July she took part in seven meetings in eleven days, including garden parties, at-homes, and open-air meetings in Hyde Park and elsewhere. Two clouds hung over this suffrage work. One was the increasing militancy of the WSPU and its antagonism to the labour movement. This encouraged members of the Labour Party, such as MacDonald, who was already ambivalent towards women's suffrage, to make scathing attacks on the militants. Fearing that such hostility would 'irritate the earnest women like Miss Ford and not instruct the thoughtless', Katharine Bruce Glasier wrote to criticize MacDonald, but her worries were groundless.[39] The militants' persistent disruption of meetings whenever there was a Labour Party speaker removed the last shred of Isabella's sympathy and she became far more critical of their actions.

At the ILP conference, WSPU members had disturbed a suffrage meeting, and Isabella could not wait to tell Millicent Fawcett about Hardie's speech in support of the NUWSS, 'which I see all the papers have omitted

[37]Isabella Ford to Millicent Fawcett, 1 Feb. 1914, Correspondence Files, Fawcett Lib.
[38]I. O. Ford, 'The International Textile Workers Congress at Blackpool', *CC* 19 June 1914.
[39]Holton, 'Feminism and Democracy', p. 243.

of course'. According to Isabella, Hardie had claimed that 'the militant section forms but a *fraction* of the women's movement & the NUWSS is carrying on, as the L.P. carries on, the only kind of work which is as we all believe really effective – in fact, educational work'. In the midst of the disturbances, she wrote, 'the women were put out with great care . . . we all watched anxiously & the WSPU will *lie* when they say otherwise. The men I must say were chucked out anyhow! You see they had to be put out – no speeches were possible. MacDonald was ill . . . and couldn't stand it all – no more could Snowden and Hardie was quite done up – I was on the platform near him.'[40]

With this experience fresh in her mind, Isabella supported a resolution, put to a meeting of the national council at the end of the month, which aimed to prevent any society from affiliating to the NUWSS if it enrolled members of a group committed to a policy of violence.[41] It was not only their opposition to the Labour Party which irritated Isabella, but also the way in which the militants gave all suffrage workers a bad name. After an attack on Adel Church she wrote to tell Millicent Fawcett that 'we live in terror now about Adel Church and people will say we've done it. The Yorkshire Post will & others – the YP is not ignorant – we've told the editor in private correspondence how things are & he knows . . .' Expressing concern for Millicent Fawcett, who was about to speak in Hyde Park, she lashed out at Christabel Pankhurst who 'couldn't face, doesn't face, these angry crowds'.[42]

The other difficulty Isabella helped to deal with was internal to the NUWSS. The increasing closeness with the ILP, a source of such excitement to some women, caused growing suspicion among others who did not have labour sympathies. They were worried that the EFF committee was becoming too involved in labour politics and that members were making decisions before they had the backing of the national council. Eleonor Rathbone, for example, described the anti-government stand of the NUWSS as 'constitutional coercion'. Hoping to calm down the critics before things got out of hand, Isabella persuaded the executive committee to call a special meeting before deciding on specific policies for the next general election. She thought their actions could only be effective if they had the backing of the membership.[43]

Worries were exacerbated further, however, when the Labour Party decided to campaign for an Adult Suffrage Bill. Isabella moved a resolution in support of the bill at the April meeting of the NUWSS' executive committee. This met with opposition from members who feared that the

---

[40]Isabella Ford to Millicent Fawcett, 14 Apr. 1914, Correspondence Files, Fawcett Lib.
[41]Minutes of NUWSS Quarterly Council Meeting, 28–29 Apr. 1914.
[42]Isabella Ford to Millicent Fawcett, autumn 1914, Correspondence Files, Fawcett Lib.
[43]Minutes of NUWSS executive committee, 5 Mar. and 2 Apr. 1914.

Labour Party would drop the women's suffrage clauses if they jeopardized the success of the bill. Isabella tried to reassure them by pointing to the commitments made by the Labour Party's annual conference, and the resolution was narrowly passed.[44] These conflicts within the NUWSS took place against a background of increasing international tension. As the threat of a European war loomed closer the majority of women's groups, from both the suffrage and labour movements, united in calling for peace. The declaration of war in August, however, was to put the solidarity of women to its severest test yet. Active work for women's suffrage almost ceased, and the NUWSS faced further internal conflicts over its stand on the question of peace and war, an issue that was to prove just as divisive for women as the relationship between suffragists and socialists.

[44]Ibid., 2 Apr. 1914.

10

Peace Campaigner, 1914–1918

My whole mind and soul is bent on Peace work . . .

Isabella's political activities took a new direction when war was declared in August 1914. She threw herself into work for peace with the same energy that she had shown in the years of agitation for the vote. Her priorities may have changed, but this was largely a question of emphasis. Isabella's involvement in the peace movement can be seen as a logical extension of all her previous campaigns. Drawing on a framework of ideas that had guided her actions for over twenty years, she argued that war harmed the interests of women and workers and that it was crucial for both groups to act together to bring it to an end. Unity, therefore, between women of all classes and between the feminist and socialist movements continued to be the principle which informed her political activities. She maintained this stand despite the fact that war, to an even greater degree than the suffrage campaign, divided women and exacerbated the conflict between the sexes at the work-place.

Although the First World War was to provide the context in which the government finally accepted a measure of women's suffrage, in 1914 such a possibility seemed remote. As tension mounted between Britain and Germany, the first reaction of women in the labour and suffrage movements was to put their weight behind demands for peace. The International Suffrage and Socialist congresses of the pre-war years had brought women together from many different countries, fostering close friendships and encouraging them to believe that women had common interests which crossed national boundaries. The basic philosophy of the mainstream suffrage movement was against the use of force to achieve social change, and all women's groups, with the notable exception of the WSPU, were united in their desire for peace in the summer of 1914.

When the Women's Co-operative Guild and the Women's Labour League suggested that a women's peace rally should be organized to put pressure on the goverment to make a stand against a European war, both the NUWSS and IWSA, the International Women's Suffrage Alliance, readily gave their support. Rosika Schwimmer, now working in the London office of the IWSA, and Helena Swanwick helped to organize the rally which took place in London on the fateful day of August the 4th. Representatives from a wide variety of women's groups turned up at the Kingsway Hall to hear Millicent Fawcett condemn this 'insensate devilry' in which women had played no part. None the less, as they left the hall they knew that Germany had not replied to Britain's ultimatum and that war would be declared that very night.[1]

The immediate reaction of the NUWSS was to suspend all suffrage activity, but stunned members still had to decide what action to take next. At the peace rally, women had been able to unite in support of two resolutions; one urging that neutral countries should mediate to bring an end to the conflict, the other calling on women's organizations to 'offer their services to their country'.[2] From the start, however, there were disagreements about how these policies should be interpreted and acted upon. Millicent Fawcett encouraged NUWSS members to concentrate on relief work – a supposedly non-controversial area of activity. On the other hand, a significant group within the executive committee, including Isabella, Catharine Marshall, Helena Swanwick, and Maude Royden, wanted suffragists to direct their energies towards the more positive goal of securing peace.

In the first few weeks of the war, they met to thrash out their ideas in Isabella's London *pied à terre*; on one occasion, when they were discussing Lloyd George's failure to resign from the Liberal government, Rosika Schwimmer recalled that Isabella was furious: 'that man has not a grain of pride . . . how fine he was during the Boer War, how decent. And to lend himself now to the humiliating role of a puppet in Grey's hand.' Normally so broadminded and full of humour, Isabella was now very angry indeed, 'having just come from a wrangle with a fish-blooded pacifist'.[3] Her own pacifism was so deeply rooted in her Quaker upbringing that 'anti-militarism was in her blood'. It was the one issue most likely to rouse her to make fighting speeches and to bring out her 'intense indignation against injustice'.[4] During a debate at the 1914 annual conference over what part the NUWSS should play in the war, Isabella 'declaimed against co-operation with the government for war purposes with a pugnacity of word and gesture which took everyone's breath away, and then, having had her say,

---

[1] For a discussion of the women's peace movement, see A. Wiltsher, *Most Dangerous Women: Feminist Peace Campaigners of the Great War* (Pandora, 1985), chs. 1, 2. See also J. Liddington, 'The Women's Peace Crusade: The History of a Forgotten Campaign', in D. Thompson, ed., *Over Our Dead Bodies: Women Against the Bomb* (Virago, 1983).

[2] Wiltsher, *Most Dangerous Women*, p. 23.

[3] R. Schwimmer, 'Women's Age of Innocence', typescript, R. Schwimmer-Lloyd Coll., New York Public Lib., p. 109.

[4] B. Turner, 'Miss I. O. Ford: An Appreciation', *Yorkshire Factory Times*, 24 July 1924; 'I. O. Ford', *New Leader* (NL), 25 July 1924.

stamped off the platform and down the hall in almost ferocious style'.[5]

Although she was impatient with the stand being taken by the NUWSS, Isabella took heart from the movement for peace which seemed to be developing in other countries. Late in August, Rosika Schwimmer, whose name left her open to attack in England as an enemy alien, decided to carry on her peace work from the comparative safety of America. Her first step on arrival was to organize a petition urging President Wilson to end the war by negotiation. On 21 September she sent a cablegram to Bessie and Isabella asking them to distribute copies of the petition to known pacifists, including Vernon Lee, Kier Hardie, H. N. Brailsford, and Catharine Marshall. Isabella quickly sent Rosika a further list of people likely to support the peace manifesto, while her sister distributed copies of the cablegram. Bessie allowed herself to be optimistic in her note to Hardie. 'It is a cablegram that gives one some hope, isn't it?'[6]

Isabella's commitment to peace was increasingly at odds with the official attitude of the NUWSS and its president. She was reluctant, however, to contribute towards any open split in the organization to which she had belonged for so many years. Her relationship with Millicent Fawcett made her dilemma as much a personal as a political one. The two women were on such intimate terms that just before the war began, Millicent Fawcett confided to Bessie and Isabella that her sister, Elizabeth Garrett Anderson, was suffering from a hardening of the arteries. The news made the two sisters 'very sad', and Isabella pledged that 'we shall never mention it to anyone but our two selves. Bessie and I thank you for trusting us about it'.[7] She was torn apart, therefore, at the thought of any rupture in this close friendship.

Replying to a letter from Millicent Fawcett concerning a meeting on women's work in time of war, to be held at the Kingsway Hall on 20 October, Isabella was particularly conciliatory, promising that she would

> never be disloyal to any course of action that *you* laid down & at the meeting I will say nothing that wd. be of a disloyal nature. I will do just what you wish Milly. . . . Say all that you think – all you write to me, about Germany, I shan't look tiresome – & I shan't feel hostile dear Millie – that's not the word – I shd so hate to think my presence made you say anything by what you *wish* to say. I will only speak about working women & their employment . . .

In her own speech for the meeting, Isabella intended to point out that none of the belligerent countries allowed women to vote and that 'our movement, being International & democratic, we are the future hope of the

[5]'I. O. Ford', *NL*.

[6]R. Schwimmer, 'Women's Age of Innocence', p. 109; letter from Bessie Ford to Keir Hardie, enclosing cablegram, 21 Sept. 1914, Francis Johnson Coll., LSE.

[7]Isabella Ford to Millicent Fawcett, autumn 1914, Correspondence Files, Fawcett Lib.

world which can only be saved from future wars by these two agencies'. If Millicent did not approve of what she was going to say, Isabella was prepared to stick to the subject of unemployment and war work. None the less, in her heart she must have known that a clash would come and hinted at this towards the end of the letter: 'I know you will understand, if I ever feel I must take some other line than what you approve – I shall only do it because I must – not because of any other reason – I will always tell you & ask you, first . . . I only wish I could feel as you do.'[8]

At the Kingsway Hall meeting, Isabella kept to her word. She 'spoke of the international character of the women's movement', which 'transcended caste, and sex, and race', and pleaded for 'love rather than revenge in our attitude towards other countries'. She told a 'touching story' of kindliness between French and German soldiers, and the audience visibly responded to this 'note of sympathy'. Speeches from other participants, however, revealed that the gulf in attitudes was growing wider. Although Millicent Fawcett was critical of the way in which war caused immensed suffering, she was also positive about the gains it could bring to women. The government was at last recognizing that women could make a valuable national contribution; they were in the envious position of being called on not to 'spread death, destruction . . . and sorrow untold', but 'to serve the State by saving life rather than by destroying it'.

Other speakers supported these sentiments by giving detailed accounts of the relief work already being undertaken. It was left to Maude Royden to introduce a note of warning. She recognized that such activities had to take place, but 'if relief work were to be the whole contribution made by suffragists to this great national crisis, she thought they no longer deserved to be suffragists at all'. It was their duty to think of the causes which led to the war, not just to deal with the results, and to help form public opinion so that when peace came 'it should not contain the seeds of war'.[9]

The two sets of views seemed to be irreconcilable. None the less, executive members still tried to work together. Five days after the meeting, Isabella wrote to Catharine Marshall to urge her not to think of resigning yet from the NUWSS.

> I am recovering from the appalling horror which seemed to destroy everything in one at first – and am eager for work . . . I consider we women must not combine with Morel & Co. yet . . . But, of course, as you know well, Mrs Fawcett is our stumbling block. She is not so bad quite as I expected for she and Agnes were most unspeakable during the Boer War . . . I intend to take more definite action – I want to visit branches and address them on 'Women's work in time of War' – a most misleading title I assure you! . . . I shall resign if Manchester and Newcastle resign, then we can consider matters.

[8]Isabella Ford to Millicent Fawcett, Oct. 1914. ibid.
[9]Common Cause (CC), 23 Oct. 1914.

Isabella showed quite clearly how relief work could never satisfy women who wanted to take action to secure peace. She was 'horribly tied up with C. Council work and Lord Mayors' Committee, because for the sake of Woman with a big W. & all that, I had to do it. Now I am trying to find tactful ways of shirking it for my whole mind and soul is bent on Peace work'. In contrast to her conciliatory letter to Millicent Fawcett, written three weeks earlier, Isabella seemed prepared to take a more determined stand: 'If the NU hangs back the cause of W. Suff. will be irrevocably damaged in the future. Do you agree with this? My mind is absolutely firm . . . your loving Aunt Isabella.'[10] For the time being, however, a split in the NUWSS was averted. Suffragists who were 'bent on peace work' satisfied their urge to do something by joining with 'Morel & Co.' in the Union of Democratic Control.

The UDC was formed in November 1914 at the initiative of the chairman of the ILP, Ramsay MacDonald, and the radical liberals C. P. Trevelyan, Norman Angell, E. D. Morel, and Arthur Ponsonby. It brought together pacifists, who thought that the use of force to settle disputes could never be justified, with all those who opposed this particular war and sought non-violent solutions to conflicts whenever possible. As Isabella made clear in a letter to Millicent Fawcett, her own opposition to the war was on pacifist grounds. 'I hate Prussianism as heartily as you do – & I long for it to go – But I do not think that war ever destroyed war – & real salvation can only come to people & nations from within.'[11]

The main aim of the UDC was to secure peace by negotiation. This policy had a broad appeal for ILP socialists, liberal radicals, and suffragists who wished to bring a speedy end to the conflict by constitutional means rather than by more controversial methods of direct action to stop the war. They were attracted by UDC proposals for the avoidance of future wars. These included the democratic control of foreign policy, provision for a plebiscite before any country was transferred from one government to another, a drastic reduction in armaments, and the establishment of an international council to create treaties of arbitration which would be enforced by international courts.

After Helena Swanwick had joined the executive committee, a resolution was passed confirming that 'the UDC, convinced that democracy must be based on the equal citizenship of men and women, invites the co-operation of women'.[12] This was a logical extension of the argument which had already become widespread in the suffrage movement before the outbreak

[10]Isabella Ford to Catherine Marshall, 25 Oct. 1914, quoted in Wiltsher, *Most Dangerous Women*, pp. 63–4.
[11]Isabella Ford to Millicent Fawcett, Oct. 1914, Correspondence Files, Fawcett Lib.
[12]Minute book of General Council of UDC, 9 Feb. 1915; see also inaugural meeting, 17 Nov. 1914. UDC papers, Hull University.

of war: that the campaign for the vote was part of a wider struggle for the right of all men and women to participate in decision-making in every area of their lives. This commitment to parliamentary democracy of the broadest kind, as the best way to ensure a 'moral regeneration of society', had underpinned the alliance between radical liberals, ILP socialists, and suffragists in the pre-war years. Their common interest in securing peace, both now and in the future, and their continuing faith in parliamentary democracy, brought them together once again and strengthened the links between them.

Isabella's sisters and nearly all of her close friends from the suffragist and socialist movements, with the notable exception of Millicent Fawcett, became members of the UDC. One of Emily's friends, the author Vernon Lee, was a leading UDC propagandist, dividing her time during the war between Adel Grange, where she wrote the *Ballad of Nations*, and rooms in Chelsea. She was able to keep the Ford sisters in touch with leading pacifists in London, including Morel, Ponsonby, Bertrand Russell, and Desmond MacCarthy, the literary critic. The MacCarthy family had been friends with the Fords since the late nineteenth century. Desmond's father had been the agent for the Bank of England in Leeds, and his mother, Isa, had often stayed at Adel Grange.[13]

This network of friendship was of vital importance in sustaining the small group of peace campaigners as they carried out propaganda for their very unpopular cause. Olive Schreiner, living in London when the war began, was widely shunned for her anti-war views and had never known such loneliness. Confined to bed with kidney trouble she saw no-one for three weeks, 'except once Isabella Ford, once my brother for a few moments and once dear Dolly Radford. But it's not the loneliness of never seeing or speaking to anyone that matters, it's the sense of being entirely cut off from one's fellows.'[14] As an effective platform speaker, which Olive Schreiner was not, Isabella could compensate to some extent for this feeling of isolation by joining with others to take action to promote peace.

A heavy cold kept Isabella at home in the first few weeks of 1915, but by February she was well enough to resume her share in the campaign for peace. She worked closely with Vernon Lee and Emily Hobhouse, a Liberal friend who had written a report on conditions in South Africa during the Boer War which was highly critical of the government. The three women distributed leaflets and addressed open-air meetings, often facing abuse from the audience. It took a great deal of courage to take a stand against the war at a time when patriotic fervour was sweeping the country, but Isabella was

[13]P. Gunn, *Vernon Lee: Violet Paget, 1856–1935* (Oxford: OUP, 1964), p. 206; information on Desmond MacCarthy was kindly provided by H. P. Cecil.

[14]Olive Schreiner to Havelock Ellis, 14 Dec. 1914, quoted in S. C. Conwright-Schreiner, *The Letters of Olive Schreiner, 1876–1920* (T. Fisher Unwin, 1924), p. 344.

used to facing hostile crowds, having been 'stoned and pelted' time and again for her labour and suffrage views.[15]

The internal politics of the NUWSS also took up a great deal of her time. As the February meeting of the national council drew closer, in order to clarify her own views, which were close to those of her UDC colleagues, she commented on the various resolutions that had been put forward about the war.

> I do not think that N.U. should make any pronouncement or undertake work, about the rights or wrongs of *this* war. An opinion about this war is not possible for us to express. But all propaganda against war in general, and in favour of substituting in the future arbitration of some sort between nations in order to settle disputes for war, I heartily and strongly support. It is absolutely essential.[16]

Anti-war suffragists were able to take heart from the resolutions passed by the council which seemed to commit the NUWSS to work more actively for peace. One of the resolutions supported the principle that 'social relations should be governed not by physical force but by recognition of mutual rights'. Another called on societies and members of the union to 'take every means open to them for promoting mutual understanding and goodwill between nations and for resisting any tendency towards a spirit of hatred and revenge'.[17]

Passing resolutions, however, was not the same as acting on them. Accusing the executive of failing to do anything positive for peace, Kate Courtney and Catharine Marshall resigned from office, although they remained on the executive. Isabella still suppressed some of her views because of her personal feelings for Millicent Fawcett. On the other hand, she was more and more anxious to do something for peace and wrote to reassure Rosika Schwimmer that she agreed that loyalty to principles was more important than loyalty towards persons. She did not put 'small things before great ones', and was hopeful that 'besides the Labour women & the Socialist women others are coming into line'. Before taking any decisions, she intended to go to London to see what other UDC members in the NUWSS were planning to do. In the meantime she was concentrating on peace work in Leeds, because all she could think about was stopping the war: 'so near to it all as we are here, it is *unbearable*'.[18]

Differences of opinion within the NUWSS executive were finally brought to a head by the announcement that an International Women's Peace congress would be held at The Hague in April. Members of the IWSA, including Dr Aletta Jacobs from Holland and Carrie Chapman Catt,

[15] *Jus Suffragii*, May–June, 1920.
[16] Isabella Ford's Council Address on 'Attitudes to the War, 1915', M50/2/9/17, Suffrage MSS Manchester Central Lib.
[17] 'Statement by Retiring Members and Others', *CC* 14 June 1915.
[18] Isabella Ford to Rosika Schwimmer, 28 Feb. 1915, Schwimmer-Lloyd Coll.

the American suffrage leader, had thought of the idea and hoped that the meeting would include representatives from neutral and belligerent countries alike. Their intention was not to discuss the origins of the present conflict, but to find a way for women from all countries to contribute towards bringing about a just and lasting peace.

The controversial issue was whether the NUWSS would support the congress. In February Isabella had been anxious to do some international work but had thought that a congress was 'probably impossible'.[19] At the executive committee meeting of 8 March, however, she joined Catharine Marshall in moving a resolution in favour of supporting the proposed peace gathering. The resolution was not carried, and the committee declined to send delegates to the congress. At the next meeting, held ten days later, the executive ruled that affiliated societies were also not at liberty to send their own representatives.

During the next two months, supporters of the peace congress took every opportunity to explain their position at public meetings and through letters to the press. They had to counter Millicent Fawcett's influential view that women had a duty to relieve suffering in this fight against the evil of Prussianism, and that by this contribution they were likely to achieve the suffrage. In doing so, they raised arguments that were not only tactical, but were rooted in a more fundamental set of beliefs about the relationship between feminism and peace. When one member of the executive committee claimed that the peace movement had nothing to do with the suffrage campaign, Isabella retorted that, on the contrary, the peace settlement had everything to do with women's suffrage, since the suffragist cause was opposed to militarism. She took an entirely opposite view to Millicent Fawcett, arguing that peace propaganda would

> strengthen our W.S. cause immensely and would clearly explain to the public that our whole raison d'etre is the substitution of moral and spiritual force for physical force. If we do not urge this, we give the lie to all our former suffrage work – we belittle the great Pilgramage [sic] and we give away our opposition to the militant methods of the W.S. & P.U. But this propaganda need not in any way concern *this* war.[20]

In their efforts to draw a link between feminism and peace, anti-war suffragists, including Helena Swanwick, Isabella, and Maude Royden, used the same arguments about women's special qualities which had underpinned their demand for the vote before the war. They insisted that women, because of their role as mothers, were more likely than men to oppose

[19]Isabella Ford's Council Address on 'Attitudes to the War, 1915', M50/2/9/17, Suffrage MSS.
[20]Ibid. See also minutes of executive committee of the NUWSS, 8 and 18 Mar. 1915., NUWSS papers, Fawcett Lib.

militarism and the use of force to achieve social change. Isabella pointed out that female socialists had been the only ones in the socialist movement in Europe to make a collective stand against the war and spelt out the reasons.

> Women have more to lose in this horrible business than some men have; for they often lose more than life itself when their men are killed; since they lose all that makes life worth living for, all that makes for happiness . . . the destruction of the race too is felt more bitterly and more deeply by those who through suffering and anguish have brought the race into the world.[21]

It was for this reason that they saw the peace movement as so inextricably linked to women's suffrage. Only when women had a say in their country's foreign policy could they use their influence to achieve peace. At a public meeting held in the Caxton Hall at the end of March to defend the Hague congress, Isabella claimed that the women of Europe were seeking 'a worthy peace', not 'peace at any price'. Now was the time to draw up peace terms, before they were coloured with revenge. 'Women represented the other side of the nation's life and . . . the combination of both men's and women's wisdom was necessary in the governance of the world.'[22] In a collective statement, the resigning members of the executive committee also raised the connection between women's suffrage and peace. 'The real cleavage of opinion in the Union lies between those who consider it essential to work for the vote simply as a political tool, and those who believe that the demand for the vote should be linked with the advocacy of the deeper principles which underlie it.'[23]

Despite protests from some provincial societies, the executive decision was not reversed. On 15 April, therefore, fourteen executive members, including Isabella, Maude Royden, Margaret Ashton, Kate Courtney, and Catharine Marshall, resigned. Isabella did so with 'deep regret', for 'I value highly, as one of the best things in my life, the past twenty years or more of work with honoured and beloved colleagues.' It was not just the peace congress that had led to her decision; she now felt that she differed 'from the majority of the Committee as to the meaning of the suffrage movement, and also about the best way of fulfilling that meaning'.[24]

Throughout the month of April, those who had resigned from the executive committee attended meeting after meeting to publicize the congress and to gain support from other women. At the suggestion of the UDC, a women's conference was held on the 14th at the Central Hall in Westminster to discuss the basis of a permanent peace settlement. Delegates from a wide variety of labour and suffrage groups came to hear eloquent

---

[21] *Leeds Weekly Citizen* (LWC), 12 Mar. 1915.
[22] *Labour Leader (LL)*, 1 Apr. 1915.
[23] Statement by Retiring Members', p. 121.
[24] Minutes of Executive Committee of the NUWSS, 15 Apr. 1915. NUWSS papers.

speeches from a host of well-known suffragists and socialists. Isabella had been closely involved in trying to get large numbers of Belgian refugees to Britain and, in seconding a resolution calling for Belgium to be restored to its place among the nations, she was able to tell the audience some of the Belgians' own views about the invasion of their country. She also seconded a resolution which urged women to join the UDC.[25]

As a result of all the publicity and discussion, 180 women, including Bessie Ford from the Leeds branch of the UDC, put their names forward to attend the Hague congress. However, the government allowed only 24 – among them Isabella – to have the necessary passports. In the event they were all left stranded at Tilbury Docks on 24 April, unable to cross the channel because shipping had been suspended, and the congress took place without them. Only Kate Courtney and Catharine Marshall, who had travelled to Holland at an earlier date, and Emmeline Pethwick Lawrence, who had come directly from the USA, were able to represent Britain at the congress, but it was still regarded as a success. In a glowing report, which must have been based on the impressions of the British delegates who *did* attend, Isabella claimed that 'the conference has proved that international understanding is possible for the future'. As always, she raised the need for women to have the vote.

> When the women of all the nations have a voice in the affairs of their various governments . . . this understanding will grow more and more rapidly . . . As the mothers and educators of the human race, the bond which unites us is deeper than any bond which at present unites men. These are the conclusions arrived at by the congress, and expressed in the resolutions passed at it.[26]

Isabella's views on the war, however, were informed by her socialist ideas as much as by her feminist ones. Believing that the origins of the war lay not only in secret diplomacy, but also in the commercial rivalry of capitalist economies, she looked to socialists throughout Europe to lead the movement for peace. She joined Katharine Bruce Glasier, Maude Royden, and others in sending a May Day message from British women to their comrades abroad. Her greetings to the workers and women of Europe were sent with 'sincere and heartfelt gratitude and admiration for the noble manner in which, amidst all the horror and ruin around us, they have kept alive and are still bravely and successfully spreading the spirit of Internationalism'. Speaking especially to German and Austrian women, she claimed that only 'when the women of the world stand together unitedly,

[25]Other speakers included Catherine Marshall, Helena Swanwick, Charlotte Despard, and Margaret Bondfield; H. M. Swanwick, *Builders of Peace: Being 10 Years History of the UDC* (P. Swarthmore, 1924), pp. 55–6. For an account of the work of Isabella, Mary Sheepshanks, and Dr Elsie Inglis to help Belgian refugees, see S. Oldfield, *Spinsters of this Parish* (Virago, 1984), pp. 183–4.

[26]I. O. Ford, 'The Hague Peace Conference', *LWC* 28 May 1915.

demanding that nations shall arbitrate . . . then wars will cease'. The slogan 'my country right or wrong' was a false patriotism, she claimed, the creed only of 'the commercial and ruling classes', and therefore women had to become international in their work for socialism and the women's movement.[27] She received a note from Adelheid Popp, leader of the Socialist Women of Austria, which recalled happier days in 1913 at the IWSA conference at Budapest when they had visited a children's home together: 'When the same efforts and the same ideas brought us together we, indeed, never thought that so soon we should become "enemies"!' Adelheid concluded with encouraging words: 'Rest firmly assured that today, exactly the same as then, we are united with you in the desire for peace and the brotherhood of nations.'[28]

After an exhausting and exciting few weeks in London carrying out propaganda for the peace congress, Isabella returned to Leeds. She spent the next three months in the West Riding, talking to a number of local suffrage societies to clear up any misunderstandings they might have about the Hague congress. The retiring members of the executive committee had not given up hope of returning to their positions. They were willing to stand for re-election as long as the resolutions submitted to the June council by the Manchester branch, reaffirming support for the proposals carried in February, were carried. They felt, quite correctly as it turned out, that the rank and file were confused about the conflicts at the centre. Early in June the resigning group wrote a long explanation of their actions in the *Common Cause*. They did not believe that the union could survive unless 'it recognises the great principles for which it stands, and continues to uphold the ideals of supremacy of moral force in human affairs'. Confining the union to suffrage and relief work could not for long remain non-controversial, and if the union's watchwords were 'safety' and 'non-controversy', it would never be able to lead the women's fight for the vote after the war.[29]

Although several compromise positions were suggested to the June council, Millicent Fawcett gained the support of the smaller, country societies for her policy of concentrating on relief and suffrage work, and the internationalists finally gave up their bid for re-election. At this stage Isabella remained on friendly terms with Millicent Fawcett. In a letter sent at the end of the month, thanking her for some press cuttings, Isabella told Millicent: 'I don't think I can ever get away from my Quaker upbringing, but it doesn't touch my deep & enduring love for you & gratitude for all I owe to you in my life & your concluding words in your letter have consoled me greatly & I thank you so much dearest Millie.'[30] At some point,

[27]*LL* 29 Apr. 1915. Other contributors included Vernon Lee and Charlotte Despard.
[28]*LL* 26 Aug. 1915.
[29]'Statement by Retiring Members', p. 122.
[30]Isabella Ford to Millicent Fawcett, 23 June 1915, Correspondence Files, Fawcett Lib.

however, the two women stopped corresponding. This may have been when Isabella and the other retiring members of the NUWSS executive turned their energies to a new organization, the Women's International League, which was formed as the result of the peace congress at The Hague.

The British section of the WIL was formally established in September. Key offices were held by suffragists from the NUWSS: Helena Swanwick was the chairman, and Maude Royden, Margaret Ashton, and Kate Courtney were the three vice-chairmen. Isabella was elected on to the executive committee of the new organization where she joined many old friends from both the NUWSS and the ILP, including Charlotte Despard, Katharine Bruce Glasier, and Margaret Bondfield.

The declared objectives of the WIL were to achieve a negotiated peace settlement based on terms that would ensure a continuing peace, the democratic control of foreign policy, and a change in public opinion towards support for international understanding and against the use of force to settle disputes. These aims and objectives were similar to those put forward by many other peace groups, and in this context it might have seemed unnecessary to set up a separate oganization for women. But the members of the WIL saw their potential contribution in trying to bring about peace as unique simply *because* they were women. Women could not vote, and therefore had played no part in causing the war; moreover, the common experience of motherhood cut across national boundaries. As non-combatants they had a greater right than men to meet and discuss peace, and 'as guardians of the race they have the duty'.[31] The WIL thus put greater emphasis than other peace groups on the need for women's suffrage, and could also draw on international links already established during the pre-war suffrage campaign.

The WIL did co-operate closely, however, with the UDC, the ILP, the No-Conscription Fellowship, and other groups which aimed to secure peace. Women socialists and suffragists were often members of all these different groups; initially they were willing to speak at meetings, distribute literature, and attend conferences for any one of them. But time was limited, and eventually women had to make choices about where to commit most of their energies. Catharine Marshall, for example, became secretary of the No-Conscription Fellowship and reduced her involvement in the WIL, whereas for Isabella the WIL remained the focus of her peace work. With so many causes claiming women's support, it was difficult to keep the executive of the WIL stable, and Isabella was among those judged by Helena Swanwick to have done the most work at headquarters.[32]

[31]'The Women's International Manifesto', *LL* 25 Mar. 1915.
[32]H. Swanwick, *I Have Been Young* (Victor Gollancz, 1935), p. 280. Among the others cited as active at headquarters were Maude Royden, Margaret Ashton, and, for a while, Ethel Snowden.

As always, Isabella was determined to play her part in building up grass-roots involvement in the cause in the provinces. She helped to form a Leeds branch of the WIL which immediately attracted seventy-five members. Among them were Bessie and Emily, who once again joined forces with their younger sister in a common cause. Although nearing seventy, Bessie was so horrified by the war that she attended meetings, helped to organize leaflets and petitions, and became a member of the general council of the WIL. Emily carried out practical relief work in Leeds, helping to develop a scheme for communal kitchens which was funded by the Lady Mayoress's Executive Committee. A cook was employed, and the centres provided hot meals for people to take away in their own jugs and basins. Emily's main interest, however, was in the plight of refugees, in particular Serbians and Belgians, and she encouraged many of those who had fled the fighting to stay at Adel Grange.[33]

Isabella used her talents as a public speaker to the full, addressing countless peace meetings at a local and national level; it must have been exhausting. Helena Swanwick, who had a similar speaking schedule, found that 'travelling in war-time was an arduous affair. Trains were erratic; sometimes shunted to allow of the passage of troop trains, so that one missed one's connection and had hours to wait. Carriages packed with soldiers, often lying all along the corridors.'[34] Isabella also used her skills as a writer to provide an alternative internationalist perspective to the narrow chauvinism being preached on all sides. In one letter to the press, she expressed indignation about the government's suggestion that goods should only be bought from the Dominions or the Allies, rather than from neutral countries.

> The idea of not buying butter from Denmark is . . . quite horrible to me, as a Suffragist. When we remember that the first International Women's Suffrage Conference held in Europe was held in Denmark and that our colours were formerly red and white, because such are Danish colours, I feel shocked at the notion of boycotting that country's butter.

She was appalled that 'suffering and ruin' would befall countries who were 'guiltless of this International crime'.[35]

Although Isabella gave priority to the peace movement during the war, she still related this activity to the other causes that she had supported over many years; women's suffrage, socialist politics, and the welfare of working women. From the beginning, she took an interest in the impact that the war was having on conditions of employment and living standards. At the Leeds May Day rally in 1915, for example, she supported a resolution calling on

---

[33]E. Ford, 'Communal Kitchens', *CC* 20 Apr. 1917.
[34]Swanwick, *I Have Been Young* p. 293.
[35]*CC* 22 Oct. 1915.

8. Isabella Ford at the Leeds Labour Demonstration, 7 May 1915 (*Leeds Weekly Citizen*). (*British Library, Newspaper Library, Colindale*)

the government to control key industries, regulate the supply of food, and end secret diplomacy. She also served on the City Council Distress Committee, took part in wage assessorships, and sat on the Leeds Lady Mayoress's Committee, which dealt with the pay of female workers. Finding all this very tedious, she admitted that she took part 'solely for w s sake to keep that end up before my fossil-like men colleagues'.[36]

In the pre-war years, most debate on the 'woman question' within the labour movement had been preoccupied with political equality. The war shifted the focus of attention to women's paid employment and once more Isabella found herself engaged in battles on behalf of the female worker. The demand for war materials and the recruitment of men to the armed services led to a labour shortage which was largely filled by women. Many took up jobs already identified with female labour, such as clerical work, retailing, and nursing, but others entered trades which had formerly been seen as male preserves. It was here that controversy was greatest. Only a small number of women were substituted directly for male labour; the majority were introduced into male work that had been altered in some way, either by subdivision or by mechanization, and were paid on lower rates. This 'dilution' of labour took place most extensively in the munitions industry, where over a quarter of a million women were introduced. They encountered fierce hostility from skilled male workers, who feared that their own position would be undermined by the use of cheap labour.

The influx of women workers into the Leeds labour force prompted Isabella to take an interest once more in their trade union organization. At the Leeds Trades Council meeting of July 1915, she warned male trade-unionists that the number of female workers was likely to increase. It was imperative, she said, in the interest of both sexes, that male trade-unionists should organize women and demand that 'for the same amount of work women shall have the same pay as the men they have displaced'. She hoped they would take a firm stand 'as firm as the South Wales miners – (hear, hear) – who made Mr. Lloyd George go down and say "What do you want?"' a remark that was greeted with laughter.[37] She was supported by a delegate from the National Union of Railwaymen, but the Trades Council secretary, Owen Connellan, was less sympathetic. He thought that most unions already admitted female members, and that women did not place enough value on their own work. None the less, he agreed to refer the matter to the executive committee for consideration.

Isabella was used to receiving a mixed reaction from trade union colleagues over the issue of female labour; as usual she tried to reconcile differences, and throughout the war showed a sympathetic understanding of the problems faced by both sexes. She found it 'difficult to bear in silence

[36]Isabella Ford to Millicent Fawcett, n.d. (wartime), Correspondence Files, Fawcett Lib.
[37]LWC 30 July 1915.

the continued jibes which are levelled at the workers who demand higher wages at this moment', and was outraged to hear the criticisms of trade-unionists made by Lloyd George at the September TUC. The thought that perpetually haunted her, she said, was not that of shirkers and unco-operative workers, but 'the tired faces of the women coming home from long hours of work, the haggard look creeping round the men's eyes, who are working through Sundays as well as weekdays'.[38]

Although often at odds with Labour MPs and trade union leaders who were enthusiastic in their support for the war effort, she drew even closer to ILP colleagues who shared her own views on the need for a negotiated peace. At the beginning of the year she sent a New Year's greeting to the ILP in which she said that her heart was full of pride at the stand it was taking 'in this present crisis'.

> I have always been thankful that I had the good sense to be a socialist, and now am more so than ever . . . in the midst of all this chaos and ruin, of the nonsense talked about this war ending all war, the ILP and its leaders, Mr Keir Hardie, J. R. MacDonald, Bruce Glasier and the rest have stood calmly upholding those principles of sense and justice which alone will save us and all humanity. How proud it makes me to remember that for four years I had the honour to be their colleague on the NAC.[39]

Philip Snowden had come back from a foreign speaking tour and was 'fighting splendidly in the House'. Hardie's health, however, caused con-cern. As early as February, Isabella had thought he looked very ill,[40] but his death in September 1915 none the less came as a shock. When his colleagues came together to pay tribute to his memory, they poured out their feelings both about Hardie and about the war he had hated so much. Isabella felt his death as an 'irreperable loss . . . His extraordinary sympathy with the women's movement, his complete understanding of what it stands for, were what first made me understand the finest side of his character . . . we women can never forget what we owe him.'[41] Speaking alongside ILP leaders at a memorial meeting in London, she described Hardie as a 'man of visions' who could never die 'for he has left his spirit behind in all of us – and we shall win, of course we shall win'.[42] At a similar meeting in Leeds held in October, she claimed that the war had killed him. None the less, she ended on the hopeful note that 'Hardie had left behind a precious spark of his spirit for us all', and said she felt inspired by him to carry on the struggle to promote international understanding.[43]

---

[38]I. O. Ford, 'When Will Women Rebel', *CC* 29 Apr. and 24 Sept. 1915.
[39]*LWC* 15 Jan. 1915.
[40]Isabella Ford to Rosika Schwimmer, 28 Feb. 1915, Schwimmer-Lloyd Coll.
[41]*LL* supplement, 30 Sept. 1915.
[42]Ibid., 7 Oct. 1915.
[43]*LWC* 15 Oct. 1915.

As 1915 drew to a close, members of the ILP, the WIL, and the UDC turned their attention to the government's proposal to introduce conscription. In December, Isabella travelled to London to take part in a WIL meeting against conscription at which her friend Helena Swanwick delivered a rousing speech on the WIL's aims: 'We stand for Democracy, and Conscription everywhere helps the Government to hold down the people. We stand for the emancipation of women, and militarism is the greatest enemy of women's freedom.'[44]

After Christmas, Isabella made her contribution to the campaign against conscription and in favour of a negotiated peace by speaking to a wide variety of organizations, both in London and in the provinces. In March 1916 she had to turn down an invitation from Rosika Schwimmer to attend a 'people's mediating conference' in Stockholm, funded by the millionaire automobile manufacturer Henry Ford, because she was 'so busy with anti-war work here. I fear our first duty is to educate our people here and to tell them the truth . . . we have all the newspapers' lies to counteract.' But rising prices were beginning to have an effect on Isabella's income, and she was finding it more difficult to finance all her propaganda work. As she wrote to Rosika Schwimmer, 'I thank you and Mr. Ford . . . for your most handsome offer about Stockholm and funds. My own means are terribly reduced by the war. But I feel too I must use my own funds for the work in order to silence criticism.'[45]

Isabella had to tread carefully now that her views were out of step with those of the mainstream labour movement. Speaking at an anti-conscription meeting on Woodhouse Moor in May 1916 with her friend John Arnott of the Leeds ILP, she honoured the men who considered it right to go and fight as well as supporting those who went before tribunals and said they could not kill their fellow men. She was not prepared, however, to go along with members of the labour movement, including the Leeds Labour MP James O'Grady, who talked about 'crushing Prussianism'. In a letter to the local labour press she pointed out that 'in the old days when it was preached that those who made a nation great were its thinkers rather than its fighters we used to preach that salvation, therefore, comes from within and not from without. It followed then, I supposed, that a nation, like an individual, must evolve its own righteousness.' Reminding her readers that Abraham Lincoln had refused to shoot deserters because 'he had never noticed that killing a man reformed him', she argued that this should apply both to Germany and to Ireland. The section of the German population who wanted to give up Belgium and France should be encouraged rather than hindered in spreading their ideas, she said,

[44]*LL* 23 Dec. 1915.
[45]Isabella Ford to Rosika Schwimmer, 8 Mar. 1916, Schwimmer-Lloyd Coll. See Wiltsher, *Most Dangerous Women*, pp. 157–8 for further details on the Ford Peace Conference.

but each time our speakers and writers urge the continuation of war in order to crush Prussian militarism, that party in Germany receives a slight setback. Would it not be a wiser policy to help that party to grow strong, by preaching the common-sense of internationalism and leaving the crushing of Prussianism to the nation who lives under it.[46]

All those campaigning against conscription and a 'fight to the finish' attitude were engaged in a losing battle during 1916, despite support from many sections of the labour movement. Political pressure was directed towards securing a more vigorous prosecution of the war, and as demand for recruits for the armed services grew, conscription was steadily extended. On the other hand, progress at last seemed to be taking place on women's suffrage. The franchise issue was re-opened towards the end of 1915 when it was realized that a significant proportion of soldiers would no longer be registered to vote because of their absence from home and would be unable to take part in any post-war election. In May 1916, therefore, a group of MPs raised the possibility of creating a special register based on war service. This revitalized the suffrage campaign. Millicent Fawcett wrote to the prime minister, pointing out on behalf of the NUWSS that women were also engaged in war work and that their claims should be considered. The WIL also sent Asquith a letter, signed by suffragists (including Isabella), Labour MPs, and female trade-unionists, declaring that it was 'essential, both for justice and expediency', that women should be placed on the register of voters.[47] Asquith's response to all these requests was surprisingly sympathetic and convinced suffragists that when a Franchise Bill was eventually introduced women had a good chance of being included.

This encouraged Isabella to draw attention once again to the links between political equality and the welfare of working women, the cornerstone of her pre-war suffrage propaganda. Realizing that suffragists might be 'called upon at any moment now to begin active Suffrage work again', Isabella was anxious to remind her colleagues that the needs of the industrial woman worker was the strongest argument that they had for the vote. In an attempt to revive the labour–suffrage alliance of the pre-war years, she wrote an article in the *Common Cause* which sought to remove middle-class prejudices against trade unions. Taking a sensitive approach to the fears of male trade-unionists faced with an influx of cheap female labour, she argued that 'it has appeared to them to be . . . a plan designed to lower the wages of the skilled worker'. 'It seems to me perfectly natural', she added, 'that the men should feel bitter dismay, when what had taken them and their fathers long years to achieve was, they imagined, threatened with extinction.' Trade-unionists might have been 'stupid . . . not to grasp at once that the way out of it all is to admit the women into their unions', but women also

[46]*LWC* 2 June 1916.
[47]Women's International League, *Annual Report*, 1915–16, pp. 12–13.

had to share the blame. Female workers, in particular middle-class women, should feel in honour bound to join a trade union and not to betray men fighting in the trenches by accepting a lower rate of pay for the jobs that they had vacated.[48] In private Isabella was more critical of the actions of male trade-unionists. In a letter to Millicent Fawcett she claimed that Leeds female munitions workers were becoming more alive about women's suffrage, partly because of their opposition to the Munitions Wages Orders '& partly because of the men's trade unions & their truly disgusting behaviour to women – & partly because of the good behaviour of some of the unions – everything is so mixed'.[49]

After her resignation from the executive committee Isabella had still remained as chairman of the West Riding Federation. Now that a Franchise Bill was being discussed she played her part once again in trying to revive interest in women's suffrage. She spoke more often on the subject of the vote, especially in the West Riding. It was not easy, however, to reawaken women's commitment to the suffrage in the midst of war. Isabella found the Leeds Women's Suffrage Society particularly depressing. As she wrote to Millicent Fawcett some time in 1916, 'I have suppressed all my tiresome war opinion & loyally worked with them all, but only about 4 of them turn up at committees & no one will have any meetings – Bandaging and such work have got on their brains . . . Mrs Grosvenor Talbot is our Hon. Sec. but I have been doing the work lately.' Irritated by this lack of interest, Isabella confessed that 'an evil part of my mind . . . wants some of our WS Society in Leeds never to have votes, but to see all the other women having them. To think that an annual subs of 1/- saves them from all their work is so horrid.'[50]

This letter was in fact a response to one sent by Millicent Fawcett, and marked a reconciliation betweeb the two women. Isabella wanted Millicent to know that she loved her as much as ever '& never forget the great debt I owe you about oh so many many things . . . It is a pleasure to be in communication with you dear Millie once more . . . Much love from both of us to you both "*warmly*" Bessie calls out from her bureau.' At Christmas time the two pairs of sisters exchanged books as presents. Isabella, writing on behalf of herself and Bessie, sent theirs sealed with wax as 'a token of lasting friendship in spite of all changes. I am so glad you understood it so – I knew you would.'[51]

The year 1917 was to prove a turning point for many of the causes that Isabella and her sisters had supported for so long. The vote was at last within reach. When the Speaker's Conference reported in January, it was

[48]I. O. Ford, 'Standing By the Men: Women and Trade Unions', *CC* 19 May 1916.
[49]Isabella Ford to Millicent Fawcett, n.d. (wartime) Correspondence Files, Fawcett Lib.
[50]Ibid.
[51]Isabella Ford to Millicent Fawcett, 22 Dec. 1916, Correspondence Files, Fawcett Lib.

recommended that women over thirty or thirty five should be enfranchised. Although suffragists greeted the age limit with derision, they saw the principle as all-important. Speaking at the annual meeting of the Leeds Women's Suffrage Society in February, Isabella reminded the audience of Millicent Fawcett's argument that the placing of one red-haired woman on the electoral register would be a step towards success. '"To give the vote to women with red hair", added Miss Ford, "would be less insulting than the present proposal regarding women of 35 as only equal to what Mark Twain called the "callow kid of 21" (laughter)" . . . they must take what they could get, and then work hard to obtain more.'[52] By the end of March, the government had accepted that women's suffrage should be included as part of the Franchise Reform Bill. Although wary of being too optimistic, suffragists believed that it was only a matter of time before it became law. It was with considerable emotion, therefore, that leading members of the NUWSS, including Isabella, signed an affectionate address to Millicent Fawcett in June on the occasion of her birthday, in which they paid tribute to her inspired leadership of fifty years.[53]

Now more than ever, with suffrage nearly won, Isabella wanted to convince middle-class suffragists of the value of trade-unionism and co-operation between the sexes in the labour movement. In her second article on the subject in nine months, she noted how the war had undermined old conventions – in particular the notion that men should receive higher wages because they supported families – and yet women continued to receive lower pay for comparable work. If women were to achieve equal pay, they had to join trade unions. This was far more of a possibility than in the past; employers needed women's help as never before, their wages were often higher, and many male trade-unionists now realized that an organized female labour force offered the best protection against the threat of cheap labour.

She urged women to follow the example of the men and to fight hard for their industrial rights: 'Standing alone, as they have mostly done in the past, they can achieve nothing; but united with men in Trade Unions, and with the Parliamentary vote behind them, they can hold their own against all the odds in the world.' Isabella's views on the wider meaning of collective organization had not changed in over thirty years; trade unionism stood for 'something more than wages and conditions of labour . . . it . . . stands for working collectively towards the highest good of the community. It teaches its members to stand together and to trust one another as comrades in this great fight.' She was worried about young middle-class workers who had never thought along these lines and urged them to look ahead. It was foolish to accept low wages on spurious grounds of patriotism, for this could have both moral and physical ill effects.

[52]*LWC* 9 Feb. 1917.
[53]'Mrs. Fawcett's Birthday Celebrations', *CC* 15 June 1917.

Our future as a healthy, strong nation mostly depends on keeping up the standard of living, and therefore, of wages . . . and on greatness of character as well as good physique. Mind and body are strangely interwoven, and those who help to deteriorate one, ignore the other too.[54]

Isabella was concerned to link women's interests as closely as possible to the Labour Party.

We have to explain to [trade union] men that to enfranchise all men, and no women, will make women more helpless than ever against exploitation, and the condition of men will then be, indeed, terrible. If we do this with sympathy, compassion, and knowledge, and without railing, we shall win the support we need of Labour.[55]

The importance of women's war work had restored Isabella's faith in the possibility of organizing women to join trade unions. Once they had the vote as well, she was convinced that women would be able to achieve economic equality. The war did give an impetus to the organization of women and to the demand for equal pay, but Mary Macarthur and other union leaders met hostility and suspicion from male trade-unionists which proved difficult to overcome. The engineering unions never opened their doors to women, and Mary Macarthur signed an agreement that women would give up their jobs at the end of the war in favour of returning soldiers. When equal-pay agreements were negotiated they proved difficult to implement, and women's wages overall continued to be lower than those of men.

The view that women were marginal workers was in many respects confirmed rather than challenged by the conditions of wartime; their influx into male trades could be seen as a temporary measure at a time of national emergency, while the importance of their role as mothers of the next generation was underlined by the loss of so many lives. The majority of male and female members of the trade union movement and the Labour Party remained unwilling to challenge the sexual division of labour at the work-place and in the home. Isabella's hope, therefore, that trade union organization would lead to economic equality between the sexes was not to become a reality in the post-war world. Suffragists contributed to this failure; their faith in political equality as a means of bringing sweeping changes in women's industrial position underestimated the structural and ideological obstacles which confined women to a subordinate position at the work-place. Moreover, their emphasis on the importance of motherhood in the reconstruction of a new society after the war reinforced rather than challenged the existing sexual division of labour.[56]

[54]I. O Ford, 'Standing Together; The Value of Trade Unionism for Women', *CC* 16 Feb. 1917, p. 587.
[55]Id. 'Men, Women and Labour?', *Women's International League Monthly Newsletter*, 1917.
[56]G. Braybon, *Women Workers in the First World War* (Croom Helm, 1981).

Although the labour movement remained divided over the question of female labour, it was to take a more united stand on its attitude to the war after 1917. Attending the Labour Party annual conference in January, Isabella found it a 'wonderful' meeting, because of 'its vigour and its magnificent involuntary response, in spite of pre-arranged votes, when vital questions were discussed'. The conference confirmed her 'absolute belief in what democracy will achieve when its day comes'.[57] The unprecedented casualties during the battle of the Somme, mounting war weariness in the population, and the first Russian Revolution led to growing demands for a negotiated peace. These were reinforced when the government refused to allow Arthur Henderson, leader of the Labour Party, to attend a socialist conference in Stockholm. He promptly withdrew from Lloyd George's recently formed coalition, and the Labour Party was able to take an independent stand in calling for a negotiated peace.

From the beginning of the war, Labour women – notably members of the Women's Labour League – had taken part in public meetings organized by the Women's International League, in particular in the north of England. Co-operation between the two groups now became even more frequent. When the Leeds WIL held a successful meeting on Woodhouse Moor to celebrate May Day in 1917, the speakers were all women with labour connections, including Isabella, Margaret Bondfield, Mrs Annot Robinson of the Manchester ILP and NUWSS, and Maud Dightam from the Leeds ILP. A member of the WSPU before 1914, Maud Dightam did not follow the Pankhursts in their patriotic support for the war. Instead she joined her ILP colleagues in the peace campaign. The resolution put to the meeting called for peace by negotiation and was supported by all but a dozen men. However, when Maud Dightam suggested that it would have been better to send the old men out than the young ones, 'the applause only came from the women'.[58]

The WIL, however, was composed largely of well-educated middle-class women, fluent in foreign languages, who had contacts with the international leaders of the peace movement. Many, including Isabella, were in close touch with leaders of the ILP and the UDC; they were members of the 1917 Club, formed in London to celebrate the first Russian Revolution, which brought together ILP socialists, radical liberals, and suffragists who opposed the war. Individual working-class women did join the WIL in the provinces but its appeal was limited, and in this context the Women's Peace Crusade, a movement which aimed to attract mass support from working women, began to gain momentum. It was launched by two members of the Glasgow WIL at a demonstration in the city on 23 July 1917 which attracted 10,000 people. This was followed late in the summer by demonstrations in

[57]'Conference Impressions: Isabella O. Ford', *LL* 1 Feb. 1917.
[58]*LWC* 11 May 1917.

other towns, including Leicester, Manchester, and Nelson.

As demands for peace grew more widespread within the labour movement, members of the ILP became interested in extending the Women's Peace Crusade. The WPC was not identified with any one organization, but drew its strength from a range of existing groups; in Glasgow the Women's International League took the initiative, in Manchester the ILP, and in Leicester the Women's Labour League. The WPC aimed to bring together the interests of women and workers in calling for a negotiated peace and the democratic control of foreign policy. Its leaders set out to organize large, popular demonstrations to show the government the strength of feeling in the country.[59] Isabella wholeheartedly supported these aims, and in Leeds it was the WIL which organized the Peace Crusade throughout August and September of 1917. Members distributed leaflets and addressed both indoor and outdoor meetings every week. For Isabella, the main aim was to abolish war altogether, but she argued that this could only be achieved through 'constructive educational work . . . so that women may think and vote intelligently on International affairs, and by so doing may help the men of the nation to have a wider and more intelligent and humane outlook than they have had in the past.'[60]

Demonstrations throughout the provinces culminated in a public meeting at the Central Hall in Westminster. It had been feared that the meeting would be broken up by 'a band of stalwarts, 100 strong', but it passed off without interruption. In moving one of the resolutions for a negotiated peace, Isabella claimed that 'the political situation in Germany, rightly handled, gives opportunity for a democratic peace', and she deplored the 'incessant shifting of ground' by the Western powers. Other speakers gave details of the Crusade in the various provincial centres. The meeting was brought to a close by Ethel Snowden, who had re-joined the ILP in 1915 and was one of the WPC's most ardent supporters; in 1917 she had addressed thousands of people on the subject of peace by negotiation.[61]

In a context of mounting war casualties and ever more urgent calls for a negotiated peace, the achievement of votes for women, which finally became law in January 1918, was almost an anti-climax. By chance, Alf Mattison met Isabella at a bus terminus just after the news had been announced; her one remark was 'So Mrs Mattison's got the vote now'. A few days later, however, she wrote to him to express her 'immense joy' and the belief that 'the great tasks that lie before us, Peace, Reform and all the rest, will be so much easier to work at. We shall have a weapon in our hands & hitherto we have had none. Her peace work was taking her all over the country, and she found that women were awakening to their new position.

[59] Mrs. P. Snowden, 'The Women's Peace Crusade', *The UDC*, 2/11 (Sept. 1917).
[60] *LWC* 24 Aug. and 2 Nov. 1917.
[61] Women's International League, *Annual Report*, 1916–17, pp. 14–15.

None the less, she was too much of a realist not to have some doubts about what women would do with the vote. 'Will they save us? Will they? I am glad Edward said we should. Some will, but some won't.'[62]

Isabella managed to find time in her heavy schedule of peace meetings to attend the International Suffrage Rally at the Kingsway Hall, London, on 9 March to celebrate the suffrage victory. As a former member of the executive committee she joined her colleagues in writing a message in the *Common Cause* to mark the occasion of the achievement of the vote.

> It is indeed wonderful when one wakes in the morning to remember that now, at last, one is considered to be a real, complete human being! After thirty years of endeavor to make men understand they were only half the world . . . the price we have paid for our enfranchisement is too heavy, some of us find, to allow us to rejoice in the light-hearted, happy fashion we used to picture in old days, but we are filled with a deep and earnest thankfulness.[63]

In the pre-war suffrage movement, it had been assumed that women, because of their common oppression and their role as 'carers', would use their vote to promote reforms on behalf of their sex. The achievement of the franchise, however, was to prove divisive for the women's movement and to call into question the extent to which women would act as a group to protect their interests. In welcoming the franchise, the WIL urged all women to use their vote to promote peace. Other peace campaigners, in particular Labour Party members, were keen to start gaining the allegiance of women for their own cause. They agreed with suffragists that women shared special characteristics as voters, but assumed that their natural home would be the Labour Party. Speakers at the May Day rally in Leeds welcomed the enfranchisement of women on just these grounds, and in June Mrs Anderson Fenn, Jeannie Arnott, and Maud Dightam led a special campaign week in Leeds to persuade women to support the Labour Party. They claimed that Labour was the only group sincerely committed to building a new world after the war. Mrs Anderson Fenn opposed the proposal put forward by ex-members of the WSPU that there should be a Women's Party based on patriotism, on the ground that true patriotism could only be found in a party in which both sexes worked together for the good of each other and the whole community. This was an argument which had been the cornerstone of Isabella's political ideas since she first became involved in the labour movement.[64]

Alongside these attempts to gain the allegiance of women voters, peace

[62]Alf Mattison's Notebook No. 1, 28 Jan. 1918, Brotherton Lib. Leeds Univ. Isabella Ford to Alf Mattison, 1 Feb. 1918. Alf Mattison's Letter Book, in the possession of E. P. Thompson.

[63]*CC* 15 Mar. 1918.

[64]*LWC* 10 May and 7 June 1918; minutes of Executive Committee of WIL, 8 Nov. 1918, WIL papers, LSE.

campaigners redoubled their efforts to achieve a negotiated and just peace. As the war dragged into its fourth year the Leeds WIL and WPC continued to hold joint peace meetings. At a May Day rally on Woodhouse Moor, Isabella and Mrs Pethwick Lawrence condemned Lloyd George for turning down the offer made by Austria in the previous year to negotiate for peace. In July the Ford sisters hosted a meeting of the Yorkshire Federation of the UDC at Adel Grange where E. D. Morel was the chief speaker. Isabella continued to carry out propaganda work in the West Riding until October, when she went to London for a meeting of the executive committee of the WIL. By 9 October she was back in the West Riding to speak in Sheffield under the auspices of the UDC, where she supported a resolution condemning Lloyd George for not taking Germany's recent peace proposals seriously.

Less than a month later, the armistice had been signed and the war was over. Although thankful that the fighting was at last at an end, peace campaigners were bitterly disappointed they had failed to achieve peace by negotiation earlier in the war. The terms of the peace settlement were also based on the very principle of revenge that they had wanted to avoid. Their only hope for a more just settlement lay in the possibility that there would be a new government after the general election which was to take place in December. Women would be able to vote for the first time, and Helena Swanwick, on behalf of the WIL executive, sent letters to local branches urging women to support candidates who best promoted WIL objects, that is, the pursuit of democracy and international peace. As an executive member of the WIL, Isabella also had to promote a non-party political stand; she urged members to attend the meetings of all parliamentary candidates and to ask questions, offering to give women advice on the issues they should raise.

In a personal capacity, however, Isabella was active in supporting labour candidates. Her long years of service to the labour movement were recognized when she was asked to stand as a candidate herself, but she declined what she saw as a great honour on the grounds of age and ill health.[65] The results of the election again brought disappointment to all those who sought to promote international understanding. Lloyd George, who at one point in the campaign had declared that they must demand the whole cost of the war from Germany, was returned at the head of a coalition government comprising 484 MPs. The Labour Party came second with 59 MPs; some of its more well-known leaders, including MacDonald, Snowden, and Henderson, were unsuccessful, but the increase in the party's vote, from under 0.5 million to almost 2.5 million, gave some cause for optimism.

The peace movement may have failed in its immediate objectives, but it did provide a basis on which internationalists could build once the war was

[65]*LWC* 8 and 29 Nov. 1918.

over. Suffragists and liberal radicals had been able to join with ILP socialists in a common campaign, and for many it had provided the final impetus for them to join the Labour Party. Despite the upheavals of war, Isabella continued to keep faith with the principles that had guided her actions in the pre-war years. Her involvement in the peace movement developed naturally out of her work for socialism and women's suffrage; she asumed that both women and workers, if their views were more fully represented in political decision-making, would use their influence to promote peace and social reform. In common with her generation of ILP socialists, she remained committed to seeking change through Parliament and argued for the return of a Labour government. Although fully aware of the Labour Party's imperfections, Isabella never wavered from the view that it was the only choice for men and women like herself who wished to reconstruct society on the basis of peace, sexual equality, and freedom for members of the working class.

11

Citizen of Tomorrow

I am in a hurry to begin to construct a new world.

The post-war world was very different to the one that had gone before. The labour movement and the women's movement now had to confront economic depression, unemployment, the rise of fascism, and the Bolshevik revolution, all of which caused them to modify or change many of their pre-war assumptions and policies. On the other hand, issues which had preoccupied socialists and feminists in the pre-war years – the relationship between gender and class politics, women's economic equality in the work-place, and the question of equal rights versus women's special needs – continued to be important, even if played out in a very different context.

With the achievement of the vote, the women's movement lost some of its momentum and unity; former suffragists became more fragmented in their interests and worked within a variety of organizations. Many women, described by some historians as 'new feminists', focused their attention on social welfare; the health and housing conditions of working-class women and the economic dependence of mothers became major areas of concern. 'New feminists' worked for their aims mainly from within either the Labour Party or the NUWSS, renamed in 1919 the National Union of Societies for Equal Citizenship. The demand of 'new feminists' for protective legislation which would reflect women's special needs as mothers led to internal conflicts within the Union. Many former suffragists disliked the emphasis on domesticity at the expense, as they saw it, of women's right to work, and there was a formal split between the two groups in 1926.[1]

Ill health and advancing age meant that Isabella took a far smaller part in these controversies than she would have done before the war. Instead, her main concern in the few years before her death was to continue to promote peace and international co-operation through work for the WIL. She was at home in the League, working alongside old suffrage friends, and felt

[1] See the discussion of new feminism in O. Banks, *Faces of Feminism* (Oxford; Martin Robertson, 1980) and J. Lewis, *Women in England, 1870–1950* (Brighton: Harvester–Wheatsheaf, 1984).

comfortable with its aims and methods, which reminded her of earlier, suffrage days. Although the war was over, League members still felt that there was plenty of work to be done. The terms of the peace settlement had to be opposed, and there were the practical problems of famine and destitution in post-war Europe, especially in Germany and Austria. One of the first actions of the WIL was to raise money to pay for a million rubber teats to send to starving German babies. Isabella played her part by writing to the *Leeds Weekly Citizen* in January 1919 to appeal for contributions, and the million teats were eventually sent.[2]

Although the league was successful in generating support for specific appeals, it remained only a small organization with a limited membership. Isabella was often exasperated at the complacent attitudes of many of her colleagues and was always making suggestions about ways to give the league more mass appeal. As a member of the organizing committee, she sent a letter to the executive meeting in November 1918 to urge headquarters to organize more public meetings so that membership and funds could be increased. In January 1919 she joined Mary Sheepshanks, a suffragist and secretary of the Fight the Famine Council, in writing to the executive to open up the question of the WIL's relationship to the Socialist International and the Labour Party. After a long discussion it was decided that affiliation to the Labour Party would limit the WIL's role and that it should aim to convert the middle classes. It was further suggested that international feminism could make the greatest contribution to current world politics and that therefore there was an urgent need for a strong, progressive, feminist movement.[3]

Such arguments recalled those of the pre-war suffrage movement. Isabella would have agreed with the emphasis on a strong, international feminist movement, but she continued to believe that it could only be effective in building a new world based on sex equality, peace, and freedom for working people if it linked with the labour and socialist movements of each respective country. The relationship between the women's movement and the labour movement, therefore, remained at the core of her activities and propaganda, but was now expressed in her work for peace rather than for the suffrage or for trade-unionism. In the first few months following the armistice, the WIL held demonstrations designed to gain public support for President Wilson's fourteen peace points. It also aimed to put pressure on the government to raise the blockade against Germany and to organize the feeding of Europe.[4] Isabella's contribution to this attempt to increase public awareness was largely made at a local level. As secretary of the Leeds branch

---

[2]*Leeds Weekly Citizen (LWC)*, 24 Jan. 1919.
[3]Minutes of executive committee of the WIL, 7 Nov. 1918; 2 Jan. 1919. During the war Mary Sheepshanks edited the IWSA journal, *Jus Suffragii*, and held anti-war views.
[4]International Congress of Women, 1919, *Report*, pp. 422–4.

of the WIL she organized a series of meetings at the beginning of 1919 on topics such as the League of Nations and the freedom of small nations.

An international Congress of Women held in Zurich in May gave Isabella the chance to re-establish contact with old friends in the international women's movement. Attending the conference as a delegate from the British section of the League, she found the journey to Zurich difficult in the new conditions of post-war Europe. 'It is a long and wearisome journey nowadays, very different from old times. We had our passports examined so often that we were sick of the sight of them! In Paris we found everything very dear; and there was much less food allowed for each course than formerly, and no milk. There was a curious feeling of tension some-how in the air.' Isabella moved a resolution that all prisoners of war should be repatriated as soon as possible, but otherwise did not take a large part in the formal proceedings. She made sure, however, that colleagues at home in the labour movement knew what the women were doing. In the middle of the proceedings she wrote to the *Leeds Weekly Citizen*: 'Our resolutions are to protest against the Peace terms . . . to abolish conscription and armaments, to raise the blockade, and all the rest with which we ILP people are familiar.'[5]

As always, she wanted to find out from women at first hand about their experiences during the war and was moved by stories of individual hard-ship. As Ethel Snowden recalled,

> tender hearted Isabella Ford flitted from one woman to another, busying herself in particular with the frail and underfed women from the ex-enemy lands, saying here and there the comforting helpful word to lonely souls inclined to half bitterness . . . Isabella came to me the second morning with her eyes full of tears. 'Dear Isabella, what is the matter?' I enquired. She showed me a telegram just received by her German neighbour announcing the death of her only daughter. 'She is heartbroken', said my friend, 'She was an only child. And it was through hunger that the decline set in. She cannot speak to us this morning. And I do not wonder.'[6]

The major disagreement at the congress was over the League of Nations. There were those who thought that its present constitution was so rotten that it should not be recognized, whereas others argued that it should be accepted and then women could work to amend it. This argument was continued at the executive meeting of the British section of the WIL in June when Isabella seconded a resolution to defer the decision to the next council meeting. Three days later, on 22 June, she joined her colleagues to speak at a meeting at Trafalgar Square in which a resolution was passed protesting

---

[5] I. O. Ford, 'Women's International', *LWC*, 30 May 1919. The WIL changed its name a number of times before settling on the Women's International League for Peace and Freedom.
[6] Mrs P. Snowden, *A Political Pilgrim in Europe* (Cassell, 1921), p. 82.

against a 'peace of violence' and pledging the meeting 'to work for a peace
of reconciliation based upon freedom, self-determination and economic
justice'.[7]

Shortly after this meeting, Isabella received a blow from which she never
fully recovered; on 11 July Bessie died in their London flat. She had always
been Isabella's closest friend and source of emotional and practical support.
They had shared so many views – on independent labour politics, peace,
women's suffrage and the importance of art, music, and literature – that
Isabella was moved to write 'a piece of myself has gone'.[8] She wrote almost
immediately to Henry Salt: 'I feel stunned yet. It's Bessie – she was taken ill
suddenly – all in a rush last Tuesday evening. Blood vessels in her brain
burst & she became unconscious & never once revived – on Friday, with
a tired sigh she left us – a smile seemed to be on her face . . . Will you tell
Edward?'[9] As soon as Edward Carpenter had been informed, he wrote to
comfort his old friend, who was still unable to believe it had really
happened. 'I don't yet realise it – I keep thinking "I will ask Bessie", or "I
will show her this" . . . she must be free & happy I feel sure – I don't
think I want her here with me because she was always suffering & though
her faith was undiminished all this famine & the rest made her v. sad'.[10] In
her many letters to Edward Carpenter, Isabella desperately tried to believe
that there was some kind of life after death. 'Of course she can't be snuffed
out & be nowhere. I am more than sure souls aren't extinguished – they
can't be – you see nothing else one possesses really matters in the least.'[11]
When Carpenter's own sister Alice died in November 1921, Isabella returned once more to this theme. 'Alice was unhappy I think you said,
physically restless. If so she will be glad to be resting now & at peace. But
oh how I wish one knew something really about it all. There must be
something to know about surely.'[12]

After cremation at Golders Green, Bessie's ashes were interred at the
Friends' Burial Ground, Adel. She had never taken such a public or
prominent part in political affairs as her sister, but her contribution behind
the scenes was not forgotten. Millicent Fawcett paid tribute to her 'un-
quenchable zeal for justice' and applied to her the lines of George Meredith,
'She can wage a gallant war / And give the peace of Eden.' Most other
tributes came from members of the suffrage and labour movements in
Leeds who remembered her quiet and selfless work for women's equality
and for socialism. Alf Mattison recalled that the New Briggate ILP Club
was founded largely through Bessie's generosity and claimed that among

[7]WIL, *Annual Report*, 1918–1919.
[8]Isabella Ford to Edward Carpenter, 2 Aug. 1919. Carpenter Coll. Sheffield Ref. Lib.
[9]Isabella Ford to Henry Salt, 13 July 1919, Carpenter Coll.
[10]Isabella Ford to Edward Carpenter, 2 Aug. 1919, Carpenter Coll.
[11]Isabella Ford to Edward Carpenter, 2 Aug. 1919, Carpenter Coll.
[12]Isabella Ford to Edward Carpenter, 22 Nov. 1921, Carpenter Coll.

the early socialists there was 'none more earnest, none whose enthusiasm was so tempered with sound judgement and action . . . More especially now than ever, when the world is under a great shadow and the outlook is full of dread uncertainties, our loss is all the keener.'[13]

Isabella found it very difficult to come to terms with the loss of her sister. She gave some of Bessie's personal things to close friends – Katharine Bruce Glasier received her silk shawl – and for the rest of the year she was kept 'extremely busy' dealing with household affairs. War-time inflation had reduced the sisters' income and they were finding the Grange increasingly expensive to run. During the summer of 1919 Isabella and Emily had to sell the motor car and unneccessary furniture, both at Adel and at their London flat.[14] This took up a great deal of time, but in October Isabella was able to get away for a few days to stay with Edward Carpenter and his friend George Hukin at Millthorpe. After the visit she felt more like her old self: 'You have done ever so much good – all of you have somehow given me some hope – I feel as if I can put on my harness more easily & be less cross & horrid here, since I have been with you – the peace & loveliness of it all, still hangs round me . . . I feel so sad without you & George & the stream.'[15]

At Millthorpe, Isabella's thoughts had turned to happier days in the past. She was encouraged to reminisce still further by Millicent Fawcett, who wanted to know what her friend could remember about key events in the suffrage campaign so that she could include them in a new book. Isabella described what was said when a deputation met Asquith in 1907, but 'I wish I could remember exactly. How peaceful the most fiery of those days seem now.' After reading a draft of the book, she declared that she thought it all 'a delightful account.' 'It brings it back vividly to my mind. I agree warmly with your estimate of Asquith & his attitude to Suffrage. It is excellent I think.'[16]

Isabella was never quite so active again in public affairs after Bessie's death. She still turned up occasionally to executive meetings of the WIL and helped to deal with the League's financial problems. These came to a head early in 1920. At a meeting on 19 February, members of the executive agreed to approach likely sympathizers for a contribution; Isabella was to contact Arnold Rowntree, a member of the Quaker manufacturing family who had a strong interest in social questions, but she also argued that the WIL would be stronger if it had a broader basis of support. She suggested, therefore, that the executive should meet in Leeds or in other provincial

---

[13]M. Fawcett, 'Miss Bessie Ford', *Common Cause (CC)*, 25 July 1919; A. Mattison, 'The Late Miss Ford', *LWC* 1 Aug. 1919.

[14]Isabella Ford to Millicent Fawcett, Autumn 1919, Correspondence Files, Fawcett Lib. I am grateful to Clare Collins for the reference to Bessie's shawl.

[15]Isabella Ford to Edward Carpenter, 23 Oct. 1919, Carpenter Coll.

[16]Isabella Ford to Millicent Fawcett, 10 Aug. n.d., and autumn 1919, Correspondence File, Fawcett Lib.

centres where a public meeting could be held to raise funds, and agreed to put forward a more definite plan for the next meeting of the organizing committee.[17] During the course of the year she began to appear once more on public platforms, usually speaking on a subject relating to peace. Standing in the pouring rain at the Leeds May Day rally, she argued strongly in favour of disarmament 'as the only security against war.' In urging support for the International she reminded the Labour Party that 'the exploiter was busy in all lands', and that the 'only power to stop the exploitation was the united power of labour, standing not only for nationalisation and higher wages, but also for a decent and happy living for the workers in all countries'.[18]

Her other major interest lay in doing something practical to relieve the post-war famine in Europe. She was interested in the work carried out by the Society of Friends; her own niece Sibelle had been a relief worker in France during the war and after the armistice joined a Friends' relief unit in Austria. Joint membership was common between the WIL, the Friends' Emergency Relief Committee, and the Fight the Famine Council, and in June 1920 Isabella went on a deputation from all three groups to Cecil Harmsworth, a conservative MP who had accompanied Lloyd-George to the Paris Peace Conference in 1919, to ask that food should be sent to Germany.[19] Immediately afterwards she travelled to Geneva to take part in the first Women's International Suffrage congress since the war. She was full of hope because it would 'include women of all sorts and ranks and colour . . . it is a great and splendid thought that whilst here we are working for social reforms, women all over the world are also working with us for these things, and it will surely inspire us to continue our work ceaselessly and fearlessly.'

On the first day of the congress she wrote a glowing report for the *Leeds Weekly Citizen* describing the discussions as 'absorbingly interesting'. She was particularly impressed by the intelligence and enthusiasm of the assembled women, which made her feel sure that 'the human race has a great future'. She could now die in peace, she said, knowing that 'a new and higher order for both men and women is slowly coming to the world'.[20] This characteristically optimistic statement chose to ignore the serious divisions of opinion between delegates about the kind of reform programme that enfranchised women should now support. The most contentious issues – the endowment of motherhood and protective legislation for women – were not included in the final list of agreed resolutions and were left to be resolved at a later date.

---

[17]Minutes of Executive Committee of the WIL, 19 Feb. 1920., WIL papers, LSE.
[18]*LWC* 7 May 1920.
[19]Emergency and War Victims Relief Committee, *Reports*, 1914–19, 1921.
[20]I. O. Ford, 'Women of the World: The Great Geneva Conference', *LWC* 18 June 1920.

Isabella had suffered from a long bout of influenza before the congress but she had been determined to go to Geneva because, as she later wrote to Millicent Fawcett, 'I was made into a full delegate by the NU (I can't get into the new name) as well as being a fraternal delegate'. She reported that she had 'a very interesting time', although she 'specially missed' Millicent; 'it wasn't the same thing at all to me since *you* weren't there'. Her illness also spoilt some of the enjoyment. None the less, she still thought the congress was a great success and had done her 'no end of good'. Emily had also been abroad, wrote Isabella, on a visit to Serbia, where she had had a 'splendid time'; while there she completed an official painting of the Crown Prince and was given the Order of Saint Salvan for all the work that she had done on behalf of Serbian refugees. Isabella was delighted with the medal and wanted Emily to wear it all day: 'She deserved it for she has slaved & toiled for Serbians – And for Belgians too – & she had a regal time there too amidst grateful families.' Isabella herself went on to visit Berne and Basle, where Anna Lindemann helped her to organize women's suffrage meetings. She then travelled extensively in Germany and was overwhelmed with the kindness she received. She told Millicent Fawcett that the visit to Germany was one she felt that she had to make. I 'wanted to see how things were & because I want to help, – (such conceit, as if I could! but *you* won't misunderstand I know & think I felt any such foolishness).' The starvation was terrible, and she found that Germany's financial position was having a serious effect on British trade. The USA was advancing money to German exporters and therefore getting all the trade for itself. The trip could not completely take her mind off Bessie's death, however; 'I kept feeling as if Bessie's thoughts were with me in Germany & it helped me – But I wonder if the pain of bereavement ever leaves one – but I am going on working, for it is the happiest thing left.'[21]

The visit to Germany certainly appeared to give Isabella a new lease of life. On her return she began to speak more regularly to labour and women's groups on the need for international understanding; at the end of August, for example, she spoke at a joint Labour Party and Trades Council demonstration in Leeds in support of a resolution to form a Council of Action to stop any war with Russia. Isabella's reaction to the two Russian revolutions of 1917 was not recorded; a lifelong opponent of the Tsarist regime she must have welcomed the change of government, and her opposition to any intervention in Russian politics was consistent with her support for self-determination in international affairs. She was concerned, however, about some aspects of Bolshevism and expressed worries in a letter to Rosika Schwimmer. The Bolshevist element, she said, 'is strangely irresponsible and devoid of any plans – they purely declaim against capitalism & capitalists & have no definite plan how to do it in a practical manner.

---

[21]Isabella Ford to Millicent Fawcett, 9 July 1920, Correspondence File, Fawcett Lib.

9. *Peter I, King of Serbs, Croats, and Slovenes.* Painting by Emily Ford dated 1920 (*Ford Family Papers, Brotherton Library, Leeds University*)

It is no use simply to destroy – anyone can do that & urge that – it's to construct & to construct on a sound basis.'[22]

Isabella found it increasingly difficult to keep cheerful in the climate of the post-war world. In common with other suffragists of her generation, she was disappointed with the attitude of younger women to the idea that the voting age should be lowered to twenty-one. Few of them wrote letters to their MPs, while speeches were delivered to half empty halls. The WIL held weekend schools to educate younger women to take an interest in public affairs and after Isabella took part in one held in October 1920, she commented that she could not help feeling sorry that the young women did not seem to be filled with 'the spirit of revolt against injustice and the ardent love of freedom and equality which inspired the set of women who fought for the political equality of men and women'. She was heartened by the fact that women were joining the ILP and the Labour Party, but found it all far too slow. 'I am in a hurry to begin to construct a good world, and so apparently are the foreign women in those countries I have mentioned. Why are not our young women in a hurry too? What is the matter with them?'[23]

The Labour Party was also a source of disappointment and anxiety. When Isabella wrote a letter to the press in opposition to a government proposal to exact a levy on capital, because she feared that the money would be used 'to murder the whole Irish race, or to exterminate Bolshevists, or to harry the Turks and Mesopotamians . . .', she called for a change of government. She had to admit, however, that the Labour Party is 'so busy now with wearisome internal jealousies and contentions, and has not distinguished itself in the House of Commons by any display of statesmanship, that one feels rather anxious and depressed.' She could only hope that 'if we elect not merely trade union officials, but men of wide outlook, and some able Labour women, we shall do well.'[24] Similar complaints about the internal quarrels in the Labour Party were expressed in a letter to Rosika Schwimmer. 'Here, our great work at present is to get Ireland righted. But, as always happens after war, a strange apathy has settled onto people & they bear it with indifference about the horrors going on there.'[25]

Isabella's letter to Rosika Schwimmer also contained insights on a more personal level, on the difficulties associated with old age: 'Life gets harder as we get older, doesn't it – & one loses ones friends by death – I have lost Olive Schreiner who was one of my dearest friends.' Isabella still refused to lose 'courage or faith or hope', for the outlook of the world was 'improving really'. The same optimism shone through when she spoke in memory of

[22]Isabella Ford to Rosika Schwimmer, 13 Feb. 1921, Schwimmer-Lloyd Coll., New York Public Lib.
[23]I. O. Ford, 'What Are the Young Women Doing', *LWC* 10 Sept. 1920.
[24]*LWC* 21 Jan. 1921.
[25]Isabella Ford to Rosika Schwimmer, 13 Feb. 1921, Schwimmer-Lloyd Coll.

Olive Shreiner at the Third International Congress of the Women's International League for Peace and Freedom, held in Vienna in 1921. 'She quoted what Olive Schreiner had said was her support and consolation in life – the conviction that no one is alone in the Universe, and that therefore, she was not alone in her hatred of cruelty and evil, but was one amongst many who hated it and were striving to conquer it.'[26]

Isabella took a particularly active part in the proceedings of the Vienna congress. She reported on the work of the British section of the WIL, pointing out how they had laboured on Ireland's behalf to a much greater extent than they had been given credit for in the newspapers, and concluded that their efforts were having a real effect on public opinion. She also claimed that the Labour Party's growing support for international co-operation was partly due to to the influence of all the WIL members who had joined the party. Later in the congress Isabella moved a key resolution calling on the WIL to reaffirm its conviction that peaceful international relations would never be assured unless they were based on self-determination and government by consent, and until the peace treaties were revised.

Meetings held outside the congress hall also occupied Isabella; one evening she spoke in German to a meeting of working women on the subject of 'War, Peace, and Women'. Four days later she addressed a gathering of war victims and former combatants on the evils of unemployment and the need for all women to unite in their opposition to war.

As always, Isabella was keen to ensure that members of the labour movement in England should be aware of international events, and on her return home she spoke to as many groups as possible, including the East Leeds Socialist Society and the East Hunslet Labour Party, about her experiences in Vienna. During the last three months of 1921, however, most of Isabella's time was spent in organizing a move from Adel Grange – her home for over fifty years.

The house and grounds had always been difficult to maintain, but war-time inflation had greatly increased the running costs. Now that Bessie was no longer there to supervise the housekeeping, Isabella and Emily finally decided to give up their struggle to keep the Grange and to move into Adel Willows, a small cottage nearby. Before Christmas they were occupied in going through 'the awful accumulation of three generations – letters etc. It is terrible. We are selling lots of things of course,' wrote Isabella to Edward Carpenter in her letter to commiserate with him over the death of his sister.[27] Sorting through all their possessions took longer than Isabella and Emily had expected. They had to catalogue books for sale, contact booksellers and find a home for many of their paintings – the National Portrait Gallery, for example, was approached to take a large portrait of Robert

[26]International Congress of Women in Vienna, 1921, *Report*, pp. 142–3.
[27]Isabella Ford to Edward Carpenter, 22 Nov. 1921, Carpenter Coll.

Carr. Writing in despair to Millicent, Agnes, and Phillippa Fawcett in this period, Isabella expressed the wish that they had already moved; they were simply 'so tired of all the turning out of drawers & reading old letters, that our one desire is to be away in the Willows'.[28]

When the move finally took place in January 1922, Isabella heard that Edward Carpenter was about to leave Millthorpe. This represented the end of an era and she remembered her first visits to his cottage when his sister Alice was also there; 'I have thought a great deal about you and Alice lately – I wish you weren't going.' She had fewer misgivings about her own move to Adel Willows, for 'life will be easier there than it is here'.[29] On the other hand, in a letter to Millicent Fawcett she expressed warm feelings about the Grange and all that it had meant to her family. 'Any small help we may have been to anyone or, more than us, what our mother did, was pure enjoyment to us – we delighted in having such nice people here & those who weren't nice are an endless source of amusement to us. It has been such a nice life for us – & I feel somehow grateful to the dear house – we are taking Agnes' fire grate, but alas, we cannot take the mantel shelf – there is no place for it.'[30]

Isabella may not have been sad about leaving the Grange, but most of her friends regretted the move; letters flooded in to thank the sisters for their hospitality over so many years. In her obituary of Bessie, written two years before, Millicent Fawcett summed up the views of other friends when she wrote that 'to many of us Adel Grange will ever remain in our memories as one of our sacred places. It breathed peace and restfulness to those who were weary, while it also inspired new courage to go on with the necessary fight to obtain a nearer approach of fair play for the woman worker and the woman citizen.'[31]

The move to Adel Willows prompted Isabella to give more financial support to the WIL; apart from paying regular subscriptions of £5, she lent £15 when the League was trying to raise money to establish an International House. In January 1922, once the house had been set up, she gave a donation of £50. She was now less active than before, but was still prepared to turn up to conferences, open-air meetings, and demonstrations to forward the cause of peace. She had spent most of her adult life speaking at such meetings, 'but her sympathies were not shop-worn'. 'Her early enthusiasm never flagged. To the last she was youthful in spirit.'[32] In July

---

[28]Isabella Ford to Millicent, Agnes, and Philippa Fawcett, 21 Dec. 1921, Correspondence File, Fawcett Lib.
[29]Isabella Ford to Edward Carpenter, 15 Jan. 1922, Carpenter Coll.
[30]Isabella Ford to Millicent, Agnes, and Philippa Fawcett, 21 Dec. 1921, Correspondence File, Fawcett Lib.
[31]M. Fawcett, 'Miss Bessie Ford', CC 25 July 1919.
[32]M. E. S. 'Isabella O. Ford', Woman's Leader (WL), 1 Aug. 1924; J. Arnott, 'Isabella O. Ford: An Appreciation', LWC 19 July 1924.

10. Emily Ford at her home, Adel Willows, near Leeds, shortly before her death (*Yorkshire Post*, 5 May 1930). (*British Library, Newspaper Library, Colindale*)

1922 she helped to organize a women's procession in Leeds as part of a 'No More War' campaign to strengthen the League of Nations. In December she attended an International Congress in The Hague which brought together delegates from trade union, socialist, and peace organizations to discuss how to promote peace. They argued for the need to train young people in pacifism and for a revision of history textbooks, as well as passing resolutions condemning the Treaty of Versailles. On her return Isabella reported her impressions of the conference to local socialist groups and also spoke at a special women's day, organized by the Leeds Labour Party in June 1923, where she urged the withdrawal of French troops from the Ruhr. In August she was involved once again in a No More War demonstration and took exception to remarks from the chairman, who said that he was not a 'peace at any price' man, for as far as she was concerned no evil could be as great as war.[33]

Despite all her misgivings about the performance of the Labour Party in the House of Commons, Isabella still believed that it provided the best hope for the achievement of international co-operation and social reconstruction. She therefore continued to urge all women to vote for Labour candidates. Chiding workers at the May Day rally in Leeds in 1922 for sending men and women who did not look after their interests to Parliament, she called on all voters, especially the women, 'to rally round the Labour banner'.[34] Isabella went to North Islington to support Edith Picton Turbervill who was standing as a Labour candidate in a by-election; other 'gallant helpers' were Maude Royden and Lady Balfour, a conservative who for the first and only time in her life appeared on a labour platform – putting the cause of women before personal political loyalties.[35] The general election held in November 1922 showed that the Labour Party, now with 142 MPs, had made important gains. When Isabella reported on the 1922 Hague Congress to a meeting of Labour women, she emphasized the importance of building on this advance. Although unable to agree with everything that Radek, the Russian Bolshevist, had said at the congress, she 'endorsed his statement that if the people want peace they must get rid of capitalist Governments. The electors of Britain had taken a step in this direction at the General Election, but they must go still further.'[36]

The Conservative Party was now in power, but the issue of trade protection led to the declaration of yet another general election towards the end of 1923. Isabella of course gave her support to the Labour Party. Despite the cold weather she helped to campaign for her old friend Philip Snowden, and many thought that in doing so she overtaxed her strength.[37] Her heart was weakened by a severe cold and cough at the beginning of the

[33]*LWC* 4 Aug. 1922.
[34]Ibid., 12 May 1922.
[35]E. Picton-Turbervill, *Life is Good* (Frederick Muller, 1939), p. 157.
[36]*LWC* 19 Jan. 1923.
[37]M. Fawcett, 'Isabella Ormston Ford', *WL* 25 July 1924.

new year, but by March she felt much better: 'I can do everything I want to do if I do it slowly.' She had been staying with suffrage friends who lived in Saxmundham, and every day they visited Aldburgh or Southwold or Orford and 'sat in the sun beside the sea in that divine air'.[38]

Confident of a full recovery, Isabella was looking forward to a trip to Washington in May for the next Women's International Congress. She told Millicent Fawcett that she would have preferred to see more of Europe and something of the East; 'still, when one is elected as a delegate & some of the expenses paid, it is nice to see some of the less interesting places in the world, & Washington will be more interesting than New York'. The Labour Party had been returned as a minority government, with her old friends Ramsay MacDonald and Phillip Snowden in the positions of prime minister and chancellor of the exchequer, and she took the opportunity to reflect on their victory. 'I am greatly moved when I think that the Labour men I have known so well like Snowden are in power. But I hear from him in particular how immense their difficulties are – both amongst their own MPs & constituents & the other parties . . . their inexperience makes things hard. I feel Miss Bondfield is a great asset.'[39]

She hoped to stay with Millicent Fawcett in London after her visit to Washington and wrote again two days later to thank her for her warning about how exhausting America could be. Trying to reassure her friend, she claimed that 'Jeannie was distinguished & I am *not*. No one has invited me to do anything, nor has anyone . . . shown any particular interest in my visit.' She could not afford to see very much of the country and did not intend to take part in the very long train journey that some delegates had planned. Tongue in cheek, she expressed amazement at how foreign women never seemed to get tired. 'The worst are the new small nations, which lie around Poland and Russia . . . They are never tired in the very least & wear us all out. It was a great mistake to create them!'[40]

The trip to America, however, never took place. Isabella's 'rather serious illness' prevented her from attending a meeting in April to honour Francis Johnson, secretary of the ILP. She sent a contribution of £1 to the ILP's treasurer, expressing her gratitude to Francis Johnson for his 'unfailing kindness' to Bessie and herself, but her shaky handwriting suggests how far her health had deteriorated.[41] Only three months later, on 14 July 1924, she died in her sleep at Adel Willows. 'Shortly before her death she said: "I feel I should like a little sleep and to be left alone", and with a wealth of bloom in her bedroom she dropped into unconsciousness and passed peacefully away.'[42]

[38]Isabella Ford to Millicent Fawcett, 16 Mar. 1924, Correspondence Files, Fawcett Lib.
[39]Isabella Ford to Millicent Fawcett, 16 Mar. 1924, ibid.
[40]Isabella Ford to Millicent Fawcett, 18 Mar. 1924, ibid.
[41]Isabella Ford to J. Macnair, 16 Apr. 1924, Francis Johnson Coll., LSE.
[42]*Yorkshire Evening Post*, 15 July 1924.

Over 400 people, including working women from the Mill Hill school, gathered at the Friends' Meeting House to offer prayers. They heard tributes to her work from representatives of the local ILP, Labour Party, Women's Suffrage Society, and the Adel Parish Council, many of whom had been her personal friends. Among them were Joseph Young, Allen Gee, Walt Wood, Alf and Florence Mattison, Alderman D. B. Foster, and Tom Duncan, all of whom had all been with her in the early days of the socialist revival in Leeds. Her ashes were then taken to Lawnswood Cemetery to be buried beside those of Bessie. Local friends later organized a lasting memorial by opening a fund which enabled one of Isabella's post-war initiatives, the awarding of annual prizes to Leeds schoolchildren for essays on peace, to continue.[43]

More well-known friends from the Women's International League and the National Union of Societies for Equal Citizenship expressed their tributes to Isabella at a memorial meeting held in London on 28 July. Millicent Fawcett spoke of a friendship which had lasted over fifty years, while Margaret Bondfield remembered the power of Isabella's influence. 'She had the gift, Christ-like in its nature, of getting at the inner meaning of the lives of those with whom she came in contact. The workers accepted her not as a middle-class woman, but as one of themselves.'[44]

The 'scorn and abuse' that Isabella had encountered in the late nineteenth century when she had taken part in strikes and helped to organize working women was glossed over in the obituaries in the local and national press. Instead she was praised for selflessly helping others less fortunate than herself and for fighting against injustice. Lovable, witty, gentle, and broad-minded were adjectives used time and again, both before and after Isabella's death, to describe her personality. The keynote of her character was given as 'keen pity for all suffering creatures', and in a poem to her memory E. D. Morel captured the tone of nearly all the appreciations written of her life:

> A great heart beating for the poor and stricken;
> A brave, gentle, tender spirit, God given;
> A soul to every test rising nobly;
> A humour rich, varied, ever kindly.[45]

Isabella would hardly have recognized herself, however, in this idealized portrait and would have felt much more comfortable with John Arnott's perceptive assessment of her complex personality.

---

[43]Information on Isabella's organisation of peace prizes kindly supplied by Ursula O. Ford in a letter to Joyce Bellamy, 26 June 1983.

[44]'Isabella O. Ford: In Memoriam', *WL* 1 Aug. 1924.

[45]E. D. Morel, 'To I. O. Ford', *Foreign Affairs*, Aug. 1924.

She had pity, but she was no weak sentimentalist. She had great courage and a full share of the shrewdness which members of the Society of Friends are said to possess . . . She was an excellent judge of character and soon detected pretence. Her own straightforwardness made her ill-at-ease with those who played to the gallery. At times she may have been a little unjust to them.

Unlike many of her contemporaries, 'her early enthusiasm never flagged. To the last she was youthful in spirit.' She had acted as a bridge, in both her ideas and in her actions, between 'the great humanitarian movement' of the early nineteenth century and the socialist movement which was its successor. Her political outlook was a holistic one in which the national and international movements of which she was a part were all 'in her mind . . . branches of one great tree'.[46]

Isabella had argued from the beginning that if socialism did not mean more than a change in economic and political structures, then it was not worth fighting for; in her vision of the future, socialism would bring beauty and justice into the lives of ordinary people, provide the potential for full human development and transform personal relationships. Such ideas were out of tune with the preoccupations of the labour and women's movements in the post-war years as they battled for specific social reforms in the face of unemployment, fascism, and the threat of war. They were to re-emerge as relevant, however, to a new generation of socialists and feminists in the 1960s and 1970s.

Isabella's faith in the power of the vote and her emphasis on a moral regeneration of society may sound old-fashioned today, but in other respects she was forward looking. Her attempt to relate gender and class oppression, her insistence that women must have a say in all issues that affected their lives, and her recognition of the political implications of personal experience would have been instantly familiar to the revived women's movement of the 1970s. The importance of her ideas and work for future generations was recognized, appropriately enough, in a sympathetic tribute from her beloved ILP, written shortly after her death: 'Isabella Ford's conception of Socialism was broad and human. She identified herself with every movement for freedom. She was international through and through, she loved animals scarcely less than human beings, she loved beauty and music, and sought a society in which all men and women would have an opportunity to develop into full human beings. She was indeed, a citizen of to-morrow.'[47]

[46]J. Arnott, 'In Memoriam: Isabella O. Ford: An Appreciation', *LWC* 19 July 1924.
[47]*New Leader*, 25 July 1924.

Select Bibliography

Place of publication is London unless otherwise stated.

Primary Sources

1. Collections of Papers

Josephine Butler Collection, Fawcett Library
Correspondence Files, Fawcett Library
Edward Carpenter Collection, Sheffield City Library
Ford Family Papers, Brotherton Library, Leeds University
Isabella Ford's Scrapbook, Leeds City Archives
Francis Johnson Collection, British Library of Political and Economic Science, LSE
J. R. MacDonald Papers, British Library of Political and Economic Science, LSE
Alf Mattison Collection, Brotherton Library, Leeds University
Alf Mattison Letter Book (in the possession of E. P. Thompson)
National Union of Women's Suffrage Societies Papers, Fawcett Library
Schwimmer-Lloyd Collection, New York Public Library
Suffrage MSS, Manchester Central Library
Union of Democratic Control Papers, Hull University
Walt Whitman Papers, Library of Congress, Washington, DC
Webb Collection, British Library of Political and Economic Science, LSE
Women's International League Papers, British Library of Political and Economic Science, LSE
Women's Labour League Papers, Labour Party Archives
Women's Trade Union League Papers, Trades Union Congress
Yorkshire Ladies' Council of Education Papers, Leeds City Archives

2. Minutes and Annual Reports

Only major sources are listed here; for other sources see footnotes.

Election Fighting Fund, Executive Committee Minutes
Emergency and War Victims Relief Committee, Annual Reports
International Congress of Women, Reports 1915, 1919, 1921
International Women's Suffrage Alliance, Annual Conference Reports
Labour Party, Annual Reports

Ladies' National Association, Annual Reports
Leeds Labour Representation Committee, Annual Reports
Leeds Trades Council, Minutes
National Union of Women's Suffrage Societies, Annual Reports
National Union of Women's Suffrage Societies, Executive Committee Minutes
National Union of Women's Suffrage Societies, Quarterly Council Minutes
National Union of Women Workers, Leeds Branch Minutes
West Riding Federation of Suffrage Societies, Annual Reports
Women's International League (British Section), Annual Reports
Women's International League (British Section), Executive Committee Minutes
Women's Labour League, Annual Reports
Union of Democratic Control, Executive Committee Minute Book
Union of Democratic Control, General Council Minute Book

3. *Journals and Newspapers*

Bradford Observer
Common Cause
Co-operative News
Daily Citizen
Daily News
Humanitarian
Jus Suffragii: International Women's Suffrage News
Labour Chronicle
Labour Leader
Leeds Daily News
Leeds Express
Leeds Forward
Leeds Mercury
Leeds Weekly Citizen
Shafts
UDC
Woman's Herald
Woman Worker
Women's Franchise
Women's Trade Union Review
Women's Union Journal
Yorkshire Evening News
Yorkshire Evening Post
Yorkshire Factory Times
Yorkshire Owl
Yorkshire Post

4. *Works by Isabella Ford*

In date order:

Fiction

Miss Blake of Monkshalton (John Murray, 1890)
On the Threshold (Edward Arnold, 1895)
Mr. Elliott (Edward Arnold, 1901)
'Our Jane Annie', *Labour Leader*, 29 Nov. 1902
'Maria On Strike', *Labour Leader*, 4 Apr. 1903
'Mother and Daughter: A Fragment of Life', *Labour Leader*, 27 May 1904
'Aunt Caroline's Christmas Eve', *Labour Leader*, 23 Dec. 1904
'In the Days of the Press Gang', *Labour Leader*, 15 Dec. 1905
'The Children', *Labour Leader*, 2 Mar. 1906 (Dostoevsky story, trans. from German)
'Of Witches', *Englishwoman*, 6 (May–July 1910)
'The Gold Fish', *Englishwoman*, 18 (Apr.–June 1913)

Non-Fiction

'Factory Legislation for Women', *Yorkshire Factory Times*, 10 Apr. 1891
Women's Wages (Humanitarian League, 1893)
'Women Inspectors of Factories and Workshops', *Woman's Herald*, 16 Mar. 1893
'Industrial Conditions Affecting Women of the Working Classes', *Yorkshire Factory Times*, 17 Mar. 1893
'Why I Joined the Leeds ILP', in J. Clayton, ed., *Why I Joined the Independent Labour Party: Some Plain Statements* (Leeds ILP, *c*.1896)
Women as Factory Inspectors and Certifying Surgeons (Women's Co-operative Guild, *c*.1897)
'Particulars for the Tailors', *Women's Trade Union Review*, Apr. 1897
'Unsatisfactory Citizens', *Women's Industrial News*, Mar. 1898
'Organisation in Bradford', *Women's Trade Union Review*, Oct. 1899
Industrial Women and How to Help Them (Humanitarian League, *c*.1901)
'Women and the Franchise', *Labour Leader*, 1 Mar. 1902
Women and Socialism (ILP, 1904, 1906)
'Woman As She Was And Is', *Labour Leader*, 13 May 1904
'The Late Mr. G. F. Watts: The Recollection of an Afternoon', *Labour Leader*, 8 July 1904
'In Praise of Married Women', *Labour Leader*, 2 Sept. 1904
'The Marriage of Mr. Phillip Snowden and Miss Ethel Annakin', *Labour Leader*, 17 Mar. 1905
'Women and the Legislators', *Labour Leader*, 19 May 1905
'At Milan: Inside the Congress', *Labour Leader*, 7 July 1905
'Women's Suffrage Convention', *Labour Leader*, 27 Oct. 1905
'The Textile Congress at Milan', *Women's Trade Union Review*, Oct. 1905
'Women's Votes; Conference of MPs', *Labour Leader*, 23 Feb. 1906

'Women at the Gate', *Labour Leader*, 2 Mar. 1906

'Exeter Hall and Trafalgar Square', *Labour Leader*, 25 May 1906

'Life in a Swiss Village', *Labour Leader*, 13 July 1906

'Women and the Transvaal Constitution', *Labour Leader*, 10 Aug. 1906

'A Council of War', *Labour Leader*, 9 Nov. 1906

'The Yorkshire Caravan', *Common Cause*, 17 June 1909

'Women's International Congress', *Labour Leader*, 26 June 1908

'The Lessons of the Women's International Conference', *Labour Leader*, 2 July 1909

'Women Workers in the Wholesale Clothing Trade', *Englishwoman*, 2/6 (July 1909)

'A Day with the Mountains', *Labour Leader*, 24 June 1910

'Women in Industry: Wages in the Textile Trade', *Standard*, 9 Nov. 1911

'A Personal Testimony', *Common Cause*, 19 Sept. 1912

'Women in the Labour Movement', *Labour Leader*, 9 Jan. 1913 (Special Suffrage Supplement)

'A Deputation and its Answer', *Common Cause*, 25 April 1913

'Why Women should be Socialists', *Labour Leader*, 1 May 1913

'Factory Girls and Gambling', *Common Cause*, 15 Aug. 1913

'On Girl Guides', *Common Cause*, 5 Sept. 1913

'The International Textile Workers' Congress at Blackpool', *Common Cause*, 19 June 1914

'When Will Women Rebel?', *Common Cause*, 29 Apr. 1915

'The Hague Peace Congress', *Leeds Weekly Citizen*, 28 May 1915

'War Work on the Land', *Common Cause*, 1 Oct. 1915

'Standing by the Men: Women and Trade Unions', *Common Cause*, 19 May 1916

'Standing Together: The Value of Trade Unionism for Women', *Common Cause*, 16 Feb. 1917

'Men, Women and Labour', *Women's International League Monthly Newsletter*, 1917

'Women's International', *Leeds Weekly Citizen*, 30 May 1919

'Women in Other Lands: Their Part in Public Life', *Leeds Weekly Citizen*, 9 Apr. 1920

'Women of the World: The Great Geneva Conference', *Leeds Weekly Citizen*, 18 June 1920

'What Are the Young Women Doing', *Leeds Weekly Citizen*, 10 Sept. 1920

5. Books, Pamphlets, and Articles

A.J.R., ed., *Suffrage Annual and Women's Who's Who* (Stanley Paul, 1913)

Anon., 'Women's Suffrage Comes of Age: Yorkshire Memories of the Stirring Militant Days', *Leeds Mercury*, 16 Mar. 1939

Anon., 'Some Eminent Trade Unionists: Miss Isabella Ford', *Leeds Weekly Citizen*, 12 June 1914

Carpenter, E., *My Days and Dreams* (Geo. Allen & Unwin, 1916)

Clayton, J. ed., *Why I Joined the Independent Labour Party: Some Plain Statements* (Leeds ILP, *c*.1896)

Collet, C., 'Women's Work in Leeds', *Economic Journal*, 1/3 (1891)

Dilke, E., 'Trade Unionism for Women', *New Review* (Jan. 1890)

——'The Seamy Side of Trade Unionism for Women', *New Review* (June 1890)

Fawcett, M., *The Women's Victory and After: Personal Reminiscences, 1911–1918* (Sidgwick & Jackson, 1920)

Ford, E. S., *Rejected Addresses: An Episode* (Leeds, 1882)

——*Careers: A Comedy* (Leeds, 1883)

——*The Fisherman's Discontented Daughter* (Leeds: Dodson, 1891)

——*The Golden Goose* (Leeds: Dodson, 1891)

——*Our School: A Comedy in Three Acts* (Leeds: Dodson, 1896)

——*A Perfect Character: A Sketch* (Leeds, n.d.)

——*Women and the Regulation System: Impressions of the Geneva Congress of September 1908* (Ladies' National Association, 1909)

——'Communal Kitchens: An Experiment in Leeds', *Common Cause*, 20 Apr. 1917

Ford, H. C., *Short Diaries of Two Visits to London, May 1887 and September 1889* (Leeds Reference Library)

Foster, J., comp., *Pease of Darlington (1891)*

Illustrated Report of the Proceedings of the International Workers' Congress Held in London July 1896 (Labour Leader, 1896)

Independent Labour Party, *Manifesto to the Women's Social and Political Union* (ILP, 1906)

Labour Who's Who, The (1924)

Maguire, T., *Machine Room Chants* (Labour Leader, 1895)

Mallon, J. J., 'Isabella Ford', *Woman Worker*, 7 Aug. 1908

Mattison, A., 'A History of the Leeds Labour Party', pts ii, v, and vi, *Leeds Weekly Citizen*, 11 Jan., 1 Feb., 8 Feb. 1918

Mattison, A., and Carpenter, E., eds., *Tom Maguire: A Remembrance* (Manchester: Labour Press, 1895)

Pease, E. R., *The History of the Fabian Society* [1918] (3rd edn. Frank Cass, 1963)

Royden, M., *Votes and Wages* (NUWSS, 1911)

Schreiner, O., *Woman and Labour* (T. Fisher Unwin, 1911)

Sherard, R. H., *The White Slaves of England* (James Bowden, 1897)

Snowden, E., *The Feminist Movement* (Collins, 1913)

Snowden, Mrs. P. [E. Snowden], 'The Women's Peace Crusade', *UDC*, 2/11 (Sept. 1917)

——*A Political Pilgrim in Europe* (Cassell, 1921)

Stoddart, A. M., *Elizabeth Pease Nichol* (J. M. Dent, 1899)

Swanwick, H. M. *Women and War* (UDC, *c.*1915)

Teufelsdroch, 'Letters to Notables. ix. Miss Isabella Ford', *Labour Leader*, 30 Jan. 1904

Turner, B., *The Heavy Woollen District Textile Workers' Union* (Dewsbury: Yorkshire Factory Times, 1917)

——*Short History of the General Union of Textile Workers* (Heckmondwike: Pioneer and Factory Times, 1920)

——'Looking Backwards', *Socialist Review*, 23 (Feb. 1924)

Women's Freedom League, *Verbatim Report of the Debate on December 3rd 1907. Sex Equality (Teresa Billington Greig) versus Adult Suffrage (Margaret G. Bondfield)* (Manchester: Women's Freedom League, 1908)

Secondary Sources

Banks, O., *Faces of Feminism* (Oxford: Martin Robertson, 1980)

——*The Biographical Dictionary of British Feminists*. vol. i, *1800–1930* (Brighton: Wheatsheaf, 1985)

Beith, G., ed., *Edward Carpenter: An Appreciation* (Geo. Allen & Unwin, 1931)

Bell, E. M., *Josephine Butler* (Constable, 1962)

Bland, L., 'Marriage Laid Bare: Middle-Class Women and Marital Sex, c.1800–1914', in Lewis, ed., *Labour and Love*.

——'The Married Woman, the "New Woman" and the Feminist Sexual Politics of the 1890s', in Rendall, ed., *Equal or Different* (1987)

Bondfield, M., *A Life's Work* (Hutchinson, 1948)

Bornat, J., 'Lost Leaders: Women, Trade Unionism and the Case of the General Union of Textile Workers', in John, ed., *Unequal Opportunities* (1986)

Boston, S., *Women Workers and the Trade Unions* (Davis Poynter, 1980)

Braybon, G., *Women Workers in the First World War* (Croom Helm, 1981)

Briggs A., and Saville, J., eds., *Essays in Labour History* vol. i (Macmillan, 1960)

Brockway, F., *Inside the Left* (Geo. Allen & Unwin, 1942)

——*Socialism Over Sixty Years: The Life of Jowett of Bradford* (Geo. Allen & Unwin, 1946)

Buckman, J., *Immigrants and the Class Struggle: The Jewish Immigrant in Leeds, 1880–1914* (Manchester: Manchester University Press, 1983)

Bussey, G., and Tims, M., *The Women's International League for Peace and Freedom* (Geo. Allen & Unwin, 1965)

Caine, B., 'Feminism, Suffrage and the Nineteenth-century English Women's Movement', *Women's Studies International Forum*, 5/6 (1982)

Chew, D. N., *Ada Nield Chew: The Life and Writings of a Working Woman* (Virago, 1982)

Clayton, J., *The Rise and Decline of Socialism in Great Britain* (Faber & Gwyer, 1926)

Conwright-Schreiner, S. C., *The Letters of Olive Schreiner, 1870–1920* (T. Fisher Unwin, 1924)

Cresswell, D'Arcy, *Margaret McMillan: A Memoir* (Hutchinson, 1948)

Crick, B., *George Orwell: A Life* (Harmondsworth: Penguin, 1982)

Ellis, Mrs Havelock, *The New Horizon in Love and Life* (A. & C. Black, 1921)

Davin, A., 'Imperialism and Motherhood', *History Workshop Journal*, 5 (1978)

Drake, B., *Women in Trade Unions* (Labour Research Department, 1920)

Farran, D., Scott, S., and Stanley, L., eds., *Writing Feminist Biography*. Studies in Sexual Politics, nos. 13–14, Department of Sociology, Manchester University, 1986

Fawcett, M. G., and Turner, E. M., *Josephine Butler* (Association for Moral and Social Hygiene, 1927)

Francini, S., *Sylvia Pankhurst, 1912–1924* (E. T. S. Universita, 1980)

Fraser, D., ed., *A History of Modern Leeds* (Manchester: Manchester University Press, 1980)

Fulford, R., *Votes for Women* (Faber & Faber, 1958)

Garner, L., *Stepping Stones to Women's Liberty: Feminist Ideas in the Women's Suffrage Movement, 1900–1918* (Heinemann, 1984)

Gawthorpe, M., *Up Hill to Holloway* (Prebscot, Maine: Traversity Press, 1962)

Gunn, P., *Vernon Lee: Violet Paget, 1856–1935* (Oxford: Oxford University Press 1964)

Hamilton, M. A., *Remembering My Good Friends* (Cape, 1944)

Hannam, J., 'The Employment of Working-Class Women in Leeds, 1880–1914', Ph. D. thesis, University of Sheffield, 1985

——'Usually Neglected in Standard Histories: Some Issues in Working on the Life of Isabella Ford, 1855–1924', in Farran, Scott, and Stanley, eds., *Writing Feminist Biography* (1986)

——'"In the Comradeship of the Sexes Lies the Hope of Progress and Social Regeneration": Women in the West Riding ILP, *c.*1890–1914', in Rendall, ed., *Equal or Different* (1987)

Hendrick, J., 'The Tailoresses in the Ready-Made Clothing Industry in Leeds, 1889–99: A Study in Labour Failure', MA Thesis, University of Warwick, 1970

Hill, C., *God's Englishman: Oliver Cromwell and the English Revolution* (Harmondsworth: Pelican, 1972)

Hinton, J., *Labour and Socialism: A History of the British Labour Movement* (Brighton: Wheatsheaf, 1983)

Hobsbawm, E. J., *Labouring Men* (Weidenfeld & Nicolson, 1968)

Howell, D., *British Workers and the Independent Labour Party, 1888–1906* (Manchester: Manchester University Press, 1983)

Holton, S., 'Feminism and Democracy: The Women's Suffrage Movement in Britain, with Particular Reference to the National Union of Women's Suffrage Societies, 1897–1918', Ph. D. thesis, University of Stirling, 1980

Hume, L. P., *The National Union of Women's Suffrage Societies, 1897–1914* (Garland Publishing, 1982)

Jeffreys, S., *The Spinster and Her Enemies: Feminism and Sexuality, 1880–1930* (Virago, 1985)

Jenkins, I., 'The Yorkshire Ladies' Council of Education, 1871–1891', Thoresby Society Publications, 56 (1978)

John, A., ed., *Unequal Opportunities: Women's Employment in England, 1800–1918* (Blackwell, 1986)

Johnson, G. W., and Johnson, L. A., eds., *Josephine Butler: An Autobiographical Memoir* (Bristol: J. W. Arrowsmith, 1911)

Levine, P., *Victorian Feminism, 1850–1900* (Hutchinson, 1987)

Lewenhak, S., *Women and Trade Unions* (Ernest Benn, 1977)

Lewis, J., *Women in England, 1870–1950* (Brighton: Harvester–Wheatsheaf, 1984)

——ed., *Labour and Love: Women's Experience of Home and Family* (Blackwell, 1986).

Liddington, J., 'The Women's Peace Crusade: The History of a Forgotten Campaign', in D. Thompson, ed., *Over Our Dead Bodies* (1983)

——*The Life and Times of a Respectable Rebel: Selina Cooper, 1864–1946* (Virago, 1984)

Liddington, J. and Norris, J., *One Hand Tied Behind Us: The Rise of the Women's Suffrage Movement* (Virago, 1978)

MacKenzie, N. 'Percival Chubb and the Founding of the Fabian Society', *Victorian Studies*, 23/1 (1980)

MacKenzie, N., and MacKenzie J., *The First Fabians* (Quartet Books, 1979)

Malmgreen, G., 'Anne Knight and the Radical Subculture', *Quaker History*, 71 (Fall, 1982)

Mappen, E., *Helping Women at Work: The Women's Industrial Council, 1889–1914* (Hutchinson, 1985)

Middleton, L., ed., *Women in the Labour Movement* (Croom Helm, 1977)

Miller, E. H., *et al.*, eds., *The Correspondence of Walt Whitman,* vols. ii–iv (New York: New York University Press, 1961)

Mitchell, H., *The Hard Way Up: The Autobiography of Hannah Mitchell, Suffragette and Rebel* (Virago, 1977)

Oakley, A., 'Millicent Garrett Fawcett: Duty and Determination', in Spender, ed., *Feminist Theorists* (1983)

Oldfield, S., *Spinsters of this Parish* (Virago, 1984)

Pafford, E. R., and Pafford, J. H. P., *Employers and Employed: Ford Ayrton & Co. Ltd.* (Edington, Wilts.: Pasold Research Fund Ltd., 1974)

Pankhurst, E. S. *The Suffragette Movement* [1931] (Virago, 1977)

Phillips, A., *Divided Loyalties: Dilemmas of Sex and Class* (Virago, 1987)

Picton-Turbervill, E., *Life Is Good* (Frederick Muller, 1939)

Rendall, J., *The Origins of Modern Feminism: Women in Britain, France and the United States, 1780–1860* (Macmillan, 1985)

——ed., *Equal or Different: Women's Politics, 1800–1914* (Blackwell, 1987)

Rosen, A., *Rise Up Women!* (Routledge & Kegan Paul, 1974)

Rowbotham, S., and Weeks, J., *Socialism and the New Life: The Personal and Sexual Politics of Edward Carpenter and Havelock Ellis* (Pluto Press, 1977)

Sarah, E., 'Christabel Pankhurst: Reclaiming Her Power', in Spender, ed., *Feminist Theorists* (1983)

Snowden, P. *An Autobiography*, vol. i (Nicholson & Watson, 1934)

Spender, D., ed., *Feminist Theorists* (Women's Press, 1983)

Squire, R., *Thirty Years in the Public Service* (Nisbet, 1927)

Stanley, L., 'Olive Schreiner: New Women, Free Women, All Women', in Spender, ed., *Feminist Theorists* (1983)

——*Feminism and Friendship: Two Essays on Olive Schreiner*. Studies in Sexual Politics, No. 8, Department of Sociology, Manchester University, 1985

Strachey, R., *The Cause* [1928] (Virago, 1978)

——*Millicent Garrett Fawcett* (John Murray, 1931)

Swanwick, H. M., *Builders of the Peace: Being 10 Years History of the UDC* (Swarthmore Press, 1924)

——*I Have Been Young* (Gollancz, 1935)

Taylor, B., *Eve and the New Jerusalem* (Virago, 1983)

Thomas, J., *A History of the Leeds Clothing Industry*. Yorkshire Bulletin of Economic and Social Research Occasional Paper No. 1. (1955)

Thompson, D., ed., *Over Our Dead Bodies: Women Against the Bomb* (Virago, 1983)

Thompson, E. P., *William Morris: Romantic to Revolutionary* (Merlin Press, 1977)

Thompson, P., *The Enthusiasts: A Biography of John and Katharine Bruce Glasier* (Gollancz, 1971)

Tickner, L., *The Spectacle of Women: Imagery of the Suffrage Campaign, 1907–1914* (Chatto & Windus, 1988)

Tolles, F. B., ed., 'Slavery and the Woman Question: Lucretia Mott's Diary of Her Visit to Great Britain to attend the World Anti-Slavery convention of 1840', *Journal of the Friends' History Society*, Supplement 23 (1952)

Tuckett, A., 'Enid Stacy', *North West Labour History Society Bulletin*, 7 (1980–1)

Turner, B., *About Myself* (Humphrey Toulmin, 1930)

Uglow, J., 'Josephine Butler: From Sympathy to Theory, 1828–1906', in Spender, ed., *Feminist Theorists* (1983)

Vellacott-Newberry, J., 'Anti-War Suffragists', *History*, 62/3 (1977)

Vicinus, M., *Independent Women* (Virago, 1985)

Walkowitz, J. R., *Prostitution and Victorian Society: Women, Class and the State* (Cambridge: Cambridge University Press, 1980)

Ward, H., *A Venture in Goodwill: Being the Story of the Women's International League, 1915–1929* (Women's International League, 1929)

White, W., ed., *Walt Whitman: Day Books and Notebooks*, vol. ii. *Day Books, December 1881–1891* (New York: New York University Press, 1977)

Wiltsher, A., *Most Dangerous Women: Feminist Peace Campaigners of the Great War* (Pandora, 1985)

Yeo, S., 'A New Life: The Religion of Socialism in Britain, 1883–1896', *History Workshop Journal*, 4 (1977)

Index